T0298929

Digital Consumer Management

Integrating consumer behaviour, digital marketing, digital platform management, web analytics, and marketing insights, *Digital Consumer Management* provides a holistic understanding—from a brand perspective—of the management of consumers and consumption in the digital ecosystem.

Chapters explore the key stakeholders in platform management, the multiple types of platforms used by brands, the various consumer-brand touchpoints, how the platforms are developed and with what goals in mind, managing consumer engagement and activities on these platforms, how the platforms are regulated, and the dark side of digital consumption. Theory is brought to life by practical examples and case studies from across sectors, and reflective questions and activities allow students to critically reflect on their learning.

Providing a comprehensive picture of digital consumption activities, digital consumer behaviour across platforms, and how brands can manage and engage with the digital consumer, this text works as core and recommended reading for students studying digital consumer behaviour, digital marketing, and marketing management. Accompanying online resources include PowerPoint slides and an instructor's manual.

Emmanuel Mogaji is an Associate Professor in Marketing at the Keele Business School, UK.

Digital Consumer Management

Understanding and Managing Consumer Engagement in the Digital Environment

Emmanuel Mogaji

Routledge
Taylor & Francis Group

LONDON AND NEW YORK

Designed cover image: Feodora Chiosea

First published 2024
by Routledge
4 Park Square, Milton Park, Abingdon, Oxon OX14 4RN

and by Routledge
605 Third Avenue, New York, NY 10158

Routledge is an imprint of the Taylor & Francis Group, an informa business

British Library Cataloguing-in-Publication Data

A catalogue record for this book is available from the British Library

Library of Congress Cataloging-in-Publication Data
Names: Mogaji, Emmanuel, author.
Title: Digital consumer management : understanding and managing consumer engagement in the digital environment / Emmanuel Mogaji.
Description: Abingdon, Oxon ; New York, NY : Routledge, 2024. | Includes bibliographical references and index. | Identifiers: LCCN 2023021336 (print) | LCCN 2023021337 (ebook) | ISBN 9781032486024 (paperback) | ISBN 9781032486031 (hardback) | ISBN 9781003389842 (ebook)
Subjects: LCSH: Information technology–Management. | Technological innovations–Management. | Industrial management–Data processing.
Classification: LCC HD30.2 .M63 2022 (print) | LCC HD30.2 (ebook) | DDC 658/.05–dc23/eng/20230630
LC record available at https://lccn.loc.gov/2023021336
LC ebook record available at https://lccn.loc.gov/2023021337

ISBN: 9781032486031 (hbk)
ISBN: 9781032486024 (pbk)
ISBN: 9781003389842 (ebk)

DOI: 10.4324/9781003389842

Typeset in Sabon
by Deanta Global Publishing Services, Chennai, India

Access the Support Material: www.routledge.com/9781032486024

Contents

Figures   vi
Preface   vii
Acknowledgements   x
The storyline   xi

1   Introduction to digital consumer management   1

2   The digital consumer   25

3   Engagement platform   45

4   Brands on platforms   65

5   Dominant platform developers   91

6   Third-party platform developers   121

7   Data analytics on digital platforms   139

8   Regulating digital consumption   161

9   Dark side of digital consumption   187

10 Contemporary issues of digital consumption   211

Index   233

Figures

1.1 The triad of digital consumption. 5
1.2 Demystifying digital consumption. 7
1.3 The conceptual framework for digital consumption. 11
3.1 The relationship between devices and platforms. 50
3.2 Graphic illustration of how a device can handle many platforms. 52
3.3 Data emerging from consumers' interaction with brands on digital platforms hosted by the devices and supported by the Internet. 55
5.1 Push notifications on a mobile phone. 94
8.1 The role of stakeholders in regulating digital consumption 180
9.1 The connections between the developers, brands, and consumers, their engagement on digital platforms, and the role of regulators in managing the dark side 206
10.1 The future aspirations and contemporary issues for developers, brands, and consumers as they engage on digital platform. 228

Preface

Digital Consumer Management: Understanding and Managing Consumer Engagement in the Digital Environment is a comprehensive guide for students—final year undergraduate and early postgraduate students, with relevant insights for start-up founders, and brand managers responsible for digital transformation.

The book begins with an introduction to digital consumer management, emphasising the importance of a clear approach to the topic. The subsequent chapters provide a multi-faceted approach to understanding digital consumers, their behaviour, and the challenges brands face in engaging with them. The role of digital platforms in facilitating digital consumption is also discussed, with a focus on their benefits for both consumers and brands. The book concludes with a discussion of brands' activities on digital platforms and the importance of investing in digital platforms to remain competitive and relevant.

The book offers strategic directions for brands, such as focusing on customer experience, leveraging data analytics and artificial intelligence, and collaborating with other brands and third-party providers. Overall, the book provides readers with a comprehensive understanding of how to effectively manage consumer engagement in the digital environment, including leveraging data and technology, providing a seamless omnichannel experience, and building trust and authenticity through transparent communication and social responsibility.

In this fast-paced environment, it can be difficult to navigate the ever-changing landscape and stay ahead of the curve. That's where this book comes in. Here are some unique approaches that I believe make the book different and very engaging while still offering much-needed theoretical and practical knowledge about understanding and managing consumer engagement in the digital environment.

Comprehensive coverage: The book offers a comprehensive exploration of managing consumer engagement in the digital environment, covering the basic concepts and unique features, and understanding digital consumers, digital platforms, and brand activities. This makes it an ideal resource for students, start-up founders, and brand managers responsible for digital transformation.

Unique approach: The book takes a differentiated approach to digital consumption and digital management, demystifying complex concepts and providing a comprehensive understanding of how to effectively manage consumer engagement in the digital environment. This approach is particularly valuable for those looking to gain a deeper understanding of the unique challenges and opportunities presented by digital technologies.

Practical insights: The book provides practical insights on how to effectively engage with digital consumers, optimise digital platforms, and enhance the overall digital consumption experience. The insights provided in the book can be applied to real-world scenarios, making it a valuable resource for anyone looking to improve their digital engagement strategies.

Current and up-to-date: The book is based on the latest research and trends in digital marketing and consumer behaviour, ensuring that readers have access to the most current and relevant information. This makes it an ideal resource for those looking to stay up-to-date on the latest developments in the field.

Accessible language: The book is written in an accessible language, making it easy for readers to understand complex concepts and apply them to real-world scenarios. This makes it an ideal resource for students, start-up founders, and brand managers who may not have a background in digital marketing or consumer behaviour.

Reflective questions: Throughout the book, reflective questions are included to help readers deepen their understanding of the material and apply it to their own situations. These questions encourage readers to consider their own digital consumption habits, the impact of digital platforms on their lives, and the role of technology in shaping consumer behaviour. By engaging with these reflective questions, readers will not only gain a deeper understanding of the topics discussed but also develop critical thinking skills that will be invaluable in navigating the ever-changing digital landscape.

The storyline: The book features a unique approach to understanding digital consumer behaviour and engagement through a captivating story. This story not only makes the book stand out, but it also helps students better comprehend the topic. By following the story, readers will gain a deep understanding of the complexities and nuances of digital consumer behaviour and engagement. This approach will make it easier for students to remember and apply the concepts covered in the book to real-world scenarios.

I believe that this book provides a valuable resource for anyone looking to improve their theoretical and practical knowledge about digital engagement strategies. By offering a comprehensive exploration of managing consumer engagement in the digital environment, providing practical insights, and taking a differentiated approach, I believe that readers will be able to gain a deeper understanding of the unique challenges and opportunities presented by digital technologies.

I sincerely hope that you will find this book to be a valuable resource that inspires you to take your digital engagement strategies to the next level. I believe that by implementing the insights and strategies discussed in this book, you will be better equipped to navigate the complex world of digital marketing and consumer behaviour, ultimately leading to increased success and growth for their brands and businesses.

Emmanuel Mogaji, PhD
Staffordshire, UK

Acknowledgements

I am humbled and grateful to express my deepest appreciation to God, who has blessed me with the gift of life, knowledge, and wisdom. Writing this book has been a challenging and rewarding journey, and I couldn't have done it without His grace and guidance.

I want to extend my heartfelt gratitude to my family for their unwavering love, support, and understanding throughout the writing process. They have been my rock, providing me with the necessary balance and perspective to navigate the ups and downs of this journey. Their unwavering belief in me has been a source of inspiration and motivation.

I also want to thank my students, particularly those on my Digital Consumer module, whose passion and curiosity have been instrumental in shaping this book. Your thoughtful questions and insightful feedback have challenged me to push beyond my limits and strive for clarity in my writing. You have reminded me of the profound impact that education can have on the lives of others, and for that, I am forever grateful.

I would also like to express my appreciation to my editor and publisher, who have been my partners in this endeavour. Their expertise, guidance, and patience have been invaluable in shaping this book into the best version of itself. Their unwavering support and belief in me have been a beacon of hope and motivation, and I cannot thank them enough.

Lastly, I want to acknowledge all those who have supported me in one way or another throughout this journey. Your encouragement, prayers, and belief in me have been a source of strength and inspiration, and I am forever grateful. Thank you all for being a part of this incredible journey.

The storyline

Friday night at the club

I have always tried to illustrate subject matters through stories; you might want to check my textbook on Brand Management through storytelling. Stories are an integral part of learning and retaining knowledge and from my teaching experience, I have come to realise that engaging with a storyline helps the students to properly contextualise the topic and keep them engaged for a long duration, so I hope you will follow me through this topic on understanding and managing consumer engagement in the digital environment as I share my story around the Friday night at the club.

I will be contextualising this module around a story which reflects on a typical Friday at the Night club and at various stages in the book, I will link you back to the story to understand the key stakeholders, their responsibility in managing consumers and the environment and platforms upon which these management occurs. Ultimately you should have a full grasp of this topic at the end of the teaching.

Humans like to enjoy themselves, and most young people go to club on Friday night. It's often a culture, at least in the Western world for people to gather in a place to start the weekend and have some fun. As you can imagine, there are many nightclubs on the high street, and every club owner wants the partygoers to come to their Club and enjoy their evening. The club owners recognise that when you have more people in the Club, the revellers will pay entrance fees and spend money on drinks and food. The numbers are essential for the club owners.

In like manners, you have VIP corners at the clubs, which are different from the main dancing area; they are a different and special place for individuals to bring their groups and enjoy. Even though it's still a separate place, they are still being served by the Club, still enjoying the music in the Club, and still feeling the environment at the Club. Even though they have their space in the Club, they are still expected to abide by the rule of the Club and make sure any illegal activities are not going on in their VIP area.

It is, however, essential to recognise that the onus is on the club owners to ensure the safety and security of everyone coming into the Club. The club owners need to install CCTV around the hall to have security at the door to check ID cards and remove anyone misbehaving. The club owner needs to put reasonable security measures to ensure that people are safe. Notably, the club owners need to ensure that illegal activities are not happening in the Club.

While people have come to enjoy themselves, it is imperative to understand that there will be some bad people who may have come to harm people. They may come with bad intentions like spiking drinks and touching people inappropriately. While the club owners may not be able to remove this risk altogether, they often try to reassure the revellers that they are safe, and revellers must see that they are safe, watching out for their drinks and the people in their company. You would expect revellers to report anyone misbehaving to the security team.

In situations where there is a continued problem in a club, the police being called often to disturbance, the government can step in to close down the Club. The government can withdraw their licence, and the Club won't be able to operate, and they lose their business. Losing the business may not only be caused by the government intervention but as poor services at the Club may also discourage people from coming back every Friday night. When the atmosphere is no longer getting exciting week after week, the DJ is not playing good music, and the drinks are no longer affordable, it will not be surprising to see that many people no longer come to the Club and go to another club down the road. The party revellers go to another club that appeals to their state.

This short story illustrates the concept of digital consumption on the digital platform. Here, we recognise the Club owner as the digital platform provider. They are the GAFAM - Google Apple, Facebook, Amazon and Microsoft of this world. They create platforms that bring consumers and brands together. They all stay on that high street of the Internet and invite people to come to their Club and enjoy themselves. They want people to download their apps, buy their devices, and subscribe to their services. They need the customers to remain within their ecosystem, making it difficult for an android user to migrate to an iPhone easily; they want everyone to write in Words, design presentations in PowerPoint, and present on Teams.

The party revellers are consumers going onto the platform to engage with other people and brands and enjoy themselves. It's a regular activity every Friday night, and you expect the customers to feel safe at the Club. The platform owners who own the Club are responsible for ensuring that the customers are safe. To ensure that no illegal activities are going on, to ensure that inappropriate behaviours are not tolerated, and anyone found doing this can be sent out of the Club – you can see what Twitter did to the former president of America.

Importantly the club owners and developers need to ensure that an underaged person does not come into the Club. The security team at the Night club has the right to check people's ID cards to be sure they are of the right age. Depending on the type of Club, there are different age limits. This measure is why social media platforms must have an age limit for opening an account. Some adult content websites and alcoholic brands will ask your age before accessing their websites. It is, however, imperative to be aware that people can fake their ID cards to enter the Club, and likewise, people can put the wrong date of birth to access a website. While that's the customer's choice to get exposed to such content, the platform developers have put those measures in place as a guide and to protect the customers.

The VIP areas are like brand pages on different social media pages, where they are curating their content on the platforms created by the clubs. You see Brand XYZ having a Facebook page, and you see Brand ABC inviting you to follow them on Instagram or download their apps on the Play Store. That's the VIP area on digital platforms. The brands are allowed to invite people to their area, and people can leave the area if they have had enough fun. The staff at the Club are serving the brands, and that's why the brands can get insight and analytics about how well people are engaging on their brand pages. It is also important to reiterate that the brand needs to abide by the rule of the platform provider. If a brand doesn't act appropriately, the platform owner can remove them.

The dark sides of digital consumption are why people may not want to engage on digital platforms. For example, the wrong people coming to clubs to spike people's drink and touch people inappropriately presents a dark side that may discourage many people from going to the Club. These people causing problems are there to have fun; they are consumers and revellers but with a hidden agenda to cause harm. It is therefore crucial for the brands to know these dark sides, the platform developers (club owners) making an effort to remove the dark sides and threats, and likewise, you would expect consumers, like the (party revellers) to be mindful of their environment, not leave their drink unattended, and make sure that they don't share their details with anyone online.

Spiking drinks is not the only dark side of partying, but the lack of inclusive design is also a dark side that needs to be considered. Imagine this Club is on the first floor, which is only accessible through a flight of stairs, and there is no lift or escalator; many people with a physical disability who requires mobility assistance in a wheelchair may not be able to access the Club; instead, they will go to a club with ramps or lift. Likewise, many people are neurodivergent, and flashing lights impact them; their needs could also be accommodated in the Club through inclusive design. Therefore, this puts the onus on the platform developers to ensure an inclusive design for everyone; the developer is expected to provide equitable access to ensure everyone can access the platforms irrespective of their ability. This means the self-service kiosk at McDonald's needs to be at a level accessible for someone in a wheelchair; if not, they might not come back.

Many people may try to avoid these dark sides and have their party at home. This is when you have brands creating their digital platform. Why have a website on Shopify or Etsy when you can design your e-commerce website from scratch? Many brands will feel the need to have their own party in their house (and not at the Club) because they think they can control the atmosphere and manage things. They could also be losing from enjoying more significant numbers of revellers, security measures, and the atmosphere. Notwithstanding the approach, the most important thing is having a platform to bring consumers and brands to engage.

The government is always involved in regulating these platforms to ensure that everyone engaging in it is safe and enjoying themselves. You cannot just open a nightclub without getting the correct license and authority from the government. There are many laws and regulations that the platform developers need to be aware of and abide by to operate in the country. Like the club illustration, each Club is given a licence and permission to operate, and once these regulations are violated, their licence is withdrawn and no longer allowed to operate. The fact that you have your party in your house doesn't mean you are exempted from the regulatory expectation of the government. That means that brands having their digital platform still have some responsibilities to ensure that everyone is safe. The neighbour can complain about loud noise coming from your house every Friday night because you are having a party. Brands must be responsible for the platforms and engagement.

Digital consumption is a process that recognises different stakeholders. It is important for students and prospective managers to understand this consumption and how best to manage it, especially on digital platforms. Significantly, we recognise the role of the developers to create a party dancing hall that is safe and accessible for people. Brands want to engage, and they come to this platform as well. Keeping everyone happy and staying on the platform is the ultimate goal of digital consumption. However, it is essential to recognise that people may choose to get involved in digital consumption to detox and remove themselves from digital platforms, just as you can decide to leave a club anytime when you are no longer having fun.

So, in summary

- Chapter 1—Introduction to Digital Consumer Management introduces you to the whole concept of the club story—the club owners (platform developers), those at the VIP section inviting other revellers (the brands) and the revellers enjoying themselves on the dancefloor (the consumers). The dancefloor is the digital platform where the fun is happening.
- Chapter 2—The Digital Consumer reflects on the revellers coming to the nightclub to enjoy themselves, you want to understand who these people are, the type of music they like, the type of drink they like, and how they want to enjoy themselves.
- Chapter 3—Engagement Platform refers to the nightclub, where the activities are happening. This is the place where other revellers meet themselves, where the brands come to use the VIP section, and where the club owners take care of everyone.
- Chapter 4—Brands on Platforms refers to the brand having their VIP at the club, they could host the party in their boardroom but because they want to engage with consumers and other people, they have to come out to the club.
- Chapter 5—Dominant Platform Developers are the club owners who have invested in building the clubhouse, they have invested in the lighting, sound systems, and security, to make sure that everyone coming to the club—the brands (VIPs) and consumers (revellers) are safe and enjoying themselves.
- Chapter 6—Third-Party Platform Developers are those aspiring to have their nightclub in the downtown or high street, they want to be big but not yet, notwithstanding, they are able to bring the party to your house, and they can organise a party bus, bring DJ to your party, and make it fun, albeit on a small basis.
- Chapter 7—Data Analytics on Digital Platforms refers to the information the brands and club owners have collected about their visitors. The VIPs can observe if a customer likes a particular drink, and they can tell the bartender to give them the drink. The club owners (platform developers) know how often people come to their club and put measures in place to manage the demands.

- Chapter 8—Regulating Digital Consumption highlights the role of the government to make sure everyone having a club has the right permission to do that, and the government makes sure that the club owners have the right security in place to ensure people are safe.
- Chapter 9—Dark Side of Digital Consumption makes you recognise that bad things can happen in a club, the fact that everyone is coming to enjoy themselves doesn't mean that bad things can't happen. Drinks can be spiked, people can be touched inappropriately, and the club owners (platform developers) need to make sure that these bad people are removed from the club.
- Chapter 10—Contemporary Issues of Digital Consumption brings a closing summary to the club story. As we grow older, we may be losing interest in clubbing, choosing to spend time with the children; also with the metaverse, we might be clubbing in the metaverse wearing our headsets, and it is therefore imperative to recognise what lies ahead.

The story's context around the Friday night at the club is a way I have developed to contextualise the topic of consumer engagement in the digital environment. The analogy of the nightclub as a digital platform provider, and the party revellers as consumers engaging with brands, is offered as a creative way to explain the concept. The story also touches on the responsibility of platform owners to ensure the safety and security of their customers, similar to how club owners have to ensure the safety of their revellers.

Consider this story emphasising the importance of storytelling as a tool for learning and retaining knowledge. By contextualising the topic of understanding and managing consumer engagement in the digital environment around a story, you can better understand the key stakeholders, their responsibilities, and the platforms on which this management occurs. Overall, the story highlights the importance of engaging with a storyline to contextualise complex topics and keep you engaged throughout the learning process.

Introduction to digital consumer management

1.1 Background

It's great to hear that we are embarking on a journey to explore understanding and managing consumer engagement in the digital environment. The book's first chapter is an essential foundation for the rest of the book, as it introduces readers to the book's basic concepts and unique features. Managing consumer engagement in the digital environment is an increasingly important topic as digital technologies continue shaping how consumers interact with brands and make purchasing decisions. However, as you can see, this topic can be easily confused with other marketing and transformation management areas. Therefore, it is essential to clearly define and differentiate the approach taken in this book, which aims to demystify digital consumption and digital management and provide a comprehensive understanding of how to manage consumer engagement in the digital environment effectively. This clarification will help readers manage their expectations and gain a deeper understanding of digital technologies' unique challenges and opportunities. Overall, the book's first chapter sets the stage for an in-depth exploration of managing consumer engagement in the digital environment and highlights the importance of a clear and differentiated approach to this topic.

1.2 Learning outcomes

By the end of this chapter, you should be able to:

- Demonstrate a systematic understanding of digital consumers and consumption from theoretical and practical perspectives.
- Evaluate the triad of digital consumption and evaluate their working relationship on the digital platform.
- Synthesise and clarify various concepts related to digital consumption and demonstrate a comprehensive understanding of this complex and rapidly evolving topic.

DOI: 10.4324/9781003389842-1

- Critically evaluate the conceptual positioning of digital consumption and the key stakeholders.
- Demonstrate understanding of the underlying theories and concepts explaining consumer behaviour and their application across different platforms.

1.3 Introduction

The world of digital consumption is rapidly evolving and changing how consumers behave. With the widespread use of technology and the Internet, consumers are no longer limited by physical boundaries and have access to an endless supply of information and products at their fingertips. As a result, the way consumers interact with brands, make purchasing decisions, and seek out information has drastically shifted. To succeed in this new digital landscape, businesses must understand and adapt to these changes in consumer behaviour. This adaptation requires a deep understanding of how consumers engage with brands online and the tools and strategies to manage these interactions effectively.

With rapid technological advancements, digital consumption and consumer behaviour have significantly changed in recent years (Sheth, 2020). The emergence of new technologies such as the Internet of Things (IoT), artificial intelligence (AI), and virtual reality (VR) has revolutionised the way consumers interact with brands and products (Dwivedi et al., 2022). The proliferation of social media platforms and mobile devices has also increased consumer engagement, creating new opportunities for businesses to connect with their target audience. As a result, companies and marketers must understand and adapt to the evolving digital landscape to effectively engage with consumers and stay competitive in the market (Oosthuizen et al., 2021).

Though the book highlights the challenges and opportunities that businesses face when trying to engage with their customers in a digital landscape, offering practical insights into how companies can adapt and leverage digital platforms to create effective strategies that drive customer engagement, loyalty, and ultimately, business success, this chapter serves as an introduction to digital consumption and digital consumer, highlighting how effective digital consumer management is critical for businesses to succeed in today's digital landscape, as it allows them to adapt to evolving consumer behaviours and preferences while staying competitive in the marketplace. The chapter also emphasises the different stakeholders shaping the digital consumption ecosystem. Whether you are a student, business professional, or simply interested in the digital world, this book provides valuable insights and practical strategies for successfully navigating the digital environment.

1.4 Who is the target audience?

When writing this textbook, a specific target audience is in mind, those that would benefit from engaging with the text. It is essential to recognise that many books target different groups, but I want to clarify this from the beginning as a form of responsibility and co-creating knowledge. I expect you to take responsibility for your learning and prepare for your future career. Reading and studying this book is not enough, but recognise there are huge expectations from you—what would you do differently after completing this book?

1.4.1 Student

The book (and the module) is designed to cater to the learning needs of final-year undergraduate students and early postgraduate students in business schools. These students are typically seeking a deeper understanding of theoretical concepts related to business and management (Chattopadhyay et al., 2022). The book aims to provide them with the necessary knowledge and insights to develop their skills and competencies in this field. The content is structured in a way that is easy to follow and comprehend, making it an ideal resource for students seeking knowledge and understanding. The book covers a range of topics relevant to the business world, including strategic management, digital marketing, project management, and innovative design. By reading this book, students will gain a solid foundation in these core business areas, benefiting their future academic and professional pursuits—those ready to act and implement what they are being taught. Students move beyond just acquiring theoretical understanding and will begin recognising practical implications of their knowledge in business and digital transformation. Ultimately you want to pass your exams and get a good grade, so I expect you to be involved in reading the book, addressing the reflective questions, and providing thought-provoking questions. It would help if you looked at how to transfer this acquired knowledge to getting a job or starting your company.

1.4.2 Start-ups

As a student, it's never too early to start developing your entrepreneurial skills and exploring the possibility of starting your own business or creating innovations for the market. One of the first steps in this process is to consider whether there is a market space for your invention. With the growing number of people online, there is no doubt that there will be a need for more platforms and digital transformation for consumer engagement in the digital environment. This presents an excellent opportunity for aspiring entrepreneurs to create something new and valuable that can capture a share of this growing market. By focusing on the needs and preferences of today's digital consumers, you can develop innovative solutions that will help you stand out in the crowded marketplace. With determination and a willingness to take risks, you can turn your entrepreneurial dreams into a reality and positively impact the world of business. The number of people using Facebook is decreasing; what other alternative is on the horizon? We are very used to Zoom and Teams. Are there possible alternatives? You want to understand consumers' engagement with technology through this book, understand consumers' pain points and develop an innovative idea. When developing new ideas for business or innovation, it's important to remember that it doesn't have to be perfect from the outset. The most important thing is to be aware of consumers' needs and a desire to address those needs through technology (Dhruv et al., 2020). With this mindset, you can explore potential solutions and ideas that have the potential to make a difference in people's lives. It's essential to approach the process with an open mind and a willingness to experiment and iterate as you go along. This approach means taking risks, trying new approaches, and learning from successes and failures. With persistence and a focus on meeting the needs of your target audience, you can develop innovative solutions that have the potential to create real value in the marketplace. So, don't let the fear of imperfection hold you back from pursuing your entrepreneurial aspirations—instead, embrace the process and the learning opportunities that come with it.

1.4.3 Staff

Not everyone may want to start their own company or develop an app, but there are still plenty of opportunities to work in a business setting and contribute to the digital transformation of companies (Mogaji et al., 2022). A range of roles is available, including business analysts, business managers, and digital marketing executives. Whether employed directly by a company or as a freelancer or agency staff on a specific project, you must have the skills and knowledge necessary to engage with consumers and develop effective digital strategies. This career path requires carrying out research better to understand the needs and preferences of different customer groups and being able to ask the right questions when presenting your findings to stakeholders. Additionally, it's crucial to develop strategies tailored to the specific needs of the company and its customers (Hoyer et al., 2020). By staying up to date with the latest trends and developments in the digital world, you can help companies stay competitive and effectively engage with their customers in today's fast-paced digital environment. Your job will be to meet customers with a personalised offer at their preferred touchpoints, so you need to understand the customers and provide the needed recommendations for your boss. As a staff member responsible for selling a company's product online or managing its digital platforms, you will engage with customers and provide them with personalised offers and recommendations at their preferred touchpoints. To succeed in this role, you will need to have a deep understanding of your customers and their needs and the ability to gather and analyse data to inform your recommendations. This effort in gathering information may involve conducting market research, monitoring customer feedback and reviews, and tracking customer behaviours and preferences. By staying attuned to your customers and their evolving needs, you can identify new engagement opportunities and develop strategies tailored to their specific tastes and interests. This approach will help you drive sales and revenue for your company and also help build strong, long-lasting relationships with your customers. Ultimately, the key to success in this role is being able to anticipate and meet your customers' needs in a personalised, relevant, and engaging way.

> **Reflective questions**
>
> **Which of these target audiences do you belong to? Are you just here for the grades or looking at opportunities to develop digital platforms for consumer engagement?**

1.5 The triad of digital consumption

Digital consumption is not done in isolation, digital consumers rely on different stakeholders within the digital ecosystem to enjoy interacting on the digital platform (Morgan-Thomas et al., 2020). Imagine you are invited to a dinner—you are invited to come and consume some food; the food has to be prepared and presented on the table for you, meaning you can't consume it unless the food has been presented, and likewise, your host will be disappointed after presenting a three-course meal, and you choose not to consume the food. In digital consumption, the brands (the host who invited you to dinner) have presented the food (engagement with digital technologies) with the support of the chef (the tech developers) with the anticipation that you (the digital consumer) will enjoy the food. You should now be getting an understanding of the three stakeholders, consumers, brands, and tech companies who make the triad of digital consumption. This term can help encapsulate these three groups' interdependence and their importance in driving digital consumption forward.

As illustrated in Figure 1.1, the combination of consumers, brands, and platform developers (tech companies) can be described as the three primary stakeholders essential for digital consumption's success.

- **Consumers:** Consumers are the end-users of digital products and services; they are the digital consumer who is the primary driving force behind the demand for digital consumption. Their preferences, behaviour, and feedback are essential for brands and tech companies to understand, as they help shape the development of new digital products and services.
- **Brands:** Brands are companies that offer products or services, and they play a critical role in digital consumption by providing platforms that meet the needs and preferences of consumers. Brands must stay on top of digital trends and technologies to remain competitive and establish a strong online presence and reputation to attract and retain digital consumers.

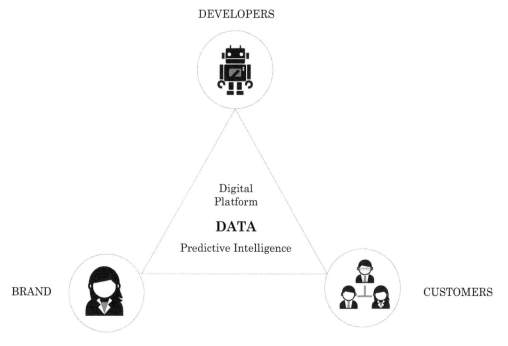

Figure 1.1 The triad of digital consumption.

- **Platform developers:** These developers can also be referred to as tech companies designing, developing, and providing digital technologies and platforms that enable consumers and brands to connect and engage with each other. They are responsible for developing the infrastructure, tools, and systems to allow digital consumption, such as social media platforms, e-commerce sites, and mobile apps.

These three stakeholders create a digital ecosystem that is constantly evolving and adapting to consumer needs and preferences. By working together, they can leverage technology to develop new and innovative digital products and services that enhance the overall consumer experience. To ensure the success of digital consumption, consumers, brands, and tech companies need to work together cohesively. Each group's interests and needs must be considered, and there must be mutual understanding and trust between them.

Consumers must be interested in the digital platforms that brands provide, as this drives demand for digital products and services (Kopalle et al., 2020). At the same time, brands must be confident that their digital offerings will meet consumers' needs and preferences and help them achieve their business objectives. Tech companies must also play a critical role in ensuring the success of digital consumption by developing and providing innovative and reliable digital platforms and technologies. They must be responsive to the needs of both consumers and brands and be willing to work collaboratively with them to improve and refine their offerings.

Cohesion and collaboration between consumers, brands, and tech companies are crucial to guarantee the success of digital consumption (Kandampully et al., 2022). Each group must work together in a mutually beneficial way to ensure that digital products and services meet the needs and expectations of all stakeholders involved. In a subsequent section, we will discuss these three stakeholders in much more detail.

We have to recognise the role of regulators in the digital consumption ecosystem. They are a crucial part of the digital consumption triad or trilogy, alongside consumers, brands, and tech companies. They help ensure that the ecosystem operates in a way that benefits everyone involved. They have an overarching responsibility. The regulators are responsible for ensuring that the interests of all stakeholders are protected and that digital technologies and platforms are used safely and responsibly (Jelovac et al., 2022). Regulators may enforce laws and regulations that protect consumer privacy, prevent fraud, and promote fair market competition. Regulators may encourage the development of new digital technologies and platforms by incentivising companies and individuals working on innovative solutions. Regulators may monitor the practices of tech companies and brands to ensure they comply with relevant laws and regulations. Regulators may bring together stakeholders from different sectors to discuss issues related to digital consumption and work collaboratively to find solutions. They also facilitate public consultations and other forms of engagement to ensure that the views of all stakeholders are considered (Flew et al., 2019). The regulators are discussed in more detail in Chapter 8.

1.6 Demystify digital consumption

Following the discussion about the target audience, it is essential to demystify digital consumption and management. Suppose you think this is about data analytics or digital marketing. In that case, you may have had similar modules and come with specific

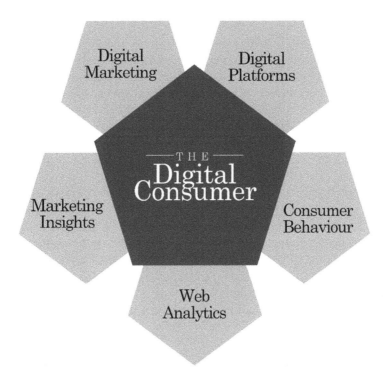

Figure 1.2 Demystifying digital consumption.

knowledge, but it is essential to manage your expectations as we move on in this book. Figure 1.2 shows the connection between digital consumption and digital management across different strands of marketing concepts, and this section discusses these strands. Demystifying digital consumption involves understanding how consumers engage with digital content, products, and services. It is a complex process that involves several key concepts that are related but distinct, including consumer behaviour, digital marketing, digital platforms, web analytics, and marketing insights.

Consumer engagement in the digital environment is the core of this book. It is described as digital consumption—where consumers engage on digital platforms and consumer information, engaging in transactions and other business activities. Digital consumption is seen here as a verb; it's a process we do regularly. You may be reading the PDF version of this book on your platform, watching a YouTube channel, or ordering a ride from Uber. You are making digital consumption on different digital platforms, and it is essential for managers of these platforms (Routledge the publishers who made the book available in PDF, YouTube for the video, and Uber providing the ride) to understand how you engage on their platform and how they can effectively manage that engagement you are having.

This digital consumption, the analytics, and tracking present an overlap for digital consumption management, and this section aims to address those overlaps. Precisely, digital consumption management cuts across these five sections; it has a significant connection, but yet digital consumption is still different. You have set expectations, but it is essential to demystify digital consumers (as subject, module, and consumer group).

1.6.1 Consumer behaviour

Digital consumer (the individual, noun) and digital consumption (the process, the verb) differ from the study of consumer behaviour. The digital bits of this consumption—using a digital platform completely changes the narrative of traditional consumer behaviour (Abdulquadri et al., 2021). Digital consumers use digital technologies and platforms to consume products and services. They are the end-users of digital technologies and platforms, and their behaviour is shaped by a wide range of factors, including their demographics, psychographics, preferences, and habits. While a large body of academic research has explored consumer behaviour, it is imperative to recognise that digital consumers exhibit different behaviour when they are online. Their access to digital platforms presents a different perspective for brands to explore. Digital consumers can easily search for information about products and services, compare prices and features, read reviews and ratings, and access a wealth of information about brands and products. This experience can lead to more informed decision-making and active engagement with brands and products. While some consumer behaviour principles apply to digital consumers, it's essential for brands, tech companies, and regulators to understand the unique aspects of digital consumption and tailor their strategies accordingly to engage with and serve digital consumers effectively (Hoyer et al., 2020).

1.6.2 Digital marketing

Digital marketing is also a common topic that can be confused with digital consumers and digital management. No doubt companies need to understand the customers before developing marketing strategies, and this understanding involves engaging with digital consumers within the digital ecosystem, but the digital consumer experience is more than just digital marketing (Chylinski et al., 2020). Managers must recognise that understanding the consumers' experiences, motivation, and challenges may be more important than just sending them an advert. The banks may keep sending an advert to a person online and need to recognise that the customers have had a bad experience with the staff in store. It's not just about advertising but about recognising the holistic. While digital marketing is a way for businesses and brands to reach and engage with digital consumers, digital consumption is the actual behaviour of those consumers as they interact with digital platforms and technologies. Digital marketing is a tool used to influence digital consumption behaviour, but it only partially encompasses the broad range of activities and behaviours that fall under the umbrella of digital consumption. Digital marketing and digital consumption are interrelated concepts important for businesses, brands, and consumers in the digital age. Understanding the differences between them can help companies and marketers better target and engage with digital consumers while delivering content and experiences that meet their needs and preferences.

1.6.3 Digital platforms

The digital platform, in this case, could mean the website, mobile app, or social media, but it is important to note that digital consumption is more than just the platform (Hein et al., 2020). Imagine going online to hire a car for your interview on Monday, and you paid for the car on the website because it said it was available; Sunday night, the website (the platform) sent you an email reminding you of the car you hire for tomorrow morning, so we can say the platform is doing well, but on getting to the hiring company, they told you there is no car, they said they could not process your order because their website was not updated to reflect the available vehicle, you ended up missing the interview because there was no car. Even though the platform worked—found a car, paid for the car, and got a reminder, the overall digital consumption has been flawed, you may not trust the company and next time, you may choose NOT to book online (no more digital consumption) but instead go to the physical address of the company, talk to someone face to face and hire a car physically. While digital platforms facilitate digital consumption, digital consumption is the actual behaviour of consumers as they engage with digital platforms and technologies. Digital platforms provide a framework for digital consumption but do not fully encompass the broad range of activities and behaviours that fall under the umbrella of digital consumption. Their experience and features as a consumer group are beyond the platform upon which they operate, and this understanding is essential for managers.

1.6.4 Web analytics

Web analytics refers to the measurement, collection, analysis, and reporting of data about the behaviour of website visitors or digital platform users. This analytics includes tracking metrics such as page views, time spent on site, bounce rates, click-through rates, conversion rates, and other user engagement metrics (more on Chapter 7 Data Analytics on Digital Platforms). Web analytics is used to evaluate the effectiveness of digital marketing strategies, identify user needs and preferences, and optimise the performance of digital platforms. Digital consumption on the digital platform allows for data generation, which managers can use to monitor and manage digital consumers, but it is imperative to recognise that understanding and managing digital consumers is more than just analysing data coming through the websites. Though websites are an integral part of digital consumption, there are many more platforms out there for digital consumers to engage and therefore managers must be aware of these options and look at more holistic data analytics. Digital consumption is not all about online purchases on websites and e-commerce; it encompasses many other forms of engagement that require digital platforms and Internet access. While web analytics provides insights into user behaviour on digital platforms, digital consumption is the actual behaviour of consumers as they engage with digital content, products, and services. Web analytics is a tool used to measure and understand digital consumption behaviour (Ponzoa & Erdmann, 2021), but it only partially encompasses the broad range of activities and behaviours that fall under the umbrella of digital consumption.

1.6.5 Marketing insights

Moving on from web analytics, marketing insights is another related concept that should be distinct from digital consumer management. Marketing insight refers to the information and data businesses and marketers use to understand their target audience, consumer behaviour, and market trends. Marketing insight can be gathered through various means, such as market research, customer surveys, social media monitoring, and data analytics. This information is then used to develop marketing strategies, create targeted campaigns, and make data-driven decisions (Olson et al., 2021). Though customers and companies are becoming interconnected, understanding digital consumers is for more than companies that need marketing insights; some other companies and organisations would want to know how people engage with their platforms. Think of the university that has installed a new attendance tracking system in the classroom; they need insight from the students and may not be marketing insights as a company wants to know how many people are using contactless payment in their stores. Beyond companies looking to sell, there are government organisations, policymakers, and no charity organisations also interested in digital consumer behaviours. Things need to be monitored and may be not just for marketing purposes. Managers need to understand that digital consumers are beyond just being a target market. While marketing insight provides insights into consumer behaviour and preferences, digital consumption is the actual behaviour of consumers as they engage with digital content, products, and services. Marketing insight is used to inform and optimise digital marketing strategies to better target and engage with digital consumers, but it only partially encompasses the broad range of activities and behaviours that fall under the umbrella of digital consumption.

Demystifying digital consumption involves understanding how these concepts are related and how they can be leveraged to create compelling digital marketing strategies and deliver engaging digital experiences to consumers. Managers are expected to have a holistic understanding of this concept as it requires businesses and marketers to stay up-to-date with the latest trends and technologies while also using data and insights to make data-driven decisions and improve the performance of their digital platforms and marketing efforts.

1.7 The conceptual positioning of digital consumption

It is imperative to set the grounds clear about the conceptual position of digital consumption, as this conceptualisation is essential for you to have a holistic understanding of the things discussed in this book. The conceptual positioning of digital consumption involves understanding the key elements that make up the concept of digital consumption and how they relate. There are reoccurring stakeholders that you need to be mindful of, different concepts that you need to understand, and some keywords that will often appear in the book. Ultimately this is about you taking the role of manager to understand your connections with the digital consumers, the values of your brand or organisation and the developers providing these platforms.

Figure 1.3 presents a graphical illustration of digital consumption, highlighting the evolving nature of the developers, businesses, and regulators while the consumers are in between being supported by the tech developers. The evolving nature of developers, companies, and regulators in the digital space is a crucial aspect of digital consumption. Developers are constantly working to create new and innovative digital platforms and tools that can meet the needs and preferences of consumers. On the other hand, businesses are focused on leveraging these digital platforms and tools to reach consumers, build brand awareness, and drive sales. The figure also highlights the dark side of digital consumption, lurking behind the scenes and waiting to cause havoc. Managers must be aware of these dark sides and implement measures to address them.

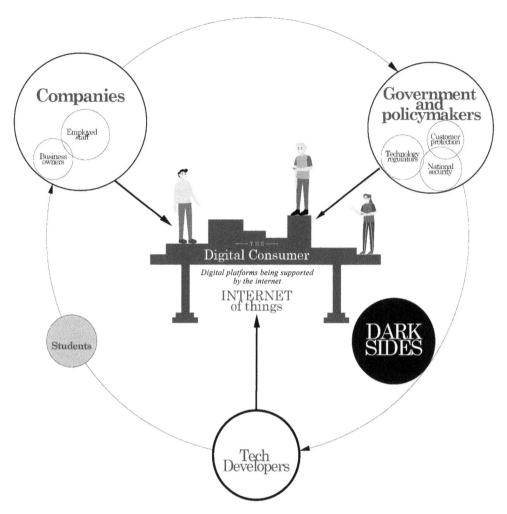

Figure 1.3 The conceptual framework for digital consumption.

1.7.1 The digital consumer

These individuals engage with digital technologies to enhance their work, leisure, and all life-around experiences (Sağkaya Güngö & Ozansoy Çadırcı, 2022). They are shopping online, attending online classes, using Automatic Number Plate Recognition (ANPR) to pay for car parking, conduct operations across different locations using robotics and the Internet. Digital consumers are in the middle of all these changes and developments. They are the ultimate beneficiaries of digital consumption, as they can access a wide range of digital content, products, and services that meet their needs and preferences. Digital consumers are often very demanding and have high expectations regarding the products and services they consume. They can access a wealth of information and quickly research and compare different products and services before purchasing. As a result, they can be quite picky and selective about the brands and products they engage with. These individuals are discussed in more detail in Chapter 2. The digital consumer population is highly diverse and heterogeneous, with variations in age, gender, education level, and experience.

This means that businesses and developers need to be aware of these differences and tailor their digital offerings to meet different consumer groups' unique needs and preferences (Dhruv et al., 2020). For example, younger digital consumers may be more tech-savvy and interested in cutting-edge technologies, while older digital consumers may be more concerned with ease of use and reliability. Similarly, male and female digital consumers may have different preferences regarding digital products and services, and consumers with different levels of education may have varying levels of digital literacy. Digital consumers are essential for brands and tech companies as the consumers generate data which can be used to inform business decisions. Managers must understand these digital consumers and adapt their strategies accordingly. This understanding may involve customising the user interface and user experience to meet the needs and preferences of specific consumer groups and developing targeted marketing campaigns and messaging that resonate with different segments of the digital consumer population.

1.7.2 The unlevelled platform

Figure 1 illustrates the uneven platform upon which digital consumers stand, illustrating that digital consumption only happens on a level platform; digital consumers have different experiences and operate on different platforms, depending on their unique needs and preferences. For example, consumers with disabilities may require specialised digital platforms that accommodate their specific accessibility needs. In contrast, other consumers may prefer platforms with a more user-friendly interface or a more comprehensive range of features and functionalities. It's essential for businesses and developers to recognise that different consumer groups may have different preferences regarding digital platforms and adapt their strategies accordingly. This may involve offering a range of different digital platforms that cater to user needs and preferences or customising existing platforms to suit the needs of specific consumer groups better (Mogaji et al., 2020). Your grandmother using WhatsApp is a digital consumer. Likewise, your niece who is using YouTube Kids. The digital platform is different for everyone. Many people will prefer to use Zoom because they find it easier to use compared to Microsoft Teams. Digital platform varies depending on the brand, the developers, the consumers, and even the regulator (see the triad of digital consumption). It is not surprising that digital platforms are not allowed in some countries. The book introduced the PESCO platform (see Chapter 4), reiterating the variety of platforms available for brands to use to engage with their digital consumers. Managers need to manage their expectations when engaging with consumers, to recognise that there are different levels of interest, abilities, and even regulatory requirements. By prioritising accessibility, inclusivity, and customisation in their digital offerings, businesses and developers can create more engaging and effective digital experiences that meet the needs and preferences of a broader range of consumers.

1.7.3 The Internet of Things (IoT)

We would not be having digital consumption if there was no Internet. As discussed in Chapter 4, the difference between a device and a platform is the Internet. You can have a mobile phone (a device) which you may use as a calculator if you don't have the

Internet to access Twitter (platform). The Internet has become an integral part of our everyday lives, and its usage continues to grow rapidly. According to Datareportal, as of January 2022, there were 4.9 billion active Internet users worldwide, representing approximately 63% of the global population. We see an organisation, transport hubs, and retail centres offering free Internet access, and many telecommunications mobile contracts now offering unlimited data on mobile contracts; you can see the growing prospects of carrying out surgical operations via robots connected to the Internet. Internet of Things (IoT) can transform many aspects of our lives—IoT-enabled devices such as smart thermostats, lighting systems, and security cameras allow homeowners to control and automate various aspects of their homes remotely, making their lives more convenient and energy-efficient. IoT-enabled wearables such as fitness trackers and smartwatches can collect data on a person's health metrics, such as heart rate and sleep patterns, and provide valuable insights to help them stay healthy and active. IoT-enabled cars can collect data on driving patterns, engine performance, and other metrics and use this data to improve fuel efficiency, safety, and maintenance. IoT technologies can create connected, intelligent cities that optimise transportation, energy usage, and other public services, making urban living more sustainable and efficient.

While IoT devices and platforms offer numerous benefits and opportunities for consumers, many people worldwide still need affordable and reliable Internet access, particularly in developing countries. The lack of Internet access creates a significant barrier to digital consumption, as it limits the ability of consumers to access and use IoT-enabled devices and services. This digital divide can have far-reaching consequences, from limiting economic opportunities and access to education to exacerbating social inequalities. As the IoT evolves, developers, policymakers, and other stakeholders must work together to address these challenges and ensure that digital consumption opportunities are accessible to all. This could involve expanding Internet infrastructure, providing education and awareness campaigns to consumers, and developing robust data privacy and security frameworks to protect consumers' rights and interests.

1.7.4 The tech developers

Tech developers are companies designing and developing platforms that support digital consumption. While it's not wrong to think of the big tech companies like Google (Alphabet), Amazon, Facebook (Meta), Apple, and Microsoft (GAFAM), there are many other companies out there making different innovations to support digital consumption—making automate self-driving electric cars, creating apps that connect people, and developing an e-commerce website. The tech developers are discussed in Chapters 5 and 6 as Platform developers, which may include the established platform developers and other third-party developers like freelancers, agencies, and boutique developers. Tech companies are crucial in providing the platform or infrastructure that enables brands to engage with their customers. They may offer various services, from developing custom solutions to providing ready-made platforms for brands to build their digital presence. In some cases, brands may work directly with tech companies to build their bespoke platform or application, while in other cases, they may use third-party developers or software solutions (Mogaji et al., 2020). Ultimately, the success of a brand's digital strategy depends on its ability to leverage technology to create engaging and personalised experiences for customers while also ensuring that their data is secure and protected.

1.7.5 The companies

Brands, organisations, and companies are increasingly turning to digital platforms to enhance their engagement with consumers. With the rise of digital technology and the ubiquity of the Internet, consumers are increasingly looking for brands that can offer seamless and personalised experiences across multiple touchpoints, including websites, social media, mobile apps, and other digital channels. As a result, businesses need to align their brand values with the ongoing trends of technology and adapt to their customers' changing needs and expectations to remain relevant and competitive in the digital marketplace (Agbo et al., 2020). This requires a deep understanding of consumer behaviour and a willingness to invest in developing innovative digital solutions that can help brands connect with customers in meaningful and impactful ways. The brands are discussed better in Chapter 4, which recognises the need to reach out to platform developers to create their platforms; for many brands that cannot afford owned platforms, they can use paid or shared platforms (see more on different types of the platform in Chapter 4). Managers working with companies need to evaluate their financial, human, and technical resources before adopting a platform for their consumer engagement strategy. For employed staff, they may present their business needs for their managers to address, but as a business owner, they would be expected to have a different approach—to bootstrap, start small, maybe from a paid media like Shopify, before migrating into their own owned media.

1.7.6 The government policies

The government and policymakers play a crucial role in shaping digital consumption by enacting regulations and policies that ensure the safety and privacy of digital consumers. For instance, governments may establish data protection laws that regulate how companies collect, store, and use personal data. They may also create policies that ensure Internet access and digital infrastructure is available and affordable to all citizens, especially those in underserved areas. Additionally, governments may engage in public awareness campaigns to educate citizens on staying safe using digital platforms and provide resources for reporting and addressing online threats and abuses. Ultimately, the government's role in digital consumption is balancing the need for innovation and economic growth with protecting citizens' rights and safety. Chapter 8 discusses regulating digital consumption. Seeing many governments blocking digital platforms operating in their countries is unsurprising. Many regulations (including GDPR) are being enforced to protect consumers as they engage on the platform. Although tech companies often advocate for self-regulation, the lingering doubts about its actual effectiveness are evident. The potential for malfunctions and the associated risks of harm are significant factors to consider. It becomes crucial for the government to step in, assuming responsibility and enforcing regulations that are both practical and enforceable, in order to ensure the safety and integrity of the technology landscape—as seen with OFCOM in the UK given new power as part of the Online Safety Bill, to regulate digital consumption. Managers must be aware of the regulations and laws governing digital consumption in their respective countries to avoid legal issues or penalties. Adhering to these regulations is not only a legal requirement but also ensures that the company is acting ethically and responsibly towards its digital consumers. This adherence will build trust and credibility with the consumers, increasing brand loyalty and customer satisfaction.

1.7.7 The dark sides

Despite the enormous benefits of these digital platforms, stakeholders must recognise the inherent dark sides of digital consumption (Mogaji & Nguyen, 2022). As illustrated in the figure, the dark side is present within the ecosystem—the tech developers working on the good can also be working on the wrong things. The dark side highlights anything that will discourage people from using digital platforms. This dark side could range from cyberbullying to harassment and misinformation. As technology advances and becomes more sophisticated, the potential for negative consequences such as cybercrime, data breaches, and online harassment also increases. Tech companies are aware of these issues and are implementing measures to address them, but staying ahead of the evolving threats is an ongoing challenge.

Additionally, some tech companies have faced criticism for not doing enough to prevent these negative outcomes, and there is a growing demand for greater accountability and responsibility from the industry (Miric et al., 2019). The dark sides are discussed in Chapter 9, challenging managers to be aware of the dark sides and make conscious efforts to address them. The dark sides are explored in the context of the triple bottom line. How it affects people, the planet, and profit, iterating how the dark sides can affect people's well-being, electric waste, desire for new devices, and power for data centres having an impact on the environment, and people disengaging from digital platforms due to harassment, misinformation, and cyberbullying can affect the profit of the company. It is imperative to recognise that dark sides are not just on social media but can also be across all the different types of media. Managers need to recognise these dark sides and effectively address them.

1.7.8 The students

As a student, understanding digital consumption and its impact on various stakeholders can be valuable for several reasons. With the increasing importance of digital platforms, there are several career opportunities in digital marketing, social media management, and data analytics (Chattopadhyay et al., 2022). By understanding digital consumption, you can identify potential career paths that align with your interests and skills. As a student, you will likely build your brand and digital presence. Understanding digital consumption can help create a cohesive, effective brand that resonates with your target audience. Digital consumption can have both positive and negative impacts on society. By understanding these impacts, you can make informed decisions about your own digital consumption habits and contribute to positive change in the digital ecosystem. Understanding digital consumption is becoming increasingly important in the modern world, and as a student, taking the time to learn about this topic can provide valuable insights and opportunities. As a student, you are acquiring the much-needed theoretical and practical understanding to shape your future. Consider yourself a prospective manager, business owner, or start-up founder. Where would you like to work? Would you be working as an employed staff in a company or have your own company? Would you be working with the government and policymakers as part of a regulatory team? Would you start your own company, developing a platform or creating mobile apps for companies? Or would you be on the dark side? Making life miserable for digital consumers on the platform? The dark side is not a place you want to be. Instead, you want to use technologies for good. You want to enhance people's well-being. I wish you all the best in any of these roles (apart from being on the dark side).

1.8 The theoretical underpinning for digital consumption

The study of digital consumption is underpinned by several theoretical frameworks that help to explain and understand consumer behaviour in digital environments. While this book and subsequent chapters may have a practical and managerial focus, it's imperative to recognise some theoretical framework upon which this digital consumption and consumer context are built. These theories can be considered formal statements, which have been tested through various research, to explain how things work and can be used to make predictions but are often still subject to multiple ongoing experiments.

Academic theories are the backbone of any academic discipline and are essential for advancing knowledge in a particular field. It is important to approach academic theories with an open mind and a willingness to learn. While some theories may be difficult to understand at first, they can become clearer and more comprehensible with time and effort. Moreover, academic theories are not set in stone; they constantly evolve and change in response to discoveries and developments. A solid understanding of academic theories is critical for students pursuing postgraduate and advanced studies. This understanding will provide a foundation for advanced research and analysis and enable students to develop new theories and concepts that could shape the future of their field. So, if you are a student, it is essential to embrace academic theories with a positive attitude, be open to learning, and stay curious. By doing so, you can unlock the full potential of your academic journey and make a valuable contribution to your chosen field of study.

Did you ask how many theories we have? Don't worry; they are numerous; there are many theories out there. Many are being disproved, and many are being approved. We can't cover all; just be mindful of the context in which you use the theories. We will spend time considering (some) theories shaping technology adoption for digital consumers.

- **The Theory of Planned Behaviour (TPB)** is a social psychological theory commonly used to explain and predict human behaviour, including technology adoption. The theory was developed by Icek Ajzen in 1985 and is an extension of the Theory of Reasoned Action. According to the TPB, human behaviour is determined by attitudes, subjective norms, and perceived behavioural control. Attitudes refer to an individual's positive or negative evaluations of a particular behaviour. Subjective norms refer to the perceived social pressure to perform or not perform a behaviour based on the beliefs of significant others. Perceived behavioural control refers to an individual's perception of their ability to perform the behaviour. The TPB suggests that these three factors influence an individual's behavioural intentions and, ultimately, their behaviour. Behavioural intentions are influenced by the individual's attitudes towards the behaviour, their perception of social pressure, and their perception of their ability to perform the behaviour. These behavioural intentions, in turn, influence the individual's behaviour. The TPB has been used in various fields, including health behaviour, environmental behaviour, and technology adoption. In the context of technology adoption, the TPB suggests that an individual's behavioural intentions to adopt a new technology are influenced by their attitudes towards the technology, the social pressure to adopt or not adopt the technology, and their perceived ability to use the technology.

■ **The Technology Acceptance Model (TAM)** is a social psychological theory developed in the 1980s to explain and predict the acceptance and adoption of new technologies. The model was first proposed by Fred Davis in 1986 and has been widely used in research on technology adoption since then. According to the TAM, an individual's intention to use technology is determined by two main factors: Perceived usefulness and perceived ease of use. Perceived usefulness refers to the degree to which an individual believes technology will help them achieve their goals and improve their performance. Perceived ease of use refers to the degree to which an individual thinks technology is easy to use and understand. The TAM suggests that perceived usefulness and ease of use directly influence an individual's attitude towards using technology, affecting their intention to use it.

Additionally, the model suggests that other factors, such as social influence and facilitating conditions, can indirectly influence an individual's intention to use technology. Overall, the TAM provides a useful framework for understanding and predicting technology adoption and has been applied in various fields, including education, healthcare, and business. The model has been updated over time, with variations such as TAM2 and TAM3 incorporating additional factors such as subjective norms and perceived enjoyment.

Reflective questions

Reflecting on the practicality of TAM, which recognises perceived usefulness and ease of use as a motivation for adopting technology, why do you prefer a MacBook instead of a PC? Do you find it more useful than PC? Or is it easier to use? Reflect on other digital technologies like the Self-Service Kiosk at McDonald's restaurants or using Uber to order a taxi.

■ **The Unified Theory of Acceptance and Use of Technology (UTAUT)** is a social psychological theory developed in 2005 to explain and predict the acceptance and use of new technologies. The model was proposed by Venkatesh, Morris, Davis, and Davis and is an extension of the Technology Acceptance Model (TAM). The UTAUT model posits that four main factors influence an individual's intention to use technology: Performance expectancy, effort expectancy, social influence, and facilitating conditions. Performance expectancy refers to the degree to which an individual believes technology will help them perform better. Effort expectancy refers to the degree to which an individual thinks technology will be easy to use. Social influence refers to the degree to which an individual is influenced by others to use or not use technology. Facilitating conditions refer to the degree to which individuals believe they have the necessary resources and support to use technology. In addition to these four factors, the UTAUT model suggests that gender, age, experience, and voluntariness of use can moderate the relationship between the four main factors and intention to use technology. The UTAUT model provides a comprehensive framework for understanding and predicting technology adoption and has been applied in various fields, including healthcare, education, and business. The model has been validated in numerous studies and has been shown to have strong predictive power.

- **The Task-Technology Fit (TTF)** theory is a conceptual framework that describes how well a technology fits the task intended to support. Goodhue and Thompson first introduced the TTF theory in 1995 to evaluate the success of information systems in organisations. According to the TTF theory, the fit between the technology and the task is determined by two main factors: Task characteristics and technology characteristics. Task characteristics refer to the specific requirements of the task, such as the complexity, interdependence, and variety of tasks. Technology characteristics refer to the features of the technology that are intended to support the task, such as its usability, functionality, and reliability. The TTF theory proposes that when there is a good fit between the technology and the task, the technology will be more effective and efficient in supporting the task.

  In contrast, when there is a poor fit between the technology and the task, the technology will be less effective and efficient and may even hinder the performance of the task. The TTF theory has been applied in various fields, including healthcare, education, and business, and has been used to evaluate the success of information systems and other technology implementations. The theory provides a useful framework for understanding how technology can be designed and implemented to support specific tasks and activities better. Reflecting on the practicality of this theory, why would you prefer to use your mobile phone to take a picture instead of the Canon DSLR digital camera? Which of these two technologies is fitter for your immediate task?

- **The Technology, Organization, and Environment (TOE)** framework is a theoretical framework used to analyse the impact of technology adoption on organisations and their environment. The TOE framework was first introduced by Tornatzky and Fleischer in 1990 to understand the factors influencing the adoption and use of new technologies in organisations. According to the TOE framework, technology adoption is influenced by three main factors: Technology, organisation, and environment. Technology factors refer to the characteristics of the technology itself, including its complexity, compatibility with existing systems, and relative advantage over alternative technologies. Organisational factors refer to the organisation's characteristics that may facilitate or hinder technology adoption, including its size, structure, culture, and resources. Environmental factors refer to the external factors that may influence technology adoption, including industry regulations, market competition, and societal norms. The TOE framework proposes that adopting and using new technologies are most successful when there is a good fit between the technology, the organisation, and the environment. For example, a new technology may be more likely to be adopted if it is compatible with existing organisational systems and processes and if there is support from external stakeholders such as regulators and customers.

The TOE framework has been applied in various fields, including healthcare, education, and business, and has been used to evaluate the success of technology implementations and inform technology strategy. The framework provides a valuable framework for understanding the complex interactions between technology, organisations, and the environment and has been influential in shaping research on technology adoption and innovation. As a prospective start-up founder, you need to understand this framework's triad and see how technology, organisation, and the environment must all work together to create an innovative platform—you may have the technology skills, able to programme, but do you have the organisational support? Are you a sole founder? Do you need to find co-founders and employ more staff to build your organisation? How about the environment? The political situation of your country, the regulations, and other policies may not allow your platform to succeed. For example, Gokada in Lagos, Nigeria, had the technology to digitalise public transportation in Lagos using a motorcycle; they had the organisation and the team, including developers and drivers, but the environment was not conducive as the government banned motorcycles in the city, so it is essential to recognise these three constructs and make sure they all align while exploring your digital platforms.

Other theories you could explore are Social Cognitive Theory (SCT), Uses and Gratifications Theory, and Consumer Culture Theory (CCT). Many of these theories provide a foundation for understanding the complex nature of digital consumption and can help marketers and other stakeholders develop effective strategies to engage with digital consumers. It is also important to remember that these theories are not universal truths and may not apply in every situation. Therefore, it is essential to approach them critically and evaluate their relevance and applicability in specific contexts.

Theories are developed based on a certain context and time period. As technology and society evolve, new theories may be needed to explain the adoption and use of emerging technologies. Theories provide a general framework for understanding individuals' attitudes and behaviours towards technology, but they may need help to fully explain the diversity of individuals' experiences and use of technology. Psychological and situational factors can influence how individuals adopt and use technology, and these factors may vary across individuals and contexts. Additionally, as new technologies emerge, applying existing theories to understand how individuals will adopt and use these technologies may be challenging. Therefore, ongoing research and theory development are needed to keep up with technological change's rapid pace and provide a deeper understanding of individuals' attitudes and behaviours towards technology. Researchers and practitioners must stay open to new perspectives and approaches and continuously evaluate and refine existing theories to ensure they remain relevant and useful in understanding technology adoption and use.

1.9 Conclusion

As we progress into the digital age, we expect that consumers will continue to rely more heavily on digital platforms for their daily needs, whether shopping, entertainment, or communication. Moreover, brands invest heavily in digital technologies to keep up with this trend. With more digital platforms available, brands are now competing with each other to offer better online experiences for their customers. This competition is not limited to online shopping websites but extends to social media platforms, mobile apps, and other digital channels. However, it's not just about offering the latest digital tools and platforms; it's also about understanding how to manage digital consumers and consumption effectively. In the digital environment, consumers have more control over their experience and expect a seamless, personalised, and engaging experience. Brands need to consider these expectations and tailor their digital strategies accordingly.

This chapter has discussed the triad of digital consumption, recognising that the digital landscape has transformed how consumers interact with brands and purchase products or services. In today's omnichannel world, consumers expect a seamless and consistent experience across all channels, including online and offline. Brands that can provide a unified and integrated omnichannel experience are more likely to win the loyalty of their customers. Moreover, developers play a critical role in meeting the needs of brands and consumers. They must be more innovative and develop platforms that provide a seamless experience across all channels. This requires a deep understanding of the customer journey and the ability to integrate various technologies and platforms to deliver a personalised and frictionless experience. In short, creating a holistic omnichannel experience is no longer an option but a necessity for brands to stay competitive in today's digital landscape.

This chapter also introduces some theories that provide valuable insights into individuals' attitudes and behaviours towards technology adoption and use. It is important to note that these theories are not mutually exclusive, and researchers often combine them to gain a more comprehensive understanding of technology adoption and use. While these theories have been influential in shaping research on technology adoption, it is essential to continuously evaluate and refine them to keep up with the rapid pace of technological change and to ensure their relevance in understanding individuals' attitudes and behaviours towards technology. These theories provide a valuable foundation for understanding technology adoption and use. Ongoing research and theory development are needed to keep up with the ever-evolving landscape of technology and its impact on individuals and organisations. By staying open to new perspectives and approaches and continuously evaluating and refining existing theories, researchers and practitioners can gain deeper insights into technology adoption and use and inform the development of effective strategies for successful technology implementation.

Understanding digital consumption is essential for any stakeholder involved in digital marketing or e-commerce. As more and more consumers turn to digital channels to research and purchase products, brands and marketers must understand how consumers behave in these digital environments. By understanding the concept of digital consumption, stakeholders can better manage digital consumers on digital platforms. This includes understanding the various stages of the consumer journey, such as awareness, consideration, and purchase, and how to tailor marketing strategies to each stage. It also involves understanding consumers' various touchpoints with brands, including social media, email marketing, and website interactions, and how to optimise each touchpoint for maximum engagement. Students and prospective managers can benefit from understanding digital consumption as it provides a foundational understanding of digital marketing and e-commerce. This knowledge can help them make informed decisions regarding managing digital consumers and developing effective digital marketing strategies.

1.10 Student activities

1. What is digital consumption, and why is it essential for companies to understand and manage it effectively?
2. How does consumer engagement on digital platforms differ from engagement on traditional platforms?
3. How has digital consumption affected traditional marketing strategies?
4. What are the different strands of marketing concepts related to digital consumption, and how do they intersect?
5. How has the growth of the Internet of Things (IoT) impacted digital consumption, and what opportunities and challenges does it present?
6. How can individuals balance digital consumption with other aspects of their life, such as physical activity and social interaction?
7. What is the role of web analytics and marketing insights in digital consumption management?
8. What role do government regulations play in shaping digital consumption, and how do businesses ensure compliance?
9. What are some of the challenges and opportunities that arise from the use of digital platforms for consumer engagement?
10. How can individuals seeking a career in digital marketing prepare themselves for the constantly evolving landscape of digital consumption?

References and further reading

Abdulquadri, A., Mogaji, E., Kieu, T. & Nguyen, P., 2021. Digital transformation in financial services provision: A Nigerian perspective to the adoption of chatbot. *Journal of Enterprising Communities: People and Places in the Global Economy*, 15(2), pp. 258–281.

Agbo, F. et al., 2020. Social media usage for computing education: The effect of tie strength and group communication on perceived learning outcome. *Journal of Education and Development using Information and Communication Technology*, 16(1), pp. 5–26.

Ajzen, I., 1985. From intentions to actions: A theory of planned behavior. In: J. Kuhl & J. Beckmann, eds. *Action Control: SSSP Springer Series in Social Psychology*. Berlin, Heidelberg: Springer. https://doi.org/10.1007/978-3-642-69746-3_2

Balakrishnan, J., Nwoba, A. & Nguyen, N., 2021. Emerging-market consumers' interactions with banking chatbots. *Telematics and Informatics*, 65, 101711.

Chattopadhyay, A., Kupe, T., Schatzer, N. & Mogaji, E., 2022. Fireside chat with three vice chancellors from three continents. In: E. Mogaji, V. Jain, F. Maringe & R. Hinson, eds. *Re-imagining Higher Education in Emerging Economies*. Cham: Palgrave Macmillan, pp. 85–96.

Chylinski, M. et al., 2020. Augmented reality marketing: A technology-enabled approach to situated customer experience. *Australasian Marketing Journal*, 28(4), pp. 374–384.

Davis, F. D., 1989. Perceived usefulness, perceived ease of use, and user acceptance of information technology. *MIS Quarterly*, 13(2), pp. 319–340.

Dhruv, G., Hulland, J., Kopalle, P. & Karahanna, E., 2020. The future of technology and marketing: A multidisciplinary perspective. *Journal of the Academy of Marketing Science*, 48, pp. 1–8.

Dwivedi, Y. et al., 2022. Metaverse beyond the hype: Multidisciplinary perspectives on emerging challenges, opportunities, and agenda for research, practice and policy. *International Journal of Information Management*, 66, 102542.

Flew, T., Martin, F. & Suzor, N., 2019. Internet regulation as media policy: Rethinking the question of digital communication platform governance. *Journal of Digital Media & Policy*, 10(1), pp. 33–50.

Gartner, 2023. What is data and analytics? [Online] Available at: https://www.gartner.com/en/topics/data-and-analytics

Goodhue, D. L. & Thompson, R. L., 1995. Task-technology fit and individual performance. *MIS Quarterly*, 19(2), pp. 213–236.

Hein, A. et al., 2020. Digital platform ecosystems. *Electronic Markets*, 30, pp. 87–98.

Hodapp, D. & Hanelt, A., 2022. Interoperability in the era of digital innovation: An information systems research agenda. *Journal of Information Technology*, 37(4), pp. 407–427.

Hoyer, W. et al., 2020. Transforming the customer experience through new technologies. *Journal of Interactive Marketing*, 51(1), pp. 57–71.

Jelovac, D., Ljubojević, C. & Ljubojević, L., 2022. HPC in business: The impact of corporate digital responsibility on building digital trust and responsible corporate digital governance. *Digital Policy, Regulation and Governance*, 24(6), pp. 485–497.

Kandampully, J., Bilgihan, A. & Li, D., 2022. Unifying technology and people: Revisiting service in a digitally transformed world. *The Service Industries Journal*, 42(1–2), pp. 21–41.

Kopalle, P., Kumar, V. & Subramaniam, M., 2020. How legacy firms can embrace the digital ecosystem via digital customer orientation. *Journal of the Academy of Marketing Science*, 48, pp. 114–131.

McKinsey, 2022. Marketing in the metaverse: An opportunity for innovation and experimentation [Online] Available at: https://www.mckinsey.com/capabilities/growth-marketing-and-sales/our-insights/marketing-in-the-metaverse-an-opportunity-for-innovation-and-experimentation

Miric, M., Boudreau, K. & Jeppesen, L., 2019. Protecting their digital assets: The use of formal & informal appropriability strategies by App developers. *Research Policy*, 48(8), 103738.

Mogaji, E., 2021. *Brand Management*. Cham: Springer.

Mogaji, E. et al., 2022. Guest editorial: Artificial intelligence in financial services marketing. *International Journal of Bank Marketing*, 40(6), pp. 1097–1101.

Mogaji, E. & Nguyen, N., 2022. The dark side of mobile money: Perspectives from an emerging economy. *Technological Forecasting and Social Change*, 185, 122045.

Mogaji, E., Olaleye, S. & Ukpabi, D., 2020. Using AI to personalise emotionally appealing advertisement. In: Banita Lal, Elvira Ismagilova, Yogesh K. Dwivedi, Shirumisha Kwayu *Digital and Social Media Marketing: Emerging Applications and Theoretical Development*. Cham: Springers, pp. 137–150.

Mogaji, E., Soetan, T. & Kieu, T., 2020. The implications of artificial intelligence on the digital marketing of financial services to vulnerable customers. *Australasian Marketing Journal*, 29(3), pp. 235–242.

Morgan-Thomas, A., Dessart, L. & Veloutsou, C., 2020. Digital ecosystem and consumer engagement: A socio-technical perspective. *Journal of Business Research*, 121, pp. 713–723.

Olson, E., Olson, K., Czaplewski, A. & Key, T., 2021. Business strategy and the management of digital marketing. *Business Horizons*, 64(2), pp. 285–293.

Oosthuizen, K., Botha, E., Robertson, J. & Montecchi, M., 2021. Artificial intelligence in retail: The AI-enabled value chain. *Australasian Marketing Journal*, 29(3), pp. 264–273.

Ponzoa, J. & Erdmann, A., 2021. E-commerce customer attraction: Digital marketing techniques, evolution and dynamics across firms. *Journal of Promotion Management*, 27(5), pp. 697–715.

Sağkaya Güngö, A. & Ozansoy Çadırcı, T., 2022. Understanding digital consumer: A review, synthesis, and future research agenda. *International Journal of Consumer Studies*, 46(5), pp. 1829–1858.

Sheth, J., 2020. Impact of Covid-19 on consumer behavior: Will the old habits return or die?. *Journal of Business Research*, 117, pp. 280–283.

Soetan, T., Mogaji, E. & Nguyen, N., 2021. Financial services experience and consumption in Nigeria. *Journal of Services Marketing*, 35(7), pp. 947–961.

Tornatzky, L. G. & Fleischer, M. 1990. *The Processes of Technological Innovation*. Pennsylvania, United States: Lexington Books.

Venkatesh, V., Morris, M. G., Davis, G. B. & Davis, F. D. 2003. User acceptance of information technology: Toward a unified view. *MIS Quarterly*, 27(3), pp. 425–478.

The digital consumer

2.1 Background

For us to consider digital consumer management, it is imperative to understand the individuals who are digital consumers. These people have decided to engage with brands on different digital platforms. They have decided to shop online instead of buying from their high street store; they have come to recognise the growing prospects of digital technology and are keen to explore its benefits fully. Understanding the behaviour of digital consumers is critical for brands that want to succeed in today's marketplace. With the increasing use of technology, consumers have become more connected, informed, and empowered, and their expectations for seamless, personalised experiences have also increased. Understanding a digital consumer requires a multifaceted approach that involves leveraging data and technology, providing a seamless omnichannel experience, and building trust and authenticity through transparent communication and social responsibility. The brands want to know you, they want to communicate with you, and they want to give you a personalised offer. So, you can start thinking about yourself as a digital consumer and what you expect from the brand. This chapter provides a background into digital consumers, describing who they are, their characteristics, and the challenges brands may face in effectively engaging with them. After reading this chapter, you will better understand the heterogeneous nature of this consumer group and their diverse needs and demands.

2.2 Learning outcomes

By the end of this chapter, you should be able to:

■ Demonstrate an understanding of digital consumers.
■ Recognise the diverse and heterogeneous nature of this group.
■ Demonstrate an understanding of digital consumer behaviours, extending your knowledge about consumer behaviours.

DOI: 10.4324/9781003389842-2

- Explain the idea of digital consumption.
- Identify the features of digital consumers.
- Recognise the inherent challenges of digital consumers.

2.3 Introduction

Technology has become an integral part of our everyday life, and we can sometimes take these technologies for granted, thinking it has often been here and there is nothing special. I am unsure if you have seen various memes on social media where people ask Gen Z about how the technology worked in the past—have you ever questioned the generally accepted icon of the save button? That is a floppy disk introduced by IBM in 1986—a small 3.5- or 5.5-in. floppy disk is capable of storing 30 to 200 Mbytes of information. For many people, that was enough to save their Word document files, but with the rate at which we generate data, the world has moved past that, and we are now storing our data on the cloud. This data generation rate suggests that humans have continuously evolved with technology, and indeed, we will keep evolving, and we expect brands to catch up with this evolution.

However, for brands to continue with this evolvement, they need to understand the needs of the consumer they are engaging with and the need to know that their innovations align with the requirements of their customers, and there is the gap this chapter aims to fill—to help understand these digital consumers, identify their unique features, and recognise their needs (Cavdar Aksoy et al., 2021). In addition, it is imperative to understand the inherent challenges of digital consumers with and on digital platforms. TikTok is trending, and very popular does not mean that all digital consumers will be on TikTok; likewise, the fact that there is a self-service kiosk at the restaurant is not a guarantee that everyone will use it.

Understanding digital consumers is crucial for brands that want to remain relevant in today's digital landscape (Khalil et al., 2022). This understanding is essential for key stakeholders to ensure that whatever innovative platform is being provided is accepted. Developers want to keep developing different innovative platforms; companies and brands want to improve their digital presence; and Governments are also keen to monitor activities on the platform—all stakeholders are interested in understanding these digital consumers. A better understanding will guarantee effective technology adoption, consumer well-being and safety on the platform, and enhance customer engagement with brands on digital platforms.

> **Reflective question**
>
> **Which of these is NOT a digital consumer? Your 5-year-old niece, your 20-year-old classmate, or your 75-year-old grandmother?**

2.4 Who is a digital consumer?

This question can be answered in many ways, and I will not be surprised if you have your definition and description of a digital consumer. Your experiences, engagement with technologies, and interaction with others may have shaped these definitions. At the same time, this may be correct, but it is imperative to acknowledge a starting point for describing a digital consumer. In this case, I have defined a digital consumer as an *individual interacting with and on digital platforms.*

Let me explain some keywords here as I expand on this definition.

Individuals are considered people who could be yourself and myself. We are very interested in things that will enhance our well-being, experiences, and interaction with others (Sağkaya Güngö & Ozansoy Çadırcı, 2022). We are willing to consume information and make informed decisions based on our knowledge. We can search for information, provide information, and curate information. However, the ability to do these things can vary depending on age, learning, and physical ability; notwithstanding, we are still human and a consumer.

Interacting 'with' suggests that in our quest for digital consumption, we can interact with others, which includes family and friends, businesses, and other organisations. Many may consider digital consumers are individuals who use digital technologies to engage with brands, products, and services. At the same time, this is right, and it is imperative to recognise that digital consumption goes beyond brands, products, and services. We can send a message to a company requesting for cancellation of services (engaging with a brand), and we can send a WhatsApp message on the family group (engaging with families and friends) and also engage with your tutors via online learning (engaging with a service). Interaction is an integral part of the consumption on digital platforms—it can be for work (with your colleagues), leisure (with your friends), or professional assistance (video call with your physiotherapist or lawyer).

Interacting 'on' refers to our activities on various digital platforms. While you choose to interact with a family member on WhatsApp, you may choose to interact with your friend on TikTok. The interaction with others needs to happen ON a platform. While the need to interact is the same, the platform and the form of interaction and engagement differ. Chatting with a friend will be different from chatting with your lecturer online. You might use Instagram DM to chat with friends, that is, interacting (chatting) on Instagram (a platform) is different from interacting (chatting) with your boss on Teams or Slack (a platform).

A digital platform refers to the ultimate destination for interaction and engagement (Chylinski et al., 2020). Digital consumers want to engage with brands and other consumers, interact with them, and share their opinions and experiences. However, this engagement must happen on the right platform and in the right way to be effective. Beyond social media, brands can also create their platforms for engagement, such as forums, online communities, and events. On these digital platforms, brands see different hacks used by their consumers—either Ikea seeing how people are recreating, reconfiguring, and reusing their furniture or Costco seeing how people buy Giftcards to circumvent paying membership fees. Both the good and the bad can happen on digital platforms, and this is why brands have to be there to know what's going on and what they can do. Ultimately, these platforms allow consumers to engage with the brand and other consumers in a more controlled and focused environment. Digital consumers need an enabling environment supporting their quest for interaction and communication. The digital platform will be discussed further in Chapter 4.

To summarise this short definition of a digital consumer, we see an individual who has become aware of using digital platforms to engage and interact with others. We know an individual who wants to buy something online, who wants to request a ride through an app, and who wants to wear a headset to escape the metaverse. Digital consumption is integral, and brands and developers must understand the intrinsic details to manage the level of consumption effectively. This management strategy may be complicated if managers are not open-minded enough to recognise this customer group's heterogeneous nature.

2.5 Demystifying digital consumers

Demystifying digital consumers involves recognising that they are not homogeneous or monolithic groups with uniform needs and expectations (Sağkaya Güngö & Ozansoy Çadırcı, 2022). Instead, digital consumers come from diverse backgrounds and have varying digital literacy and preferences. While age, gender, and location can influence digital behaviour, they are not the only determinants. For example, two people of the same age and gender from different parts of the world may have vastly different digital behaviours and preferences based on their cultural, economic, and educational backgrounds. Therefore, to effectively manage consumer engagement in the digital environment, brands must adopt a customer-centric approach that recognises and respects this diversity. They need to understand their target audience's unique needs and preferences and tailor their marketing efforts accordingly.

The definition of digital consumers is varied and diverse, and there is no one-size-fits-all approach to understanding or engaging with them (Agbo et al., 2020). Digital consumers come from different backgrounds, have varying levels of digital literacy and preferences, and use digital technologies in different ways. This section aims to demystify some notions around digital consumers, and by doing this, we can better understand digital consumers and their behaviours. This can help brands develop more effective strategies for engaging with their target audience and building strong relationships.

- It is not about age. Though we have Gen Z and Gen Y and many other variations and classifications of age groups, you cannot suggest that older people cannot be a digital consumer; the fact that your grandmother can still send a WhatsApp message makes her a digital consumer, the intensity of her consumption may however vary. While younger generations may be more tech-savvy and have grown up with digital technologies, older generations are also increasingly adopting them daily.
- It is not about gender. Digital consumption is not limited to any specific gender. Both male, female, and non-binary consumers consume digital content and use digital technologies daily. While there may be some differences in how men and women use digital technologies, it's important not to make assumptions about their digital consumption patterns based solely on their gender. For example, some studies have shown that women use social media more than men, while men spend more time playing video games. However, these differences are not absolute and can vary greatly depending on the individual. While you might think some apps (and platforms) are designed for those who identify as a woman—a period-tracking

app like Clue and Flo, you have individuals of other genders downloading this app to monitor their partners' periods.

- It is more than education. Education can also be seen as a determinant of digital consumption, but this needs to be challenged. Following the explanation of the grandmother sending a WhatsApp message, many people still need to be educated that they can still use their phones to carry out financial transactions. In managing digital consumption, you need to recognise consumers who may need to be educated enough but can still use digital platforms. Many people who cannot type in WhatsApp can use voice notes to communicate with their friends and facility. Their limited education (composing proper English) has not limited them to engage on a digital platform. Therefore, brands need to adopt a customer-centric approach and avoid making assumptions about their audience's digital consumption patterns based on gender. Instead, they should focus on understanding their audience's unique needs, preferences, and behaviours and develop strategies tailored to these insights. By adopting a customer-centric approach, brands can develop more effective strategies for engaging with their target audience, building solid relationships, and ultimately driving business growth.

- It is more than ability. It is imperative to recognise the need for inclusive design. Managers must recognise the need to develop their platform to encourage the inclusion of people with varying abilities. Digital consumption is not just limited to able-bodied individuals. People with disabilities also use digital technologies and can benefit significantly from the use of assistive technologies. For example, screen readers, which are software programs that read out text on a computer screen, can enable visually impaired individuals to use digital devices and access digital content. Similarly, Bluetooth beacons in supermarkets can assist individuals with mobility impairments or visual impairments in navigating and finding products within the store. Managers and brands must be open-minded and inclusive in their approach to digital consumption. This inclusive approach involves developing digital platforms and experiences that are accessible and inclusive for individuals with disabilities.

- It is not about location—The fact that you are in a developed country does not make you a better digital consumer, some people are in many war-torn countries, and many people in developing countries around the world are using digital technology. Despite the War in Ukraine, there are people still consuming digital content. Vynck et al. (2022) reported on a young girl singing 'Let It Go' from Disney's Frozen movie in a bomb shelter and a Ukrainian band in full combat gear offering to live-stream with pop star Ed Sheeran. Not to mention Elon Musk providing Starlink for people to access the Internet in the country (Tucker et al., 2022). So, the location may not always be an excuse for not engaging on the digital platform.

- It is not just about shopping or social media. When I teach digital consumption and digital consumer behaviour, the students often start with the assumption that digital consumption is about shopping online and using social media. While these two activities are integral to digital consumption, it is imperative to understand that there is more to digital consumption. Learning through online classes, carrying out operations using robots, and even virtual cycling on a peloton to get an immersive indoor cycling experience are all various forms of digital consumption.

- It is not just about the platform. Everyone has their favourite platform for digital consumption. Many people use Google Pixel, while others will prefer Samsung Galaxy. Many people prefer to use Google Maps. In contrast, others prefer TomTom. This preference for the platform does not stop us from engaging on digital platforms and with different brands and developers (Olaleye et al., 2022). While we recognise that digital platforms are an integral part of digital consumption, there are variations in terms of sophistication and what users can expect. As consumers are willing to engage with other fitness enthusiasts on the peloton, there are alternatives like Echelon sport smart connect bike and Apex rides. Brands will keep innovating on platforms and consumers will keep choosing their favourites. Managers working on understanding digital consumers must therefore be optimistic and open-minded about consumers' preferences for their digital platform and what the brands can provide.

- It is not always about being connected. While digital technologies have enabled consumers to stay connected 24/7, not all are always connected. Some consumers may live in areas with limited internet connectivity, while others may need the financial means to purchase and maintain digital devices (Soetan et al., 2021). Additionally, some consumers may disconnect from digital devices to focus on other aspects of their lives, such as work, family, or hobbies. Also, while e-commerce has grown significantly recently, not all digital consumers buy online. Many consumers still prefer to shop in physical stores or use a combination of online and offline channels.

To successfully manage consumer engagement in the digital environment, stakeholders—students, staff, and start-up founders, need to be open-minded and adaptable in their approach to digital consumers (Mogaji et al., 2020). This approach involves recognising that digital consumers come from diverse backgrounds and have unique needs, preferences, and behaviours regarding digital consumption. By being open-minded and receptive to these differences, individuals can develop more effective strategies for engaging with digital consumers, building solid relationships, and ultimately driving business growth. For example, students can explore emerging digital trends and technologies to understand better how digital consumers engage with brands and consume digital content. Staff working in a company can collaborate with developers to develop innovative ideas to meet the needs of their diverse customer base (Balakrishnan et al., 2021). Start-up founders can leverage customer feedback and data analytics to gain insights into their target audience's needs and preferences and develop products and services that are tailored to these insights.

> **Reflective question**
>
> **What are the implications of these consumer behaviours on brand engagement?**

2.6 Characteristics of digital consumers

Haven provided a definition of digital consumers and demystified digital consumers; we will now focus on the key characteristics of this consumer group. You must critically reflect on how these characteristics will affect your strategic management (as a prospective business manager) as you deal with the customers and introduce your digital platform.

2.6.1 Connected

Digital consumers are well connected for online interaction, they have access to the Internet, which supports their quest for social media, gaming platforms, and even exacting to the metaverse (Koohang et al., 2023). As a business manager, it is important to be present and active on these channels and to engage with customers promptly and meaningfully. Digital consumers are connected through mobile technology, supported by the Internet of Things, enhancing their expletives. As iterated earlier, the connection may be for something other than leisure for also learning, working, and other productive activities. It is unsurprising to see that many commercial centres, transport hubs, and retail centres provide free Internet through Wi-Fi for their visitors to connect and access the Internet, suggesting that they know customers like to be connected, so we help them get connected. With the rise of smartphones and mobile devices, digital consumers are increasingly mobile-first, meaning they are connected on the go; everywhere they go, they are more likely to be connected through their mobile phones (Chylinski et al., 2020). Digital consumers are expected to access digital content and services on the go. As a business manager, it is essential to develop a mobile-friendly digital platform that offers a seamless experience across multiple devices (see more on the dichotomy in digital consumption in Chapter 10). More importantly, think about access to digital consumers' locations via mobile phones and how that can inform real-time advertisement—location-based advertising (LBA), analytics, and data. Brands know where these consumers are. From their interaction online, they can be invited into the physical stores, provided the consumer has shared their data and consented to be tracked.

Reflective questions

Why do you think these companies give customers free Internet? What are the benefits these companies receive from providing free Internet? What are the benefits for the consumers when they get connected?

2.6.2 Convenience

Digital consumers are always keen on convenience, and managers need to recognise this when considering their strategies for deploying digital platforms (Minami et al., 2021). Digital consumers want their service now and now. We want our delivery today, we go to Amazon Prime, and retailers offer next-day delivery for consumers who can afford to pay more. Even though there are sustainability concerns, digital consumers are keen on their conveniences. There is online shopping, online dating, and online banking. Many consumers do not go to the banks, and now we see bank branches closing down, and people can carry out their financial transactions online. As part of the consumers' need for convenience, we no longer carry flash drives and hard drives; we are saving our files on the cloud—from Google Drive to OneDrive and Dropbox; and there are enormous benefits to accessing your data anywhere.

2.6.3 Personalisation

Digital consumers expect a personalised experience tailored to their needs and preferences (Cavdar Aksoy et al., 2021). Personalisation has become a growing need among digital consumers who want more than just a generic experience when interacting with businesses online. Today's consumers seek personalised offers and experiences catering to their specific interests, preferences, and needs. One of the main reasons for this trend is that digital consumers are often overwhelmed by the sheer amount of information and options available online. As a result, they are more likely to engage with businesses that provide a personalised experience that helps them cut through the noise and find what they are looking for. For example, suppose a consumer has purchased running shoes from an online retailer. In that case, they may expect personalised offers and recommendations for running-related products such as socks, water bottles, and apparel. This personalised approach saves the consumer time and effort in finding these products. It shows that the retailer understands their needs and is committed to providing a tailored experience. Moreover, personalised offers and experiences can also increase consumer loyalty and drive sales (Mogaji et al., 2020). When consumers feel that a business is catering to their unique needs and interests, they are more likely to continue doing business with that company and recommend it to others. As a business manager, it is essential to leverage customer data and analytics to gain insights into customer behaviour and preferences and to use this information to deliver targeted and personalised content and offers (Dangi & Malik, 2017).

2.6.4 Creators

Digital consumers are content creators (Lehnert et al., 2021). It is a common trend to see people take pictures of what they are eating, wearing, and even people they are meeting, it has become a normal trend, and via this acts, massive data are being generated which gives insight into consumers' activities; these content creation tendencies have also developed into user-generated contents where brands can invite their customers to take pictures and use their brand hashtag or share their post or comments on various posts on social media. In addition to user-generated content, there are reviewers on products, on apps, and online where consumers create information that can influence other consumers' choices. Brands invite you to rate them, drop your comments, and give them website reviews. Beyond creating content for brands, there are growing numbers of influencers, online celebrities, and YouTubers on YouTube, TikTok, and Instagram creating and monetising their content. You also need to recognise that Only Fans is also a very relevant platform for content creators.

2.6.5 Tech-savvy consumers

Digital consumers are generally tech-savvy and comfortable with using a range of digital technologies, such as smartphones, tablets, and social media platforms (Zollo et al., 2022). As a prospective business manager, it's important to develop a digital platform that is user-friendly and intuitive and that offers a seamless customer experience across multiple devices and platforms. Beyond creating content on digital platforms, digital consumers are also known to consume information online. They shop online, order food and ride from the digital platform, and read reviews to decide what to buy. Managers need to understand these characteristics of digital consumers and be able to offer contents that are relevant to their consumers. Consumers will want to keep coming to a platform that offers them something different to consume. Why do you think Netflix will keep producing more films for their platform and Disney+ will offer exclusive access to some movies on their platform? Here brands know that they need to meet the insatiable needs of consumers on a digital platform. This approach also involves a regular update to the website; for example, when there is a train strike or disruption due to the weather, consumers want to be sure that they are updated.

2.6.6 Globalised

Digital consumers are globalised, with access to information everywhere and whenever (Verbeke & Hutzschenreuter, 2021). As alluded to in the description of digital consumers, locations make little difference. Digital consumers can transact business anywhere around the world and work and learn from any part of the work. This understanding of the globalised nature of digital consumers is important for managers in developing a digital environment that can meet the globalised need of their consumers. For example, this means websites should have options for different languages, self-service kiosks at train stations should have other language options, and even virtual meetings should allow for translators for audience joining from different parts of the work. Digital consumers can access opportunities everywhere, look at many people freelancing on Fiverr and Upwork, working with clients from different parts of the world, and they do not need to travel. However, they can keep themselves in the loop with access to technology, breaking down barriers and geographical divides.

2.6.7 Empowered

Technology has provided opportunities for consumers to engage with brands on a very different level; consumers do not have to send a letter to make a complaint about a brand. Digital consumers are empowered through digital technology to share their concerns with brands through various digital and social media (Bandara et al., 2021). Digital consumers are unsatisfied with information from a single source—the brand or an influencer. These consumers have been empowered to make informed decisions through other sources like reviews, user-generated social media content, and their company research. These digital consumers are now very knowledgeable as information now abounds. They have friends, fans, a chatbot, or ask virtual assistance when deciding. Digital consumers value authenticity and transparency, and they expect brands to be honest and upfront about their products, services, and business practices. Building trust and credibility with customers is essential to be transparent and authentic in your communications and interactions as a business manager. Notably, there are growing trends of cancel culture, where consumers can share their thoughts, opinion, and reviews on social media, asking for brands to be boycotted and cancelled (Bouvier, 2020).

Celebrities and politicians are not exempted from these empowered digital consumers. Now you can send a tweet to the President of your country or send a direct message (DM) to a celebrity on Instagram. You can do a video to complain (or complement) a product and expect the brand to respond. Bournvita had to respond to a customer criticising the claims on their chocolate drink. This approach is considered deinfluencing, where consumers take to social media to critically challenge brands' claims and do the opposite of influencing and telling consumers not to buy the product. Brands are very much aware of these empowered consumers and are always keen to address their concerns before it starts trending and cause an adverse effect on the brand. Therefore, managers must improve their understanding of these digital consumers, develop strategies to manage them in digital environments, and ensure the concerns are adequately and promptly addressed.

2.6.8 Separated ecosystem

Do you have a different social media account for your family and friends and another for a prospective employer? If I search your name on Instagram, would I find your real account, or do you have a dummy account where you put the good stuff? Why do you think some people have different social media accounts for different purposes? It is imperative to recognise a growing concern about operating in different ecosystems—suggesting that what people represent online may differ from what we portray offline. Digital consumers are mindful of curating the right persona that will appeal to the right people, and there are significant implications for managers engaging with digital consumers in a digital environment. Consumers are aware that brands are targeting them; they are aware they are being tracked and their online behaviours are being monitored. It is, therefore, not surprising to see digital consumers operating in different realms. Managers need to reflect on their digital marketing strategies, asking if they are targeting consumers through their right persona or the different personas they have on digital platforms. Many digital consumers will have numerous social media accounts, emails, and avatars in the metaverse.

> **Reflective question**
>
> **What are the implications of these features for brands?**

By considering these key characteristics, business managers can develop effective strategies for engaging with digital consumers and building strong relationships. This involves developing a user-friendly and mobile-first digital platform, leveraging customer data to deliver personalised content and offers, and building trust and credibility through authentic and transparent communications.

2.7 The challenges

With your understanding of the different characteristics of digital consumers, what are the challenges for brands and tech developers? How do you expect brands to deal with these consumers? Are you a brand manager trying to develop digital marketing strategies or are you a tech start-up founder, it is imperative to recognise these challenges and find ways to address them. This section discusses some relevant challenges with digital consumers. At the same time, it may appear generic, but you are expected to reflect on how they affect your business practices and what specific ways to address them.

2.7.1 The ecosystem

Tech developers are working towards developing and expanding their ecosystem—Facebook is growing its ecosystem by focusing on the metaverse; Google, Apple, and the rest of the big tech companies are growing their ecosystem, and questions can be asked if consumers can find their ways across these ecosystems. Would you stop using an iPhone and start using Google Pixel? Do you imagine yourself now having a Gmail account and Google Drive and listening to music on YouTube? How do you envisage brands working with these different platforms? If you were to develop an app for your business, would you consider both the Apple Apps Store and Google Play Store or other app stores like Amazon Appstore, AppBrain, or GetAPK? How about consumers? How do you expect them to detach themselves from these ecosystems? Brands must have a sense of corporate digital responsibility to ensure that consumers are supported in the digital environment. As seen with TikTok introducing a daily 60-minute screen time notification to all accounts belonging to a user under 18, tech developers are being tasked to ensure the privacy and safety of their users. As a prospective tech developer or manager interested in managing consumer engagement in the digital environment, you must start envisaging how to support users on your platform. It is essential to recognise the skills, human, financial, and technical resources to make corporate digital responsibility of the companies.

2.7.2 The data control

Though data is now abundant, there are significant challenges for brands and tech developers regarding how to access and use the data. Consumers are aware they are being tracked, they are aware of brands' desire to collect their data, and the consumers ultimately (should) have control over how they use their data. No doubt, some organisations will offer services in order to get data from consumers. You have free emails from Outlook, Hotmail, and Yahoo; you have free social media profiles from Facebook and TikTok; these tech companies are offering these services to access data. There are growing concerns about how consumers manage their data, you have seen people install ad blockers, and then there are prospects of people monetising their content. Many digital consumers use these ad blockers, making it difficult for brands to reach their target audience with online advertising. Brands need to create non-intrusive and relevant ads that provide value to the user. For example, native advertising, where ads are seamlessly integrated into the user experience, can effectively engage with digital consumers without disrupting their browsing experience (Campbell & Grimm, 2019).

Tech developers can also address the challenge of ad blockers by creating ad formats that are less intrusive and more engaging. For example, Google's AMP (Accelerated Mobile Pages) technology enables publishers to create fast-loading and engaging mobile pages that are less likely to be blocked by ad blockers. How about OnlyFan—the question remains if people will choose to pay for these services and take control of their data. We have seen the strategy being adopted by Twitter, where they are selling a subscription called Twitter Blue, an opt-in, paid subscription which reduces the number of advertisements users will see. Meta is also planning to introduce paid subscription service called Meta Verified. Brands need consumers on digital platforms to share data and insights which can help with their marketing and product development. As getting much-needed data is becoming more challenging, brands must start exploring innovative ways to meet their data needs.

2.7.3 The information overload

As with the overload of data, there is an overload of information, making communication very difficult (Roetzel, 2019). Digital consumers can be overwhelmed with content, making it challenging for brands to capture their attention and engage with them effectively. How many advertisements do you think people see in a day online? How are people able to filter through all this information? There are significant implications for managers trying to understand digital consumer behaviour in a digital environment. What would you want your brand to say to stand out from the crowded marketplace? Every brand can now advertise on Facebook, every brand can use influencers, and every brand can have a website for the product and services—what can they do differently? Managers need to start exploring options to stand out from the crowd, perhaps providing personalised offers, using artificial intelligence to gain a deeper understanding of consumers' needs, and adopting precision targeting to reach out to them, moving onto the metaverse or ultimately choosing to stay out of digital media. J.D. Wetherspoon closed all the Twitter, Instagram, and Facebook accounts for its 900 outlets (Weaver, 2018). Lush tweeted that 'we are switching up social' as 'Increasingly, social media is making it harder and harder for us to talk to each other directly. We are tired of fighting with algorithms and do not want to pay to appear in your newsfeed'.

Credit goes to some tech developers for addressing information overload by designing platforms prioritising relevant and high-quality content over low-quality or irrelevant content. For example, social media platforms like Facebook and Twitter use algorithms that prioritise content based on the user's interests and engagement levels. Even though this information may be relevant, albeit too much at some time, digital consumers tend to have short attention spans. They quickly switch to other platforms if they need help finding the content engaging enough. Brands must create visually appealing, interactive content, and easy to consume (Mogaji et al., 2020). For example, using videos, infographics, and interactive content can help brands capture the attention of digital consumers and keep them engaged.

2.7.4 The digital divide

We always take pride in our technology gadgets; from the days of the Apple iPod to the Galaxy Z Flip, having the right gadget and device to access the digital environment is essential. It is unsurprising to see developers and tech manufacturers coming out with newer versions of the technology, and people keep queuing for days in front of stores to buy them. The rapid pace of technological development has resulted in a growing demand for digital devices and services. However, only some have the means or the opportunity to access these resources. This challenge creates a disparity that can lead to adverse outcomes, such as limited educational opportunities, reduced job prospects, and social exclusion (Lythreatis et al., 2022). We must recognise the inherent challenges around the digital divide—the gap between those with access to digital technology and those without. It is a significant challenge that affects not only individuals but also communities and entire countries.

The COVID-19 pandemic has certainly exacerbated and highlighted the extent of the digital divide and its impact on education. With schools and universities forced to close their physical campuses, there was a rapid shift towards online learning. However, this shift was impossible for many students in developing countries who needed access to suitable devices and Internet connectivity (Chattopadhyay et al., 2022). Moreover, while some people buy the latest gadgets, others need help accessing basic digital resources. This disparity is especially concerning in higher education, as students without access to digital technology are disadvantaged. They may miss important learning opportunities and need to catch up with their peers with access to online resources.

Accessing the metaverse through a headset and other virtual reality kits might be considered a luxury (Dwivedi et al., 2022). However, it is something to keep in mind for managers and developers considering engaging consumers in the digital environment. This is an emerging technology that needs to be recognised. Notwithstanding, it is imperative to recognise digital inequality, which could be from limited access to the right gadgets and devices or access to the Internet. Access to the Internet may be seen as a necessity for some people worldwide, but for some, it is a luxury. In the UK, we see telecommunication companies offering unlimited mobile Internet for consumers; in contrast, this may be seen as a regular thing, spare some thought for people in another part of the world where access to the Internet is expensive. They have to switch off their data overnight so that mobile apps running in the background of their phone do not consume their data. In addressing these data issues, some companies offer websites with low bandwidth for people with limited Internet data. In addition, Managers need to evaluate how this digital inequality affects digital consumption and explore what they can do to address these inequalities.

Furthermore, the digital divide is wider than access to hardware and software. It also encompasses factors such as digital literacy and the ability to use digital technology effectively. Even if someone has access to a device, they may need to learn how to use it to its full potential, thus limiting their ability to take advantage of its opportunities. We must address the digital divide to ensure that everyone has equal access to the benefits of digital technology. It is also essential to note that addressing the digital divide is not just a matter of providing devices and connectivity; it is also about ensuring that everyone can participate fully in the digital world. This requires a concerted effort from governments, organisations, and individuals to bridge the gap and provide opportunities for all to participate in the digital world. For example, providing subsidies for Internet access or offering low-cost devices to students who need them. In addition, there needs to be a focus on digital literacy training to ensure that individuals have the skills to use digital technology effectively.

2.7.5 The psychological effect

We all enjoy using technology and being digital consumers. There is nothing bad in benefiting from the enormous advantages digital technologies offer individuals and businesses. However, as responsible brands, managers, and tech developers, it is imperative to recognise the psychological effects of digital consumption and explore opportunities to address some of these issues. Using digital technology can be intimating for some people; think about the first time you used a contactless card on the bus or at the barrier at the train station, think about the first time you played the PlayStation, sometimes these we take for granted can be intimidating for many others, and organisations are expected to show some responsibility in streamlining the use of their technologies. It is not surprising to see banks introducing additional support for people to use their mobile apps and online banking during the COVID-19 pandemic when people cannot access banks. You see companies having prompts on their website to check if you need assistance to navigate. You see staff at self-checkout machines in a supermarket to support people who may need support. Beyond the immediate need for help, the psychological effect of digital technology can also be experienced when there is a service breakdown. For example, there were reports of chaos in 2021 when WhatsApp, Instagram, and Facebook went down for several hours—with users across the globe experiencing issues on the social media platforms (Waddell & Morrison, 2021). People have become used to these social media profiles and feel a gap in their life because their daily digital consumption has been disrupted. You see people leaving Instagram to use Twitter to get their dose of social media. For brands and small businesses selling on Instagram, their business is also disrupted. Even when things are working well, the dark side of social media and digital technology cannot be ignored. Some people are concerned about metrics—the number of followers, views, and likes. There are mental health implications for people feeling depressed. There are concerns about data privacy, security, and fraud. There is dark side exploitation of trolls and abuses (this is discussed in depth in Chapter 9).

It is not surprising to see digital consumers taking a digital detox, an intentional and temporary reduction or complete elimination of one's use of digital technology, such as smartphones, computers, and social media platforms. It is a consumer behaviour that has become more common in recent years as people seek to manage their digital consumption and maintain a healthy balance. A digital detox can take many forms, from a few hours of unplugging each day to an entire week or longer of abstaining from all digital technology. Aligning with Section 2.5 on demystifying digital consumers, there are growing need for consumers to detach themselves from being connected; this does not make them less a digital consumer but a way of self-regulation (see Chapter 8 on Regulating Digital Consumption). The goal of digital detox is to reduce the negative effects of digital technology on mental and physical health, including stress, anxiety, and sleep disturbances. Digital detox is a way for people to take control of their relationship with technology and find a healthier balance in their lives. Brands must be aware of digital technology's psychological effects and dark sides as they manage consumer engagement in a digital environment.

2.7.6 The geographical limitations

Though we might agree that digital technology has broken geographical barriers, we must recognise that there are still some inherent geographical limitations that managers must be aware of. Some areas still have no Internet access, and their digital consumption experience is often negatively affected. Even in developed countries, there are still areas with limited Internet access. Imagine travelling on holiday to places with no Internet, imagine travelling to places where Google Maps is not working, or imagine travelling to places where card payments are not accepted, and you have to use cash. In some places worldwide, consumer engagement on digital platforms could be improved. These challenges, however, present opportunities for brands to be innovative if they need to target people in these areas. For example, Soetan et al. (2021) reported on how vulnerable consumers in Nigeria are using Unstructured Supplementary Service Data (USSD) codes, sometimes referred to as 'quick codes' or 'feature codes', to access financial services when there is no Internet access. The political situation in some countries is also an issue that needs to be recognised when discussing the challenges of digital consumption. The society and political, legal, and regulatory environments are essential for managers.

We recognise that businesses are trying to reach different customers worldwide, but how would they reach consumers in China? Many people in China need access to platforms available in Europe or North America. WeChat is China's most popular social network; it is the closest thing to Facebook in China and has further integrated payment services to keep consumers in their ecosystem. Countries like China, North Korea, Syria, Qatar, and the UAE have put some bans on WhatsApp; even though it is the world's most-used instant messaging app, these countries have banned it and a handful of countries have banned it for security and political reasons. Likewise, in Nigeria, there was a ban on Twitter. However, as you can imagine, digital consumers will find their way around these things by using Virtual Private Networks (VPN) to encrypt their Internet traffic and disguise their online identity spoof their location in another country. Managers must know these geographical limitations and challenges, recognise that some consumers may have difficulties accessing their services, and ultimately manage their expectations.

Reflective question

How many digital consumers do we have in the world?

2.8 Beyond business to consumers (B2C)

This book and chapter may have focused on consumers (individuals), as we have discussed the demystification, characteristics, and challenges from individual consumers' perspectives. While this may be a limitation of this book, it is imperative to reiterate that you should be aware of another context of digital consumption. Though not explicitly covered in this book, you must be aware of many opportunities for business-to-business (B2B), consumer-to-consumer (C2C), and consumer-to-business (C2B) interactions. This awareness can spur further research interest, knowledge quest, and entrepreneurial zeal.

B2B interactions involve companies selling products or services to other businesses. This type of interaction often involves larger transactions and longer-term relationships between the companies (Mogaji et al., 2023). In the digital world, B2B interactions can occur through online marketplaces, e-procurement systems, and other digital platforms. Alibaba, the Chinese e-commerce giant, is an example of a successful B2B digital platform. Alibaba operates various online marketplaces that connect businesses with suppliers and manufacturers, enabling them to source products and materials more efficiently and cost-effectively. As of 2021, Alibaba had over 1 billion active users and generated over $100 billion in revenue annually.

C2C interactions involve individuals buying and selling products or services to other individuals. Online marketplaces, such as eBay and Craigslist, are examples of digital platforms that enable C2C interactions. Etsy, an online marketplace for handmade and vintage goods, is another example of a successful C2C digital platform. Etsy enables individual sellers to connect with buyers, creating a community of creators and shoppers. As of 2021, Etsy had over 90 million active buyers and 4.4 million active sellers, generating over $10 billion in annual revenue.

C2B interactions involve individuals selling products or services to businesses. This type of interaction often occurs in freelance or gig economy platforms, where individuals offer their services to businesses on a project-by-project basis. Fiverr, a freelance services platform, is an example of a successful C2B digital platform. Fiverr enables individuals to offer their services to businesses on a project-by-project basis. As of 2021, Fiverr had over 4 million active buyers and 3.5 million active sellers, generating over $200 million in annual revenue.

Beyond business to consumers (B2C), we can see the power and potential of various digital interactions. By recognising the opportunities in these different types of interactions, businesses and individuals can leverage the power of digital technology to access new markets and increase their revenue streams. It is essential to be open-minded and explore all possible avenues for digital interaction to maximise the potential benefits of the digital world.

2.9 Conclusion

Engaging digital consumers has become increasingly critical for brands and tech developers in the digital age. Understanding who digital consumers are, their characteristics, and their challenges are essential in creating an engaging and safe online environment. This chapter has explored what it means to be a digital consumer. This exploration is essential for your theoretical understanding and managerial responsibility. It is important to have a holistic understanding of the characteristics of individuals using your digital platforms and innovative solutions—to understand their struggles and challenges and ultimately to devise ways to address them.

This chapter has tried to demystify digital consumers and to open your understanding to the vast opportunities that abound when you explore the digital environment for digital consumers. You want to think beyond social media and shopping, think beyond age and location, and acknowledge the heterogeneous nature of this customer group. Digital consumers use digital technologies to interact with brands, products, and services. They are tech-savvy, connected, and mobile. They expect seamless and personalised experiences across all digital channels and devices.

However, engaging digital consumers is challenging. The rapid pace of technological change, the increasing amount of digital noise, and the rise of online privacy concerns all contribute to a complex digital landscape. The challenges have also been discussed for your knowledge, you are aware of them, and you can start reflecting on how to adjust your business operations to enhance the experiences of digital consumers. How would you seek permission and ethically collect their data? How would you manage their overload of information?

Moreover, how would you develop an inclusive design to ensure people of all abilities can engage on your platform? I expect you to reflect on these questions as you expand your knowledge about digital consumers. Brands and tech developers must be mindful of these challenges (and questions) and work with regulators to create an online environment that prioritises user privacy, security, and trust.

In closing, engaging with digital consumers requires deep understanding of their behaviours, preferences, and expectations. Brands, tech developers, and regulators must work together to create a safe and engaging online environment that prioritises user privacy, security, and trust while providing relevant and valuable content that captures and retains user attention. By doing so, they can build long-lasting relationships with digital consumers and succeed in the digital age. As a student, remember to build on your knowledge about consumer behaviour. There are certain behaviours that consumers will keep exhibiting either as digital or non-digital consumers. As illustrated under demystifying digital consumers, pay attention to the fundamental insights from the study on consumer behaviour. Also, remember that the focus might have been on business to consumers (B2C), be open-minded to recognise opportunities that abound with B2B (business to business), C2C (consumer to consumer), and C2B (consumer to business).

2.10 Student activities

1. How would you describe the difference between consumers and digital consumers? Can you identify 3–5 differences?
2. How would you explain the idea of digital consumption?
3. Which of the characteristics of digital consumers stands out for you? Critically discuss your decision.
4. Create a persona of a digital consumer based on demographic and psychographic data. What are their interests, values, and needs? How do these factors affect their online behaviour?
5. Would you consider a company a digital consumer? What are their characteristics and challenges when dealing with other digital consumers?
6. How would you address the gadget limitations being experienced by digital consumers in developing countries?
7. The Chief Executive Officer of your company has announced that all social media pages will be deleted. Would you agree or disagree with that decision? Critically discuss and justify your decision.
8. Brands have a responsibility to ensure the safety of consumers on their platforms. What measures should brands put in place to protect their consumers?
9. Critically evaluate the impact of the COVID-19 pandemic on digital consumerism. How has the shift to remote work and online shopping affected consumer behaviour? What new trends have emerged?

10. Examine the global differences in digital consumerism. How do cultural, economic, and political factors affect digital habits and preferences? What are the challenges and opportunities for multinational companies?

References and further reading

Abdulquadri, A., Mogaji, E., Kieu, T. & Nguyen, P., 2021. Digital transformation in financial services provision: A Nigerian perspective to the adoption of chatbot. *Journal of Enterprising Communities: People and Places in the Global Economy*, 15(2), pp. 258–281.

Agbo, F. et al., 2020. Social media usage for computing education: the effect of tie strength and group communication on perceived learning outcome. *Journal of Education and Development using Information and Communication Technology*, 16(1), pp. 5–26.

Balakrishnan, J., Nwoba, A. & Nguyen, N., 2021. Emerging-market consumers' interactions with banking chatbots. *Telematics and Informatics*, 65, 101711.

Bandara, R., Fernando, M. & Akter, S., 2021. Managing consumer privacy concerns and defensive behaviours in the digital marketplace. *European Journal of Marketing*, 55(1), pp. 219–246.

Bouvier, G., 2020. Racist call-outs and cancel culture on Twitter: The limitations of the platform's ability to define issues of social justice. *Discourse, Context & Media*, 38, 100431.

Campbell, C. & Grimm, P., 2019. The challenges native advertising poses: Exploring potential federal trade commission responses and identifying research needs. *Journal of Public Policy & Marketing*, 38(1), pp. 110–123.

Cavdar Aksoy, N., Tumer Kabadayi, E., Yilmaz, C. & Kocak Alan, A., 2021. A typology of personalisation practices in marketing in the digital age. *Journal of Marketing Management*, 37(11–12), pp. 1091–1122.

Chattopadhyay, A., Kupe, T., Schatzer, N. & Mogaji, E., 2022. Fireside Chat with Three Vice Chancellors from Three Continents. In: E. Mogaji, V. Jain, F. Maringe & R. Hinson, eds. *Re-imagining Higher Education in Emerging Economies*. Cham: Palgrave Macmillan, pp. 85–96.

Chylinski, M. et al., 2020. Augmented reality marketing: A technology-enabled approach to situated customer experience. *Australasian Marketing Journal*, 28(4), pp. 374–384.

Dangi, H. & Malik, A., 2017. Personalisation in marketing: An exploratory study. *International Journal of Internet Marketing and Advertising*, 11(2), pp. 124–136.

Dhruv, G., Hulland, J., Kopalle, P. & Karahanna, E., 2020. The future of technology and marketing: A multidisciplinary perspective. *Journal of the Academy of Marketing Science*, 48, pp. 1–8.

Dwivedi, Y. et al., 2022. Metaverse beyond the hype: Multidisciplinary perspectives on emerging challenges, opportunities, and agenda for research, practice and policy. *International Journal of Information Management*, 66, 102542.

Flew, T., Martin, F. & Suzor, N., 2019. Internet regulation as media policy: Rethinking the question of digital communication platform governance. *Journal of Digital Media & Policy*, 10(1), pp. 33–50.

Hein, A. et al., 2020. Digital platform ecosystems. *Electronic Markets*, 30, pp. 87–98.

Hodapp, D. & Hanelt, A., 2022. Interoperability in the era of digital innovation: An information systems research agenda. *Journal of Information Technology*, 37(4), pp. 407–427.

Jelovac, D., Ljubojević, Č. & Ljubojević, L., 2022. HPC in business: The impact of corporate digital responsibility on building digital trust and responsible corporate digital governance. *Digital Policy, Regulation and Governance*, 24(6), pp. 485–497.

Kandampully, J., Bilgihan, A. & Li, D., 2022. Unifying technology and people: Revisiting service in a digitally transformed world. *The Service Industries Journal*, 42(1–2), pp. 21–41.

Khalil, A., Abdelli, M. & Mogaji, E., 2022. Do Digital Technologies Influence the Relationship between the COVID-19 Crisis and SMEs' Resilience in Developing Countries?. *Journal of Open Innovation: Technology, Market, and Complexity*, 8(2), pp. 100–109.

Koohang, A. et al., 2023. Shaping the metaverse into reality: A holistic multidisciplinary understanding of opportunities, challenges, and avenues for future investigation. *Journal of Computer Information Systems*, pp. 1–31.

Kopalle, P., Kumar, V. & Subramaniam, M., 2020. How legacy firms can embrace the digital ecosystem via digital customer orientation. *Journal of the Academy of Marketing Science*, 48, pp. 114–131.

Lehnert, K., Goupil, S. & Brand, P., 2021. Content and the customer: Inbound ad strategies gain traction. *Journal of Business Strategy*, 42(1), pp. 3–12.

Lythreatis, S., Singh, S. & El-Kassar, A., 2022. The digital divide: A review and future research agenda. *Technological Forecasting and Social Change*, 175, 121359.

McKinsey, 2022. Marketing in the metaverse: An opportunity for innovation and experimentation [Online] Available at: https://www.mckinsey.com/capabilities/growth-marketing-and -sales/our-insights/marketing-in-the-metaverse-an-opportunity-for-innovation-and -experimentation

Minami, A., Ramos, C. & Bortoluzzo, A., 2021. Sharing economy versus collaborative consumption: What drives consumers in the new forms of exchange?. *Journal of Business Research*, 128, pp. 124–137.

Miric, M., Boudreau, K. & Jeppesen, L., 2019. Protecting their digital assets: The use of formal & informal appropriability strategies by App developers. *Research Policy*, 48(8), 103738.

Mogaji, E., 2021. *Brand Management*. Cham: Springer.

Mogaji, E., Olaleye, S. & Ukpabi, D., 2020. Using AI to personalise emotionally appealing advertisement. In: Banita Lal, Elvira Ismagilova, Yogesh K. Dwivedi, Shirumisha Kwayu *Digital and Social Media Marketing: Emerging Applications and Theoretical Development*. Cham: Springers, pp. 137–150.

Mogaji, E., Restuccia, M., Lee, Z. & Nguyen, N., 2023. B2B brand positioning in emerging markets: Exploring positioning signals via websites and managerial tensions in top-performing African B2B service brands. *Industrial Marketing Management*, 108, pp. 237–250.

Mogaji, E., Soetan, T. & Kieu, T., 2020. The implications of artificial intelligence on the digital marketing of financial services to vulnerable customers. *Australasian Marketing Journal*, 29(3), pp. 235–242.

Morgan-Thomas, A., Dessart, L. & Veloutsou, C., 2020. Digital ecosystem and consumer engagement: A socio-technical perspective. *Journal of Business Research*, 121, pp. 713–723.

Nguyen, N. & Mogaji, E., 2023. Information technology for enhancing transportation in developing countries. In: Chemma, N., El Amine Abdelli, M., Awasthi, A. and Mogaji, E. (Ed.) *Management and Information Technology in the Digital Era*. Bingley: Emerald Publishing Limited, pp. 81–94.

Olaleye, S. et al., 2022. The composition of data economy: A bibliometric approach and TCCM framework of conceptual, intellectual and social structure. *Information Discovery and Delivery*, 51(2), pp. 223–240.

Olson, E., Olson, K., Czaplewski, A. & Key, T., 2021. Business strategy and the management of digital marketing. *Business Horizons*, 64(2), pp. 285–293.

Oosthuizen, K., Botha, E., Robertson, J. & Montecchi, M., 2021. Artificial intelligence in retail: The AI-enabled value chain. *Australasian Marketing Journal*, 29(3), pp. 264–273.

Ponzoa, J. & Erdmann, A., 2021. E-commerce customer attraction: Digital marketing techniques, evolution and dynamics across firms. *Journal of Promotion Management*, 27(5), pp. 697–715.

Roetzel, P., 2019. Information overload in the information age: A review of the literature from business administration, business psychology, and related disciplines with a bibliometric approach and framework development. *Business Research*, 12(2), pp. 479–489.

Sağkaya Güngö, A. & Ozansoy Çadırcı, T., 2022. Understanding digital consumer: A review, synthesis, and future research agenda. *International Journal of Consumer Studies*, 46(5), pp. 1829–1858.

Sheth, J., 2020. Impact of Covid-19 on consumer behavior: Will the old habits return or die? *Journal of Business Research*, 117, pp. 280–283.

Soetan, T., Mogaji, E. & Nguyen, N., 2021. Financial services experience and consumption in Nigeria. *Journal of Services Marketing*, 35(7), pp. 947–961.

Tucker, E., Alonso, M. & Wattles, J., 2022. SpaceX Starlink user terminals arrive in Ukraine, officials says [Online] Available at: https://edition.cnn.com/2022/02/27/business/starlink -activated-ukraine/index.html

Verbeke, A. & Hutzschenreuter, T., 2021. The dark side of digital globalization. *Academy of Management Perspectives*, 35(4), pp. 606–621.

Vynck, G., Lerman, R. & Zakrzewski, C., 2022. How Ukraine's Internet still works despite Russian bombs, cyberattacks [Online] Available at: https://www.washingtonpost.com/ technology/2022/03/29/ukraine-internet-faq/

Waddell, L. & Morrison, S., 2021. WhatsApp, Instagram and Facebook in chaos as apps stop working in outage [Online] Available at: https://www.standard.co.uk/news/uk/whatsapp -instagram-facebook-outage-not-working-server-b958747.html

Weaver, M., 2018. Wetherspoon founder denies social media account closure is stunt [Online] Available at: https://www.theguardian.com/business/2018/apr/16/jd-wetherspoon-closes-all -social-media-accounts

Zollo, L., Rialti, R., Marrucci, A. & Ciappei, C., 2022. How do museums foster loyalty in tech-savvy visitors? The role of social media and digital experience. *Current Issues in Tourism*, 25(18), pp. 2991–3008.

CHAPTER 3

Engagement platform

3.1 Background

Building on our knowledge of the digital consumer, as discussed in Chapter 2, digital platforms play a crucial role in facilitating digital consumption by providing a means for digital consumers to interact with brands and access their products or services. These platforms can take many forms, such as websites, mobile apps, social media channels, or e-commerce marketplaces. Digital platforms provide a range of benefits to both consumers and brands. These platforms offer consumers convenience, accessibility, and a seamless user experience. With digital platforms, brands would find it easier to connect with their target audience and deliver their products or services to consumers.

Similarly, digital consumers would need more opportunities to engage with brands and access their needed products or services. Therefore, the role of digital platforms in facilitating digital consumption cannot be overstated. This chapter aims to discuss the context of the platform as a place for engagement. The platform is a central hub that enhances digital consumption, bringing together all the key stakeholders—the developers providing the platform, designing its features and functionalities, and ensuring its performance and security. Brands offering their products or services on the platform leverage its features to engage with their target audience and consumers who need to access the platform easily, navigate it comfortably, and find the products or services they need quickly. They also need to feel safe and secure when transacting on the platform. This digital platform serves as a key connection between the trilogy of developers, brands, and consumers. It is anticipated that you will reflect on this knowledge when considering the right platform to provide for consumers within the digital environment.

DOI: 10.4324/9781003389842-3

3.2 Learning outcomes

By the end of this chapter, you should be able to:

- Recognise the role of digital platforms for digital consumption.
- Understand different platforms for digital consumption.
- Understand the various features of these platforms.
- Recognise the differences between digital platforms and devices.
- Understand activities on digital platforms.
- Identify the inherent challenge with digital platforms.

3.3 Introduction

We have recognised there are digital consumers—individuals interacting with and on digital platforms, and there is a need to explore the context of the platform when it comes to their interaction and engagement in the digital environment (Sağkaya Güngö & Ozansoy Çadırcı, 2022). The diverse nature of the consumer base in terms of their preferences, needs, and behaviours requires digital platforms to be flexible and adaptable to accommodate different user requirements. For example, some consumers prefer interacting with brands through social media platforms, while others may use dedicated mobile apps or websites. Some consumers may value personalised recommendations and offers, while others prioritise convenience and speed.

It is anticipated that digital platforms will be designed with a user-centric approach that considers the needs and preferences of different user segments (Ibert et al., 2022). The success of a digital platform depends on its ability to provide a seamless and personalised user experience that meets the diverse needs of the consumer base. This requires a deep understanding of the target audience and a flexible and adaptable platform design. This deep understanding is essential for managers keen on understanding consumer behaviour in the digital environment, how they use technology, where they use technology, and if the consumers' experience can be enhanced through some changes the brands are making. This is why some business owners change their e-commerce website provider from Wix to Shopify or WordPress, looking for the right platform to streamline their business operations.

Ultimately, selecting the right platform is critical to ensure effective engagement between brands and consumers with the vast abundance of various digital platforms, including social media platforms, e-commerce marketplaces, mobile apps, and websites (Dhruv et al., 2020). This involves understanding the different types of platforms available, how people access them, and the challenges they may face when using them. Moreover, brands need to know how consumers access these platforms, such as mobile devices, desktop computers, or other devices. This understanding can help brands tailor their platform design and content to optimise the user experience for the specific device and platform. This chapter aims to explore the engagement platform and highlight the different features, activities on platforms, and the challenges that consumers may face when using the platform, such as technical issues, security concerns, or privacy issues. Overall, selecting the right platform requires careful consideration of various factors, including platform type, user access, and potential challenges. Brands must ensure that their chosen platform fits their business purpose and is optimised to deliver a seamless and engaging user experience.

> **Reflective question**
>
> What should a business owner do to ensure consumers find their platform, engage and share it with others?

3.4 Digital devices

We can't talk about platforms without discussing devices. Devices are the host for platforms. Devices are considered hardware that serves as the infrastructure that supports digital platforms (Ogundokun et al., 2020). Devices are like your mobile phones, television, laptops, virtual reality headsets, and self-service kiosks. A mobile phone is a device, while social media is a platform to upload and share pictures. The laptop is a device, while Chrome is a platform to access the Internet. The self-service machine is a device, while the platform offers the opportunity to order food. The smart speaker is a device, and Alexa (and Siri) is the platform to access the Internet. A car is a device that allows artificial intelligence as a platform for autonomous and driverless vehicles. Managers must clearly understand the difference between devices and platforms as they develop digital transformation strategies. You need to develop your platform with an understanding of the devices hosting them. That is why you want to ensure your website (platform) is optimised and designed for mobile phones (devices).

Access to devices is often not controlled, unlike access to the platform. You don't need permission or a password to access most devices, provided you can buy it as anyone can have it. Also, you don't need access to the Internet to use your devices, and you can have your smartphone and choose to use it as a calculator if there is no Internet on it. Devices are often open access and waiting for any platform. You buy your phone and choose to install any app on it. You have your smart TV and can choose to connect your Netflix or Paramount+ account to it. We also need to recognise that these devices sometimes have pre-installed platforms. You sometimes have laptops with pre-installed Microsoft Edge for browsing, Safari pre-installed on Apple iPhones, and you can already have Netflix installed on your smart TV. While there is an agreement between the platform and device developers, the devices are open to allow any other platforms.

3.5 What are digital platforms?

This is one of the main questions you should be able to answer upon completing this chapter. What does a digital platform mean? There are going to be different definitions and explanations for this. Still, it is essential to make something clear, and then you can critically evaluate where you stand regarding digital platforms. Digital platforms are technology infrastructures providing a space for brands and consumers to interact and engage (Ibert et al., 2022). They serve as a bridge between brands and consumers, enabling them to communicate, exchange information, and transact. Digital platforms can take many forms, such as social media platforms, e-commerce marketplaces, mobile apps, websites, and even the self-service kiosk at the restaurant or self-checking at hotels. Each platform provides unique features and functionalities that allow brands and consumers to engage with each other in different ways (Tafesse & Dayan, 2023).

Unsurprisingly, many students will consider social media platforms the only viable digital platform. This suggests the need for you to be open-minded and better understand the encompassing nature of digital platforms. As a manager, you want to think beyond social media as a digital platform, and you want to gain a holistic understanding of the digital environment, and identify the possible platforms that you can use and how best to support your customers on the platform.

The list of available digital platforms is vast, and it is not practical or necessary for businesses to use every platform available (Gawer, 2021). Making a strategic decision about the right platform is crucial to ensure that companies utilise the platform that best aligns with their objectives and target audience. There are many more social media platforms outside Facebook, Twitter, and Instagram, but you are not expected to use everything. Before selecting a digital platform, businesses must evaluate their goals, target audience, and budget (Abdulquadri et al., 2021). This evaluation will help them identify which platforms best suit their needs and resources. They should also consider the platform's user interface, features, functionalities, and security and privacy policies. Likewise, as a manager, you want to find out the platforms that your consumers are conversant with (remember the example of WhatsApp in China and UAE)—you cannot operate your chatbot in those countries as using WhatsApp is not allowed. You want to know where the customers are and how best to engage them. Digital platforms have become increasingly important in today's digital landscape, allowing brands to reach a wider audience and engage with their customers in real time. They also provide consumers greater convenience, accessibility, and choice when accessing products and services.

3.6 Features of digital platforms

Discussing the features of digital platforms should help you expand your horizon and better understand platforms upon which you can engage with consumers. You should reflect on these features to start compiling a long list of digital platforms and identify the suitable ones for your consumers.

3.6.1 Enabling digital consumption

Digital consumers cannot engage in digital consumption without a digital platform. There is a need for that place for consumers to interact. The digital platform offers consumers the opportunity, access, and place to carry out their digital consumption. The eLearning platform for you to learn, the streaming platform to watch that series, and the social media platform to keep in touch with your friends and families are all digital platforms.

3.6.2 Available on devices

As earlier alluded, the devices can be seen as the host for the platforms. Digital platforms are available on digital devices. The infrastructure is being supported with devices such as mobile phones, laptops, and tablets. Consider evaluating access to your company's website on Google Analytics; you can see how consumers access your website (the platform) through desktop computers, mobile phones, and tablets (the devices).

3.6.3 The gatekeepers

Digital platforms have gatekeepers. These gatekeepers ensure that no one gains unauthorised access to the platforms. This gatekeeping suggests why you need to have your sign-in details, password, one-time password (OTP), a one-time PIN, and one-time authorisation code before you gain access to your university or work email. You might have your phone (the device), but you must bypass the gatekeepers by your password to access your email (the platform). This gatekeeping is why access can be revoked when the consumers do not abide by the terms and conditions of the platform.

3.6.4 Access is not guaranteed

The fact that you have your password does not guarantee you access to a platform. Imagine if you have not paid your fees in full, you may have the correct password to your email, but your account may have been blocked. Remember Donald Trump, the former president of the United States, was kicked out of Twitter and Facebook. This suggests that managers are responsible for vetting those who come to their platform. At the same time, there is a need to engage with consumers; the managers, serving as gatekeepers, can still deny some people access to the platform.

3.6.5 Internet is essential

Often you will need the Internet to access the platform. The Internet of Things makes the differences between the platform and a device. You can have your device (mobile phone), but you can only access some platforms if you have the Internet. You might still be able to use your phone as a calculator (instead of accessing Uber to order a ride), your laptop to type Word documents (instead of joining your online classes), and TV to watch programmes from the local station (instead of watching Netflix). So, managers need to be aware of the limitations consumers may face when they don't have access to the Internet. That is why some companies, restaurants, and transit hubs offer free Wi-Fi to ensure people can still access specific platforms on their devices.

3.6.6 Analytics are integral

Data is an essential derivative of engagement on a digital platform (see more in Chapter 7 for Data analytics on the digital platform). When even consumers engage on a digital platform, they leave their digital footprints, which are essential for brands to evaluate their strategies (Gawer, 2021). The prospect of analysing these data is an essential feature of digital platforms. Brands and developers can track how many people have downloaded their apps from the apps store, and they can track how many people have signed up for the newsletter on the platform and see how many people have watched their latest advertisement on YouTube. Analytics is an integral feature of digital consumption on digital platforms, which is essential for managers to understand consumer engagement on digital platforms (Gartner, 2023). It is imperative to recognise that collecting and analysing these data is not enough but the strategic business decision made upon the analysis. Managers must be able to make informed decisions based on analytics.

3.7 Devices and platforms

There is a strong connection between devices and platforms. While this chapter may focus on platforms, we cannot have this conversation without devices. Digital devices and platforms are closely interconnected, as digital devices provide the means for users to access digital platforms. Digital devices are electronic gadgets that allow users to interact with digital content and services. In contrast, digital platforms are the online infrastructure that enables users to connect, engage, and transact with each other. Digital devices come in various forms, including smartphones, tablets, laptops, desktop computers, and wearable devices (Ogundokun et al., 2020). These devices provide users with different functionalities and features, such as touch screens, voice recognition, cameras, and GPS, enabling them to interact with digital platforms differently.

The device (seen as the hardware and physical object) serves as the platform host (seen as the software and abstract object). This connection offers an opportunity for brands and consumers to engage. Digital platforms are designed to be compatible with different digital devices, allowing users to access them from anywhere and at any time. For example, social media platforms can be accessed from smartphones, tablets, laptops, and desktop computers, providing users with a seamless experience across different devices (Agbo et al., 2020). Digital devices and platforms are two sides of the same coin, as they work together to provide users with the means to interact with digital content and services. Businesses need to ensure that their digital platforms are optimised for different devices to offer their users a seamless experience, regardless of their device. They should also remember that the digital landscape constantly evolves, with new devices and platforms emerging. They need to stay current to remain competitive in the digital marketplace.

As illustrated in Figure 3.1, the device hosts the platform upon which the engagement, interaction, and the whole digital consumption happens—through the device, users can access the platform and engage with the brand. Engagement on digital platforms can take many forms, such as likes, shares, comments, clicks, and purchases. These metrics provide businesses with data about their users' behaviour, preferences, and interests, which can be used to optimise their marketing strategies, improve user experience, and increase customer loyalty. The quality of the engagement is crucial for businesses, as it provides them with insights into how well their consumers are interacting with their platform. Notably, the engagement is paramount for managers as it indicates how well consumers interact with the platform they have provided (Chylinski et al., 2020). Managers need to monitor engagement on their digital platforms to ensure they meet their business goals and deliver value to their customers. They need to use analytics tools to track engagement metrics, such as conversion rates, bounce rates, time on site, and click-through rates, to identify areas for improvement and optimise their marketing campaigns (this is discussed in more detail in Data Analytics on Digital Platform in Chapter 7). Table 3.1 summarises the characteristics between the digital platform and devices.

Figure 3.1 The relationship between devices and platforms.

Table 3.1 The characteristics between the digital platform and devices

Features	Devices (Hardware)	Platform (Software)
Examples	Mobile phone Car Smart speaker Self-service machine Laptop Smart TV Smartwatch	Social media as a platform to upload and share pictures Artificial intelligence as a platform for autonomous vehicles and driverless cars Alexa (and Siri) as a platform to access the Internet Platform offers the opportunity to order food. Chrome is a platform for accessing the Internet. Netflix, Paramount, and Disney as streaming platforms Support operating system platforms like Apple WatchOS, Google Wear OS, and Samsung Tizen. Fitness and Health platforms such as Fitbit, Communication platforms such as messaging apps, music and entertainment platforms such as Spotify, and Navigation and location-based platforms such as Google Maps. Payment platforms such as Apple Pay and Google Pay. Smart home platforms such as Amazon Alexa and Google Assistant.
Digital consumption	You are not using the devices for digital consumption.	The platforms are being accessed through devices to ensure digital consumption.
The Gatekeepers	No gatekeeper. You can buy and use the devices; however, you may require a password/PIN (to log into your computer or phone).	Gatekeepers are needed. You need to sign up to get an account, use your password and log in details.
Access	Access is guaranteed. The device is for the consumer. You don't need anyone's permission.	Access may be denied if consumers don't abide by the terms and conditions.
Internet	Internet is not needed to use the devices. It, however, has inbuilt features which allow the device to determine its location and offer location-based features and services.	Internet is needed to access the platform.
Analytics	Analytics are not integral but may include built-in sensors and features that support monitoring and analytics. For example, smartwatches use a combination of sensors, including accelerometers, gyroscopes, and optical sensors, to track physical activity and monitor heart rate.	As data emerges from consumers' interaction on the platform. Analytics and insights are integral on platforms.

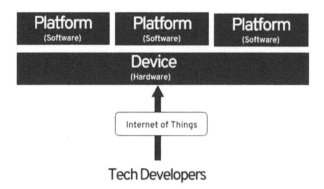

Figure 3.2 Graphic illustration of how a device can handle many platforms.

Figure 3.2 graphically illustrates how a device can handle many platforms, provided there is Internet to initiate the connection. The huge possibilities of a platform on devices present a significant challenge for managers developing platforms and evaluating consumer engagement in a digital environment. How many apps do you expect consumers to install on their phones? What's the size of their phone, and can it even take another app? How many apps do you use for Navigation—tom-tom, wave, Google Maps, and how many do you really use?

Unsurprisingly, the devices are getting bigger and with more capacity to allow more platforms to be installed. Now you have a mobile phone with about 256 GB internal storage to allow consumers to install different apps and enhance their digital consumption. Devices are making considerable advancements to meet the growing needs of consumers. For many years there was no apps store, but now there are many apps store besides Google Play and Apple Apps Store; for many years, there were phones with smaller screens and low-pixel cameras, but now device manufacturers like Apple, Samsung, and Google are competing to have the best camera megapixel. Even Chrome and Internet Explorer can operate with several tabs to meet the demands of consumers.

Many have a device, but not everyone is guaranteed access to the platform. Managers interested in understanding consumer engagement in the digital environment must keep a tab on the simultaneous progress and advancement of the devices and platforms (Sturgeon, 2021). There is a need to start reflecting on what the future holds for technology and how best to prepare for what lies ahead. What are the devices that are emerging—think about the flip phones and how you can start developing your platforms to align with those devices.

> **Reflective question**
>
> **Which is more important for a brand—their platform or consumers' devices?**

3.8 Activities on platforms

As consumers engage with digital platforms, they leave behind digital footprints that can include a wide range of information. This information may include a user's search and browsing history, social media activity, location data, purchase history, user pro-files, and cookies and tracking data. Platforms, brands, and advertisers can use this information better to understand users' preferences, behaviours, and interests and to deliver more targeted and personalised experiences. Managers are expected to understand these digital footprints to shape their strategic direction for managing consumer engagement in the digital environment. The key derivative of activities on the platform is DATA. This section addressed some of these data-driven activities and their importance to a business manager.

3.8.1 Data generation

How many pictures do you have on your phone? How many of them have you stored on Google Photos or Amazon Photos? How many tweets have you sent about a company, and how many movies have you streamed on Netflix? These insights can emerge from your activities on digital platforms as digital consumers. During digital consumption, consumers generate a lot of data. According to the listed Important Statistics About how much data is created every day, digital consumers generated 2.5 quintillion bytes of data every day in 2021, 41,666,667 million messages were sent daily on WhatsApp. In 2022, 333.2 billion emails were sent every day, and in 2022, 91% of Instagram users engage with brand videos (FinanceOnline, 2022). Consumers are generating data as they engage on digital platforms, and these data generation trends are bound to grow. With increasing access to the Internet, technologically advanced devices, and more engaging platforms, digital consumers will keep engaging with what's on offer.

> **Reflective question**
>
> You have heard about Gigabytes (your phone could be 128 GB storage) and Terabyte (Your Google Drive could be 2TB), 1,024 GB = 1 TB. How big is a yottabyte?

3.8.2 Data collection

While data is being generated on digital platforms during the engagement, it is imperative to recognise opportunities for data collection. You need to reflect on all the messages, tweets, and user-generated content from the consumers; how much of this data is being collected? Many data are generated but have yet to be collected and stored for analysis. This could be due to the company's manpower, infrastructure, or lack of awareness. At this point, it is imperative to recognise the ethical collection of the data. While it's been generated, organisations need to ensure that the data are collected ethically, with the consent of the consumers and assurance that it will be used appropriately. You might decide to take a picture of yourself using a brand; you have generated the data and shared it on your social media page; you would expect the brand to reach out to you with courtesy asking if they can feature your picture (using their brand) on an advertisement. Managers must be aware of the implication of the ethical collection of data; even though it might be readily available, data ethics forms an integral part of corporate digital responsibility for the brands.

3.8.3 Data analysis

Surely the brands are not just collecting this information for collection's sake. Tesco is not just collecting information on Clubcard users for collection's sake, and neither is Netflix collecting data for fun. The analysis of these data to shape business practices is essential. Managers need to find a way to analyse the vast amount of data to make an informed decision. This could be around precision-targeted, personalised offers, or targeted messaging. Digital consumers know that brands are collecting data about them, and they would appreciate it if the data is used to get them a personalised offer. Managers must explore opportunities to build on their data collection strategies and analyse the data to shape their business practices. Here artificial intelligence and machine learning are integral in developing algorithms that can learn from the data and enhance business operations and the customer's digital experience. Managers must evaluate their data infrastructure and human and technical resources to collect and analyse data.

3.8.4 Evaluating engagement

From the data analysis, brands can evaluate how well consumers engage with their digital platforms. This evaluation may go beyond selling to see if and how consumers benefit from digital innovations. This could be the National Health Services evaluating how people use the online appointment booking system or the University assessing how well students use the virtual learning environment. This evaluation could also involve reasons for national security, seeing people's messages, and monitoring online activities to protect against specific threats, such as terrorists or hostile states. No doubt, this evaluation should comply with stipulated data protection regulations, but in some cases, there could be justifiable reasons to adopt a 'neither confirm nor deny' (NCND) response about whether the engagement has been evaluated for national security purposes. Ultimately, managers need to keep a tab of activities on their platform, ensuring their data infrastructure is fit for purpose.

3.8.5 Dark activities

While engagement on digital platforms may be anticipated for a good purpose, it is imperative to recognise that there are inherent challenges and opportunities for this engagement and digital consumption to be jeopardised—more of this is to be discussed in Chapter 9. Dark sides exist, and bad activities are happening on digital platforms. This may involve activities around terrorism, cyber-attack, and fraud (Mogaji & Nguyen, 2022; Verbeke & Hutzschenreuter, 2021). These shady activities can jeopardise the business operations of the organisation. Likewise, individuals engaging in digital consumption are exposed to scams—people cloning their cards and making an authorised purchase, people are exposed to trolling and abuses—remember the three black football players facing racist abuse after England's Euro 2020 defeat? Managers must know these dark sides and implement measures to support their staff and customers. This could mean providing additional support and training for staff managing companies' social media accounts where angry consumers may be swearing at them. Likewise, fraudulent activities must be flagged to protect the consumers. As discussed in Chapter 2, Section 6, digital consumers are empowered, and sometimes they can use their power on the digital platform to abuse other users, brands, and platform developers (Sağkaya

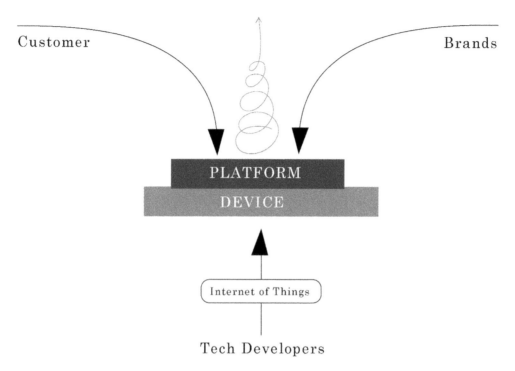

Figure 3.3 Data emerging from consumers' interaction with brands on digital platforms hosted by the devices and supported by the Internet.

Güngö & Ozansoy Çadırcı, 2022). However, they have the responsibility to remove customers perpetrating these acts and ensure the safety and well-being of others.

Summarising these activities, Figure 3.3 illustrates the engagement of these stakeholders, noting that when consumers and brands engage on digital platforms provided by tech developers and supported by the Internet of Things (IoT), it can lead to the emergence of data (Nižetić et al., 2020). This data can come from various sources, such as user interactions with the platform, IoT sensors that capture information about the environment or products, and third-party data sources that are integrated into the platform. The emergence of this data can provide valuable insights for brands and businesses, allowing them to understand their customers better and make more informed decisions about their marketing and business strategies. For example, companies can identify trends, preferences, and behaviours by analysing user data and informing product development and marketing campaigns. More of this is to be discussed in Chapter 7, which focuses on data analytics on digital platforms. The emergence of data on digital platforms and IoT devices has the potential to drive innovation and improve customer experiences, but it is essential to balance this with considerations for privacy and security.

3.9 Challenges

Digital platforms and IoT devices can benefit consumers, brands, and organisations significantly, but stakeholders must be aware and address some challenges—access, connectivity, technical skills, privacy and security, and user experience are all factors that can impact consumer engagement. The challenges discussed in this section are about access to digital platforms. Brands, organisations, and tech developers need to consider these challenges when designing and implementing digital platforms, as these considerations can enhance the experiences of digital consumers on the platform (Mogaji & Nguyen, 2022). There needs to be more than the awareness to address the challenges to increase quality engagement on the platform through the devices—creating technologies that are more accessible, reliable, and user-friendly, which can, in turn, improve consumer engagement and satisfaction.

3.9.1 Digital divide

There is a digital divide regarding access to the digital platform. There is digital poverty where only some can access platforms because of their devices. This digital divide is not just about the global north versus the global south but affordability. Until January 2022, before Blackberry's operating system for mobile phones was decommissioned, many people were accessing platforms through their Blackberry phones. However, their experiences and activities on the platform have changed. Managers must recognise that many people may be digitally excluded even when developing innovative solutions for the platform. There is a lack of support for obsolete devices like Blackberry and Nokia phones and a growing desire to keep up with emerging technologies—never devices and upgrade versions. It is not surprising to see organisations working on developing affordable digital devices for people to access the platform. There are many cheap Android phones outside of Samsung and Google. How did you dispose of your PS4 when you wanted to get the PS5? You might want to start considering donating hardware for people in need, and some people will still benefit from your old hardware. Geographical locations can also present a digital divide for people trying to access the platform—many people may not be able to access your platform by virtue of their locations. You might be using your WhatsApp in the UK but unable to use it in UAE. This challenge is not about your inability to use the platform but the virtue of your going on holiday in another country. Contractual agreements, copyright, and language issues can also reiterate the digital divide. For example, Google Maps isn't available in some regions because of contractual limitations, language support, and address formats.

3.9.2 Internet access

As iterated in the feature of digital consumers, access to the Internet can pose a challenge for consumers accessing the platform. The quality of Internet connectivity can vary widely depending on location and other factors, impacting the reliability and usability of digital platforms and devices. There are many people out there with devices who need the Internet to access the platform. Internet access can also exacerbate a digital divide where people need help with the Internet and cannot enjoy the platform's benefits. Managers should start understanding how to streamline people's experiences on platforms even when they don't have Internet access. That is why you see Facebook allowing you to send a message and promising you to send it when you connect to the Internet. You can also save an area from Google Maps to your phone or tablet and use it when you're offline. Likewise, SugarSync and Box cloud storage platforms give you access to your file when you are offline, and you can sync entire folders for offline access rather than selecting files individually. You might also have experienced a suggestion to switch off your video when making a call online; these are the platform's initiative to help digital consumers manage their expectations when they have little to no Internet access. Managers must consider if and how consumers can access the platform without Internet access. Can they offer an offline alternative or a low-bandwidth alternative? The company might also provide free Internet access (as seen at airports, Schools, and Train stations); it is, however, imperative to be mindful of ethical implications—free Internet or accessible data collection and likewise, consumers to be aware and cognizant of their vulnerability when using the free internet.

3.9.3 Knowledge and skills

The knowledge and ability to use the platform can be a challenge for prospective digital consumers. Some consumers may need more technical skills or expertise to effectively engage with digital platforms and devices, which can limit their ability to take advantage of these technologies. As alluded to in Chapter 1, digital consumers are on different levels, and the manager wants to start asking if and how digital consumers can use their platforms. How is it being designed? How about the user interface? Would it require a different cognitive skill level, or do you expect anyone to use it? There could be a need to educate consumers about the platforms and invite them to use them (Balakrishnan et al., 2021). You would require a different skill set to use Google Analytics than Facebook. Unsurprisingly, many people still find LinkedIn challenging, and likewise, TikTok. That's why you see a different advertisement to introduce the digital platforms and, in some cases, have an influencer demonstrate it.

An example is a Monday.com—project management portal which was being advertised on YouTube, and the client is demonstrating how they used it; likewise, an example of Wix.com being advertised with staff demonstrating how they are using the platform to create a website. These demonstrations help educate people and build their knowledge, awareness, and skills. Imagine your first time using your University's virtual learning environment—Moodle, Blackboard, or Canvas. Do you think it has been designed to align with your knowledge and skills? Managers must evaluate their digital platforms to ensure they provide user-friendly, engaging, and interactive platforms. Managers need to consider creating content—like short YouTube videos about how to use the platforms.

3.9.4 Ability

The ability to use the digital platform is considered different from knowledge and skills but more of the physical and mental ability to engage with the device and platform. Think of how a visually impaired person can shop online, tweet, and post pictures on Instagram; how about those with learning disabilities? Should they be excluded? Managers must start exploring inclusive design with their platform to ensure that digital consumers engage in digital consumption irrespective of their ability or disabilities. Brands have responsibilities to engage with the tech developer to address these key issues around their platform. Tim Berners-Lee, W3C Director and inventor of the World Wide Web, said, 'The power of the Web is in its universality. Access by everyone, regardless of disability, is an essential aspect. You should ask your website developers how to design your website to be inclusive and compliant with the Web Content Accessibility Guidelines (WCAG) international standard". Beyond the website, you want to consider your mobile app, self-service kiosk, and virtual reality platforms encompass all disabilities that affect access to the digital platforms, including auditory, cognitive, neurological, physical, speech, and visual. You should consider how wheelchair users will tap into their contactless card at the train station. How would they make their order on the self-service kiosk at the restaurant? How about those who are neurodivergent and dealing with colours? How would you design your mobile app? Managers must recognise these inherent challenges and improve their digital platform designs.

3.9.5 Data control

While digital consumption has led to increased data, there are inherent challenges in accessing and effectively using this data to enhance business operations. Some consumers are unwilling to share information with the company; they are not ready to be tracked or share their locations and may even drop a fake email address to bypass the website's email request. Likewise, there has been a growing concern about data privacy and security on digital platforms in recent years (Andrew & Baker, 2021). As a result, tech developers are implementing measures to control access to data and ensure that consumers' personal information is protected. For example, Google is pushing for a cookieless world, meaning it will no longer use cookies to track user activity online.

Similarly, Apple is taking control of consumer data and tracking on its iPhones by introducing features like App Tracking Transparency, which gives users more control over which apps can track their data. These developments reflect the growing importance of data privacy and security in the digital age. Regulators around the world are increasingly scrutinising how brands and tech developers collect, use, and store data on digital platforms. For example, the General Data Protection Regulation (GDPR) in the European Union and the California Consumer Privacy Act (CCPA) in the United States have set new data privacy and security standards and have given consumers greater control over their personal information. These regulations have forced brands and tech developers to be more transparent about how they collect and use data and to provide users with more control over their data. In this way, regulators are working to protect consumers' privacy rights in the digital age (Mogaji et al., 2020). With increasing regulatory scrutiny and consumer concerns about data privacy, brands need help to collect and use data from third-party sources such as social media platforms and ad networks. As a result, many brands are now turning to 'zero-party data', which refers to data that consumers willingly and proactively share with a brand. This might include information such as preferences, purchase history, and feedback on products or services. By building their data collection strategies and focusing on zero-party data, brands can create more direct relationships with consumers and gather more accurate and relevant data that can be used to drive business growth.

3.9.6 Legal and regulatory requirements

Significant legal and regulatory implications may affect access to the platform—these implications could be from an individual or a country perspective. For example, remember the case of Donald Trump, the former president of the United States, who was restricted from accessing the platform. As alluded to earlier, some countries have stopped access to certain platforms. For example, Twitter was banned in Nigeria; even though consumers are welcome on Twitter, the legal and political situation limits their participation. The legal requirement also expects brand and tech developers to put an age limit on accessing the platform (Olannye-Okonofua, 2021). Have you tried visiting Heineken's website? The website will ask you, 'When were you born?' The brands want to ensure you are an adult before accessing content on their platform. Likewise, you would expect pornography and X-rated websites to have these age limits on their websites. In addition, you will expect social media pages to have an age limit for those who want to create an account. It's, however, another conversation if these visitors are actually of that age. Heineken will not know if you have faked your birthday to access their websites, but they have done their best to ensure the right digital consumers can access their platforms. By law and regulatory requirements, most popular social media services require users to be at least 13 years of age before registering, but haven't you seen children on these pages? You would, however, be mindful that brands should have measures in place to maintain control.

Reflective question

At what age would you expect your niece to have a YouTube channel?

It is imperative to recognise that we think beyond these challenges. While managers need to be aware of these challenges, they need to find a way to address them to enhance consumer engagement in the digital environment. Table 3.2 summarises the key challenges and what brands and managers can do.

Reflective questions

What are the advantages and disadvantages of a brand having a digital platform?

3.10 Conclusion

Consumer engagement in the digital environment will be enabled through their access to devices and platforms. Brands and managers interested in managing digital consumption must know how consumers can access their platforms. Brands are investing money into developing their platform and must get consumers to engage. This chapter has looked at the differences between the devices and platforms, recognising that the devices serve as the host to the platform offers, and the different features of devices and digital platforms have been discussed.

Ultimately managers need to understand the activities on the platforms and how they can enhance their business operations. Data is a critical component of digital consumption and engagement on digital platforms. Brands and managers can leverage

Table 3.2 Key challenges and action points for managers

s/n	Challenges	Action points
1	Digital divide	■ Provide support as long as possible.
		■ Make cheap phones to bridge the digital divide.
		■ Donate hardware to those in need.
		■ Recycling hardware—Allow consumers to recycle their hardware.
2	Internet access	■ Provide free Wi-Fi at airports, Schools, and Train stations.
		■ Be mindful of ethical implications—free Internet or free data collection.
		■ Warn consumers about their vulnerability and exposure to hackers.
		■ If not free, make it affordable.
3	Knowledge and skills	■ Educating customers about the platform.
		■ Advertising the platform to expand people's knowledge.
		■ Demonstrate how it works—build trust, get demonstrators, and reassure people.
		■ Provide a user-friendly platform.
		■ Provide customers with short videos (on YouTube) showing people using it.
4	Ability	■ Inclusive design.
		■ Colour design—neurodivergence.
		■ Adaptive technology.
		■ Text descriptions.
		■ Work with developers to address the inclusive designs.
5	Data control	■ Offer transparency and give consumers control over their data.
		■ Implement measures to protect consumer data and ensure data privacy and security.
		■ Adjust data collection strategies to account for growing regulatory scrutiny and consumer concerns.
		■ Focus on zero-party data and build direct relationships with consumers.
		■ Gather accurate and relevant data to drive business growth.
		■ Develop a clear understanding of data regulations and privacy laws in the regions where the business operates.
6	Legal and regulatory requirements	■ Create yours—Donald Trump created TRUTH social media after being banned on major social media.
		■ Explore other platforms—something your target audience likes—website vs social media.
		■ Be innovative—create your device and close the ecosystem of devices—think Apple starting iPhone and Appstore.
		■ Protect users from abuse, and ensure the right people (the right age) gain access to the platform.

v to understand consumer behaviour, preferences, and needs. This can help them make more informed decisions about engaging with consumers and improving their products and services. However, managers must ensure they collect and use data ethically and responsibly, respecting consumer privacy and following relevant regulations. Data can be collected through various means, such as cookies, tracking pixels, and user accounts. This data can then be analysed to gain insights into consumer behaviour, such as what content they engage with, how long they spend on the platform, and what actions they take (Ponzoa & Erdmann, 2021). This data can also personalise the consumer experience, providing tailored content and recommendations based on their previous activity.

The chapter has also highlighted some challenges consumers may face while accessing digital platforms, such as poor connectivity, high data costs, and lack of digital literacy. Brand managers need to be aware of these challenges and take steps to address them. For example, they can work with telecommunication companies to provide affordable data packages for consumers or invest in digital literacy programmes to educate consumers on digital platforms. By addressing these challenges, brand managers can increase consumer engagement on their digital platforms and improve their overall business performance.

3.11 Student activities

1. What is your understanding of the difference between devices and platforms?
2. What is the concept of digital platforms, and how are they used in engaging customers?
3. What are your expectations for brands when consumers engage with their platform?
4. Think of a digital device you are not using; why are you not using these platforms? What are the challenges and limitations?
5. Think of a digital platform that you are not using. Why are you not using these platforms? What are the challenges and limitations?
6. How can brands and tech developers ensure digital platforms suit consumers and meet their business needs?
7. Why is it essential for brands to consider an inclusive design with their digital platform?
8. What practical action point will you expect from (i) website design, (ii) mobile app design, and (iii) self-service kiosk design regarding ability and legal requirements?
9. Why do you expect brands and consumers to engage on a digital platform?
10. How do you describe the role of Google, Amazon, Facebook, Apple, and Microsoft (GAFAM) in developing digital devices and platforms?

Reference and further reading

Abdulquadri, A., Mogaji, E., Kieu, T. & Nguyen, P., 2021. Digital transformation in financial services provision: A Nigerian perspective to the adoption of chatbot. *Journal of Enterprising Communities: People and Places in the Global Economy*, 15(2), pp. 258–281.

Agbo, F. et al., 2020. Social media usage for computing education: The effect of tie strength and group communication on perceived learning outcome. *Journal of Education and Development using Information and Communication Technology*, 16(1), pp. 5–26.

Andrew, J. & Baker, M., 2021. The general data protection regulation in the age of surveillance capitalism. *Journal of Business Ethics*, 168, pp. 565–578.

Azmoodeh, M., Haghighi, F. & Motieyan, H., 2021. Proposing an integrated accessibility-based measure to evaluate spatial equity among different social classes. *Environment and Planning B: Urban Analytics and City Science*, 48(9), pp. 2790–2807.

Balakrishnan, J., Nwoba, A. & Nguyen, N., 2021. Emerging-market consumers' interactions with banking chatbots. *Telematics and Informatics*, 65, 101711.

Chattopadhyay, A., Kupe, T., Schatzer, N. & Mogaji, E., 2022. Fireside chat with three vice chancellors from three continents. In: E. Mogaji, V. Jain, F. Maringe & R. Hinson, eds. *Re-imagining Higher Education in Emerging Economies*. Cham: Palgrave Macmillan, pp. 85–96.

Chylinski, M. et al., 2020. Augmented reality marketing: A technology-enabled approach to situated customer experience. *Australasian Marketing Journal*, 28(4), pp. 374–384.

Dhruv, G., Hulland, J., Kopalle, P. & Karahanna, E., 2020. The future of technology and marketing: A multidisciplinary perspective. *Journal of the Academy of Marketing Science*, 48, pp. 1–8.

Dwivedi, Y. et al., 2022. Metaverse beyond the hype: Multidisciplinary perspectives on emerging challenges, opportunities, and agenda for research, practice and policy. *International Journal of Information Management*, 66, 102542.

FinanceOnline, 2022. 53 important statistics about how much data is created every day [Online] Available at: https://financesonline.com/how-much-data-is-created-every-day/

Flew, T., Martin, F. & Suzor, N., 2019. Internet regulation as media policy: Rethinking the question of digital communication platform governance. *Journal of Digital Media & Policy*, 10(1), pp. 33–50.

Gartner, 2023. What is data and analytics? [Online]. Available at: https://www.gartner.com/en/topics/data-and-analytics

Gawer, A., 2021. Digital platforms' boundaries: The interplay of firm scope, platform sides, and digital interfaces. *Long Range Planning*, 54(5), pp. 102045–102056.

Hein, A. et al., 2020. Digital platform ecosystems. *Electronic Markets*, 30, pp. 87–98.

Hodapp, D. & Hanelt, A., 2022. Interoperability in the era of digital innovation: An information systems research agenda. *Journal of Information Technology*, 37(4), pp. 407–427.

Ibert, O., Oechslen, A., Repenning, A. & Schmidt, D., 2022. Platform ecology: A user-centric and relational conceptualization of online platforms. *Global Networks*, 22(3), pp. 564–579.

Jelovac, D., Ljubojević, C. & Ljubojević, L., 2022. HPC in business: The impact of corporate digital responsibility on building digital trust and responsible corporate digital governance. *Digital Policy, Regulation and Governance*, 24(6), pp. 485–497.

Kandampully, J., Bilgihan, A. & Li, D., 2022. Unifying technology and people: Revisiting service in a digitally transformed world. *The Service Industries Journal*, 42(1–2), pp. 21–41.

Kopalle, P., Kumar, V. & Subramaniam, M., 2020. How legacy firms can embrace the digital ecosystem via digital customer orientation. *Journal of the Academy of Marketing Science*, 48, pp. 114–131.

Miric, M., Boudreau, K. & Jeppesen, L., 2019. Protecting their digital assets: The use of formal & informal appropriability strategies by App developers. *Research Policy*, 48(8), 103738.

Mogaji, E., 2021. *Brand Management*. Cham: Springer.

Mogaji, E. & Nguyen, N., 2022. Managers' understanding of artificial intelligence in relation to marketing financial services: Insights from a cross-country study. *International Journal of Bank Marketing*, 40(6), pp. 1272–1298.

Mogaji, E. & Nguyen, N., 2022. The dark side of mobile money: Perspectives from an emerging economy. *Technological Forecasting and Social Change*, 185, 122045.

Mogaji, E., Soetan, T. & Kieu, T., 2020. The implications of artificial intelligence on the digital marketing of financial services to vulnerable customers. *Australasian Marketing Journal*, 29(3), p. 235–242.

Morgan-Thomas, A., Dessart, L. & Veloutsou, C., 2020. Digital ecosystem and consumer engagement: A socio-technical perspective. *Journal of Business Research*, 121, pp. 713–723.

Nižetić, S., Šolić, P., González-De, D. & Patrono, L., 2020. Internet of Things (IoT): Opportunities, issues and challenges towards a smart and sustainable future. *Journal of Cleaner Production*, 274, 122877.

Ogundokun, R., Afolayan, J., Adegun, J. & Afolabi, A., 2020. Marketing information products and services through digital platforms: Tools and skills. In: Adeyinka Tella, eds. *Handbook of Research on Digital Devices for Inclusivity and Engagement in Libraries*. New York: IGI Global, pp. 93–112.

Olannye-Okonofua, D., 2021. Twitter ban in Nigeria: A metaphor for impediment on uses and gratification theory. *International Journal of Social Sciences*, 4(1), pp. 198–206.

Olson, E., Olson, K., Czaplewski, A. & Key, T., 2021. Business strategy and the management of digital marketing. *Business Horizons*, 64(2), pp. 285–293.

Oosthuizen, K., Botha, E., Robertson, J. & Montecchi, M., 2021. Artificial intelligence in retail: The AI-enabled value chain. *Australasian Marketing Journal*, 29(3), pp. 264–273.

Ponzoa, J. & Erdmann, A., 2021. E-commerce customer attraction: Digital marketing techniques, evolution and dynamics across firms. *Journal of Promotion Management*, 27(5), pp. 697–715.

Sağkaya Güngö, A. & Ozansoy Çadırcı, T., 2022. Understanding digital consumer: A review, synthesis, and future research agenda. *International Journal of Consumer Studies*, 46(5), pp. 1829–1858.

Sheth, J., 2020. Impact of Covid-19 on consumer behavior: Will the old habits return or die? *Journal of Business Research*, 117, pp. 280–283.

Soetan, T., Mogaji, E. & Nguyen, N., 2021. Financial services experience and consumption in Nigeria. *Journal of Services Marketing*, 35(7), pp. 947–961.

Sturgeon, T., 2021. Upgrading strategies for the digital economy. *Global Strategy Journal*, 11(1), pp. 34–57.

Tafesse, W. & Dayan, M., 2023. Content creators' participation in the creator economy: Examining the effect of creators' content sharing frequency on user engagement behavior on digital platforms. *Journal of Retailing and Consumer Services*, 73, 103357.

Verbeke, A. & Hutzschenreuter, T., 2021. The dark side of digital globalization. *Academy of Management Perspectives*, 35(4), pp. 606–621.

Brands on platforms

4.1 Background

This chapter focuses on brands and their activities on digital platforms. In Chapter 2, we discussed digital consumers engaging and interacting on digital platforms, and in Chapter 3, we discussed the digital platforms that support digital consumption. This chapter focuses on the importance of recognising the role of brands on digital platforms and how they can enhance the overall digital consumption experience. Brands play a crucial role in creating a seamless and engaging digital experience for their customers. They must keep investing in their digital platforms to remain competitive and relevant. The chapter explores some motivations for brands to keep investing in their digital platform, including the need to build customer loyalty and trust, the potential for cost savings and increased efficiency, and the desire to remain competitive in a rapidly evolving digital landscape. By investing in their digital platforms, brands can differentiate themselves from their competitors, create a positive brand image, and offer customers a seamless and personalised experience. The chapter also identifies some key considerations for brands as they explore different platform options for consumer engagement, such as the level of control and ownership, the potential for cost savings and increased efficiency, and the level of customisation and personalisation. Additionally, the chapter provides some strategic directions for brands concerning their digital platforms, such as focusing on customer experience, leveraging data analytics and artificial intelligence, and collaborating with other brands and third-party providers. Overall, the chapter provides a comprehensive overview of the different platforms available to brands and the key considerations and strategic directions they should keep in mind as they invest in their digital platforms for consumer engagement.

DOI: 10.4324/9781003389842-4

4.2 Learning outcomes
By the end of this chapter, you should be able to:

- Understand why brands come on the platform to engage.
- Recognise different platforms for brands to engage.
- Explain the different brand activities of the platform.
- Identify key considerations for brands on the platform.
- Provide strategic direction for brands considering a platform for engaging digital consumers.

4.3 Introduction
Brands are aware of digital transformation around them; they see how these transformations change business operations. Business is expected to act and align with emerging digital technologies. This alignment is essential to ensure viability and sustainability. There is growing investment in technology as brands try to meet their customers' needs. The Oracle (2020) report on emerging technologies offering a competitive edge for companies found that 80% of companies use at least one emerging technology for finance and operations; companies that have used these emerging technologies have increased their annual revenue by 58% and grew their annual net income 80% than their counterparts who do not. Brands are beginning to recognise the need to 'disrupt or be disrupted'.

Brands are aware that digital consumers are meeting and congregating on platforms and want to come on board and engage (Santos et al., 2022). The brands need to know the types of platforms that are available and where to invest their resources. There is an investment in artificial intelligence, the Internet of Things (IoT), robotics process automation, augmented reality, and metaverse (Vander Schee et al., 2020). Brands are recognised that engaging with consumers on the digital platform is beneficial for their financial viability, sustainability, and brand reputation. There are inherent benefits for brands in this ecosystem, so investment is needed.

Several platforms are available for brands, including websites, mobile apps, and social media. Each platform offers unique benefits and challenges, and brands must carefully consider their goals and objectives before deciding which platform to invest in. Some key considerations include the target audience, the content and services offered, and the level of interactivity and engagement required (Hamzah et al., 2021). Managers, however, need to have justifiable reasons for the strategic decision on where and what to invest, the type of technology to use, and the platforms to engage with their customers. This may be a huge decision to make, and there is a need to have every possible knowledge.

This chapter addresses some concerns around knowledge about suitable platforms for brands, key considerations of which platform, and some inherent challenges to be aware of. At the end of this chapter, you will be able to critically reflect on which digital platform to select for your company (as employed staff), a client (as a freelancer or consultant), and your career (as a start-up founder). Overall, this chapter emphasises the importance of recognising the role of brands in enhancing the digital consumption experience and provides some key insights and considerations for brands as they explore different options for investing in their digital platform (Abdulquadri et al.,

2021; Agbo et al., 2020; Balakrishnan et al., 2021). This knowledge is important for prospective managers deciding on their digital platform and tech developers working with brands to develop their platform. You are expected to acquire the knowledge needed to make an informed decision, ask some tough questions, and reflect on your digital transformation strategies.

Reflective questions

How many platforms can you name? Should brands consider these platforms?

4.4 Motivations for brands on platforms

This section explores the motivations for brands to invest in the platform. When I refer to brands, this could mean an individual who is an influencer, a university with students from different parts of the world, or a company selling furniture. These different motivations for brands influence their investment and effort towards platform management. The challenging and reflecting questions for brands are: Why come to the platform? It is not cheap or easy to have digital platforms. It requires a strategic approach with versatile human, technical, and financial resources and capabilities.

4.4.1 Business norm

In today's digital age, it has become essential for businesses to establish a presence on digital platforms (Dhaoui & Webster, 2021). With more and more people spending time online, companies must take advantage of the opportunity to engage with their target audience and expand their reach. As a result, having a website, social media profiles, and mobile apps has become a business norm, and many innovative brands are exploring new digital platforms like the metaverse to stay ahead of the curve. By having a presence on digital platforms, businesses can stay connected with their target audience 24/7, regardless of location or time zone. Additionally, digital platforms allow companies to analyse customer behaviour and preferences, which can be used to improve their marketing strategies and increase sales. In addition, by investing in digital platforms, brands can reach a wider audience and connect with customers in different geographic locations. This can help to expand the customer base and increase sales. Digital platforms can also provide customers with a more convenient and seamless shopping experience, from browsing products to purchasing and receiving support. This can help to build brand loyalty and increase customer satisfaction (Giakoumaki & Krepapa, 2020).

The question, however, remains if brands need to come to all these digital platforms to engage. Would you expect your fashion brand targeting Gen Z to have a LinkedIn page? Would you propose to your marketing managers to have a Reddit page for the fashion brand? Would you expect your fishmonger on the high street to have a mobile app? While it is a business norm for businesses, managers must critically evaluate how the business norm for the platform and digital transformation aligns with their needs, customer expectations, and resources (Soetan et al., 2021). Managers must also decide if it is worth going away from the business norm—to do something different to make their brand stand out (Hein et al., 2020). Apple went away from the QWERTY business norms with the keyboard on mobile phones and created the touch screen phones. Primark had no e-commerce website, and customers could only purchase products from their physical stores. However, in recent years, Primark has started to explore the possibility of expanding into online sales, recognising the increasing importance of e-commerce in the retail industry; while Primark may have been slow to embrace e-commerce, the company is now taking steps to expand its online presence and adapt to the changing retail landscape, the company has come to recognise that having a digital platform like a website is a normal business necessity.

4.4.2 Meeting the consumers

Another reason and motivations for brands on the platforms are to meet the consumers. Brands are aware that their consumers are engaging on many different platforms, and they can as well come and engage (Labrecque et al., 2020). Brands know consumers are on social media, so they create their own pages and communities. Brands know that consumers will go into the metaverse, so they started buying real estate and creating experiences in the metaverse. Brands know that digital consumers want touchscreen experiences, so they started offering touchscreen self-services at restaurants. Brands want to meet those who should benefit from their products and services and showcase what they offer. Importantly, as iterated in Section 3.8 on platform activities, brands want to collect customer data. As long as you, as a digital consumer, have clicked on and accepted their terms of use and that you agree to abide by them, your data is being collected. This could also include your data via email sign-ups.

Interestingly, brands are also motivated to see what their competitors are doing and what they are providing to the customers. Meeting consumers' need for personalisation is indeed one of the key motivations for brands to invest in a digital platform. With a digital platform, brands can collect data on their customers' preferences, purchase history, and behaviour, which can be used to personalise the customer experience and offer targeted promotions and recommendations. Email sign-ups are a common way for brands to collect customer data and build their email marketing list. By encouraging customers to sign up for their email newsletters, brands can stay in touch with their customers, provide updates on new products and promotions, and gather valuable data on their customers' preferences and behaviour.

4.4.3 Channel of communication

When did you last visit a high street store to make a complaint? Often digital consumers will use the digital platform as a channel to communicate with brands (Mogaji, 2021). Likewise, brands will use digital platforms to communicate with their customers. If you have bad service with a company, you may want to tweet about your experience. Mogaji and Erkan (2019) studied how UK commuters used Twitter to complain and share experiences about their train transport companies. Likewise, when these train companies want to announce their strike actions, they share updates on their websites, mobile app, and social media. While they may have put their posters at the train stations, they want to use their various digital platforms to communicate with staff. Likewise, Universities will use Moodle and another virtual learning environment to communicate with students, Uber will update you about your driver on their apps, and Influencers will ask you to click the notification buttons to stay updated with their new content. Brands are on digital platforms to also get consumer feedback; brands can carry out brand listening on social media, carry out sentiment analysis to understand digital consumers' attitudes towards their brand, review comments on Trustpilot about the brands, and see comments on those who have downloaded their apps.

Digital platforms provide numerous opportunities for brands to connect and engage with their customers. By encouraging customers to follow them on social media or download their mobile app, brands can provide updates on new products and promotions, answer customer questions and concerns, and gather feedback from their audience. However, with these opportunities also come challenges for brands. With so many digital platforms available, it can be difficult for brands to know which ones to focus on and how to optimise their engagement strategies. To be successful in the digital space, brands must evaluate their business practices and find ways to improve their engagement with digital consumers. This may involve investing in new technology and tools to understand better and analyse customer data, developing targeted marketing campaigns that are tailored to specific segments of their audience, or collaborating with influencers and other brands to reach a wider audience. Ultimately, the key to success in the digital space is to be flexible, adaptive, and willing to experiment with new approaches to stay ahead of the competition and meet digital consumers' evolving needs and expectations.

4.4.4 Gain insights

Building on the prospects of digital platforms for communication, numerous communication channels are being opened for a consumer-brand relationship, and data are being generated. Managers must be aware of the plethora of channels and start exploring how to gain insight which will change their business operations (Miric et al., 2019). Brands are motivated to engage on the platform because they can achieve precision targeting through artificial intelligence, machine learning, and algorithm that can progress vast amounts of data from digital consumers on the platform. Gaining insight is not just about how many products you are selling or how many appointments have been booked; it may simply mean how many people click on their advert about vaccine boosters. Brands are on the platform to evaluate their investment and see how consumers use it. It is imperative that managers may seek assistance from analytics and third-party companies like Hotjar, Clicky, and Google Analytics.

Brands invest in digital platforms not only to engage with their customers but also to evaluate the performance of their digital marketing campaigns and the effectiveness of their investment. To achieve this, managers may seek assistance from analytics and third-party companies like Hotjar, Clicky, and Google Analytics. These companies provide various tools and technologies to track and analyse customer behaviour, engagement, and conversions on digital platforms. By using these tools, brands can gain valuable insights into how their customers use their digital platforms, which areas are most popular, where customers are dropping off, and what they need to do to improve their engagement and conversions. For example, Google Analytics provides a wealth of data on website traffic, user behaviour, and customer demographics. With this data, brands can better understand their audience and tailor their marketing campaigns to their needs and preferences. Hotjar, on the other hand, provides heatmaps, session recordings, and feedback polls to help brands identify areas for improvement on their website or app. Analytics and third-party companies are essential in assisting brands in evaluating their investment in digital platforms and optimising their engagement strategies. By leveraging these tools and technologies, brands can gain a competitive advantage in the digital space and provide their customers with a personalised, engaging, and seamless experience. Ogi Djuraskovic presented some of the best Web Analytics Tools in 2023, which brands can use to generate valuable insight into the performance of their digital platform (Djuraskovic, 2023).

Web Analytics Tools	Insights
Google Analytics	Turning data insights into action
Similarweb	Similarweb measures the digital world
Clicky	Analyse traffic in real-time
Matomo	Website analysis with 100% control
Finteza	Advanced web analysis and evaluation
Woopra	Understanding the customer journey
Chartbeat	Measure customer engagement
Hotjar	Understanding site traffic and data
Crazyegg	Detailed analysis of websites
Mixpanel	Web analysis and data science

Source: https://firstsiteguide.com/best-website-analytics-tools/

Digital platforms provide brands with an opportunity to not only connect with customers but also to monitor their competitors and stay abreast of industry trends. By analysing the behaviour of competitors on digital platforms, brands can gain valuable insights into their strategies, product offerings, and marketing tactics. This information can be used to adjust their strategies and stay ahead of the competition. Let us say a brand operates in the retail industry and has an online store on a digital platform like Amazon. By monitoring the behaviour of their competitors on the same platform, they can gain valuable insights into their competitors' product offerings, pricing strategies, and customer reviews (Kretschmer et al., 2022). For instance, they can track their competitors' pricing for similar products, identify their top-selling products, and analyse customer reviews to understand their strengths and weaknesses. With this information, the brand can adjust its pricing strategies, product offerings, and marketing tactics to differentiate itself from competitors and stay ahead of the curve. Additionally, they can use this information to create targeted promotions and advertisements that resonate with their target audience and drive sales. Additionally, digital platforms provide a space for brands to showcase their unique value proposition and differentiate themselves from their competitors, which can help to attract new customers and increase sales.

4.4.5 To sell

Ultimately with the amount of information collected from the consumers, it is time to sell to them. Brands are on digital platforms to meet the consumers and ultimately to sell. Why create an e-commerce website for your fashion brands and not have a payment option? Websites, apps, and social media create avenues for brands to sell to customers on their platforms. From small businesses having small shops on Instagram to the creative Christy doing customised t-shirts on Etsy and big corporations trading through their apps, brands have enormous opportunities to sell on digital platforms. A brand can afford not to have a website but rely on social media, including Instagram and WhatsApp. On a practical level, brand managers must consider the ownership and structure of their platform as they expand on their selling path (Morgan-Thomas et al., 2020). As a small business, would you want to keep selling on Instagram, or do you want to migrate to Shopify or have your e-commerce websites? Managers must reflect on the level of control, security risk, and data privacy (this will be discussed in the subsequent section under the type of platforms); mangers selling on other platforms need set to ask, what happens if Facebook or Amazon close their website? Ultimately, selling on digital platforms can reduce the brand's transaction cost of finding prospective customers.

The growing prospects of NFTs (Non-Fungible Tokens), cryptocurrencies, and metaverse wallets present significant opportunities for brands to sell on digital platforms. As consumers become more familiar with these technologies, they seek ways to use them for transactions in the metaverse and other digital spaces (Dwivedi et al., 2022). For example, NFTs are unique digital assets that can be bought and sold on various blockchain-based marketplaces. Brands can leverage NFTs to sell their customers digital collectibles, limited edition merchandise, and other unique digital products. There are emerging trends of brands going onto the metaverse (virtual platforms) to sell and engage with consumers. Coca-Cola recently created an NFT collectible that was auctioned on OpenSea, a leading NFT marketplace, and these collectibles garnered a winning bid of $575,883.61 in an online auction (Coca-Cola, 2021). Gucci launched a digital sneaker on Roblox, a popular metaverse platform, the digital pair of sneakers called The Gucci Virtual 25 that can be 'worn' in augmented reality (AR); it was sold as an NFT. The brand's creative director designed and sold the sneaker for around $12 (Campbell, 2021). As these technologies increase in popularity, we can expect more brands to experiment with them innovatively (Koohang et al., 2023).

> **Reflective question**
>
> Considering small business selling on eBay, Etsy, Facebook, and Amazon, how feasible is it for a brand to create its space within the platform to initiate customer engagement?

4.5 Typology of digital platforms for brands

The section is not about listing all available digital platforms but creating a typology or classification system for digital platforms. The section introduces the PESCO (Paid, Earned, Shared, Co-Created, and Owned) platforms, an extension of the PESO model, a well-known framework for classifying media types. The PESCO model adds a new category, Co-Created platforms, to the existing PESO framework. Co-Created platforms are digital platforms where customers, users, or brands are involved in co-creating and disseminating content. By creating this typology, this section provides a useful framework for businesses to understand the different types of digital platforms available and how they can be leveraged for marketing and engagement purposes. It also emphasises the importance of co-creation and user-generated content in today's digital landscape. It highlights the need for businesses to actively engage with their customers and involve them in creating content. It is important to emphasise that you should distinguish *platforms* from *media*. Though social media is a 'media' and 'platform', a printed newspaper is a media and not a digital platform. This section will describe the different types of PESCO platforms and their advantages and disadvantages. Table 4.1 presents a summary of these platforms.

4.5.1 Paid platforms

Paid platforms in the PESCO model refer to digital platforms that brand pay to access and use to engage with consumers. Often these platforms are only needed for a particular purpose, and the brand does not need to invest money to develop them, or they are not affordable for the company. Companies can pay for these platforms on a pay-as-you-go basis, meaning they only pay for what they use. This arrangement can be considered Software as a Service (SaaS). These paid platforms can be for project management (like Monday.com. asana.com), cloud storage (Google Drive, Dropbox), virtual learning environments for universities (Moodle, Blackboard), or e-commerce (Shopify, Wix). Imagine you are starting an e-commerce website selling sneakers. Would you want to create your own platform (e-commerce website), or do you want to use the service of Shopify? Shopify here is a paid platform where the brand owners pay a subscription fee to access the platform. You also need to remember that if you (the sneaker seller) do not pay your subscription to the platform owners (Shopify), your motivation for being on the platform (see Section 4.4.5—to sell) will be truncated. Your digital consumers may not be happy if they cannot place an order.

4.5.2 Earned platforms

These are platforms that a brand is using by virtue of their mutual agreement and activities with the brand owner. This type of platform may not necessarily be paid for but used collaboratively. Earned platforms are owned by another brand (a company or an individual), but brands can collaborate and reach a wider audience. These platforms are used when brands work with influencers, partnerships, demonstrations, and reviews of products. Content can be well planned to align with platform owners' values and ensure enough activities and engagement for consumers invited to engage on the platform. You (as brand manager) could be invited to a podcast to share information about your brand—you do not own the podcast (the platform owner is the host), but you have used that platform to engage with your customers (see Sections 4.4.2 and 4.4.3—to meet and communicate with consumers). You could also work with an influencer to create content about your brand on their platform. By virtue of your partnership with other platform owners, you get access to data, analytics, and insights (see Section 4.4.4—to gain insight)—Brands can use various digital tools and analytics to track the impact of their marketing efforts on different earned platforms. For example, they can track the number of views or downloads for a podcast episode featuring their brand or the number of people who used a unique code to purchase their products after seeing an influencer's post. This data can be used to evaluate the effectiveness of their marketing strategies and make informed decisions about future investments in digital platforms. It can also help them better understand their target audience and tailor their messaging and engagement to meet their needs and preferences. These insights may, however, be limited depending on the platform structures, owners, and analytics. Remember that you do not own the platform but rely on the host's feedback. It is, therefore, imperative for managers to critically evaluate their options concerning their earned platform.

Reflective question

Would you instead work with an influencer with 5000 followers and get 4000 sales or work with an influencer with 500,000 followers and make 40,000 sales?

4.5.3 Shared platform

Tech developers, often the dominant platform developers, own shared platforms but are open for brands to use to engage with their audiences. Examples of shared platforms include social media platforms like Facebook, Twitter, and Instagram, as well as messaging apps like WhatsApp and WeChat. Brands can use these platforms to reach a wider audience and engage with their followers by sharing content, responding to messages, and running targeted advertising campaigns. However, because a third-party provider owns these platforms, brands have less control over the platform's functionality and user experience. They may need to pay for additional features or advertising opportunities—as seen with Twitter Blue. Social media pages will often be categorised under this type of shared platform, and this is because the brands have not paid to use the platform and they are simply using it as a business norm (see Section 4.1.1) because everyone is there. Brands can create their pages on Facebook and create content for Facebook and invite consumers to come and engage with them on their page (remember the story at the beginning, VIP section in the nightclub is the brands inviting you to follow them on their page). Recognising that payment (making it a paid platform) comes with benefits and advantages is imperative. It is not surprising that Twitter is changing its pricing structure to see people now paying for Twitter Blue. The access to data and insights provided by the tech developer and platform owners is also an advantage for brands to keep using this shared platform—with Facebook pixel and Google Analytics, you can get deeper insights into how consumers engage with your platform.

Conversely, brands must be mindful of their vulnerability on these shared platforms. The brands have to abide by the terms and conditions of the platform owner—more like you are renting a room and you need to abide by the rules of the landlord, and in worst-case scenarios, you could be kicked out of the shared platform (because you do not own). If you are a small business owner selling on Amazon, your marketplace is at the mercy of Amazon; anything could happen if though they may have assured you all is well. Brands' content (to communicate and engage with consumers) may be moderated and even deleted. Remember Donald Trump (as a brand) was kicked out of Twitter (a shared platform), and not surprising that he had to go and create his own platform—TRUTH.

4.5.4 Co-created platform

These are platforms that are co-created by brands and/or consumers. Brand-led co-created platforms can share similarities with earned and owned platforms, but the structure and arrangement differ here. While a brand is hosted on an earned platform and could create its platforms, two brands can create a new one entirely. For example, when Kanye West and GAP collaborated to create a new brand, they had to have a co-created platform. Kanye (as a brand, has his own owned platform) and GAP have their platform, BUT they created a completely different website for the collaboration. In 2019, home goods brand West Elm partnered with rental service Rent the Runway to create a new home decor and bedding line called 'West Elm x Rent the Runway'. The collaboration created a new brand, and the products were sold through a new website, westelmrentals.com. The website, however, no longer functions. Ivy Park, a clothing brand co-founded by singer Beyoncé and Adidas, had a co-created platform—weareivypark on Instagram, @WeAreIvyPark on Twitter, and https://www.ivypark.com/ as their website, and these are different from the website of Beyoncé and Adidas.

These brand-led co-created platforms are created to manage the relationship and often not to impact the brands who are co-creating. These co-created platforms may often last for a short period while the co-creation and working relationship is going on, and once it is over, they can close their co-created platform and keep maintaining their platforms. Likewise, when there is a problem, as seen with Kanye West terminating his agreement with GAP, their digital platforms have to be removed. There are also challenges in managing these platforms. For example, at the time of writing, @WeAreIvyPark was last updated on Twitter on 28 October 2022; meanwhile, @adidasoriginals was updated on 27 March 2023. Commitment to these co-created platforms could be an issue for brands as companies may often feel that they are maintaining two different platforms simultaneously. They may choose to have the co-created brand with one of the companies instead of creating a new one. Nike and Tiffany collaborated to make a show, and they had to host the digital platform with Tiffany instead of just creating another platform.

Co-created digital platforms can also be consumer focused and led, developed through collaboration between the brand and its customers or other external stakeholders. These platforms are designed to facilitate customer engagement and co-create content or products. Examples of co-created digital platforms include online communities or forums where customers can share ideas, provide feedback, and collaborate with the brand on product development. Brands may also use co-creation platforms to gather customer data and insights to inform their marketing and product development strategies. Building and managing a community can be a demanding task for brands. However, it can also be rewarding as it allows brands to engage with their most loyal customers, gather valuable insights and feedback, and create a sense of belonging among their audience. Some examples of successful brand communities include Nike's NikePlus, Sephora's Beauty Insider, and Lego's Ideas platform. These communities provide a space for customers to interact with each other and with the brand, share their experiences and opinions, and participate in exclusive events and offers. In return, the brands can gather customer preferences, behaviours and need data, and use this information to improve their products and services. It is essential for brands to carefully consider their community strategy, including the platform(s) they use, the type of content they share, and the level of interaction they facilitate. They must also be prepared to invest resources in community management, including moderation, content creation, and customer service. However, the benefits of a thriving community can be significant in terms of customer loyalty, brand reputation, and revenue growth.

4.5.5 Owned platform

The brand owns this platform, and they have complete control. Brands try to have their platform to address the challenges of other platforms—the limited access to data, the fear of being kicked out, the moderation of their content, and even security and privacy. As with that Donald Trump's example, he had to create an entirely new social media company to address his challenges at Twitter. Brands can create their e-commerce website from scratch without relying on Shopify or Wix. Brands like McDonald's and KFC can have their app instead of relying on and putting all their effort into JustEat or UberEat. Brands can take control of their data, security, and content. The brands can get access to first-party data—they do not need to beg the influencers for data, they have access to everything on their platform, and they have control and can manage this process. Despite these huge advantages, it can be very expensive to create these owned platforms. Moreover, brand awareness to attract consumers may not always be there. Many people will see more options for Chinese food on Uber Eat than looking out for the Lucky Stat Chinese takeaway app. Also, consumers are now responsible for protecting the platform from cyberattacks and other security breaches. To address these challenges, some brand owners will start with a paid platform where they have a bit of control, enjoy brand awareness, and also can be covered with the security infrastructure of the platform providers. However, managers must reflect on if and when to move from a paid, shared platform into an owned one.

Platform	Description	Examples
Paid platform	The brand pays developers to use their platform for an agreed time and context.	Monday.com Google Drive Microsoft Teams
Earned	The brand earned the platform as a virtual of mutual engagement and activities.	Collaboration with partners
Shared	The brand is sharing the digital platform with other brands and other consumers.	Social media pages
Co-Created	Two or many other brands have come together to create a new brand, and therefore they have created different platforms for their co-created brands.	@WeAreIvyPark on Twitter and https://www.ivypark.com/. Adidas and Beyoncé are creating different platforms.
Owned	The brand owns the digital platforms, and it can control what goes on where and when.	Brand's website Brand's app Brand's metaverse space

4.6 Key consideration for brands

The digital landscape is constantly evolving, and brands must carefully consider their strategy for engaging with consumers in this environment. While there are many platforms available, not all of them will be a good fit for every brand, and it is essential to choose the ones that will help them achieve their business goals. Ultimately, the key is to approach digital engagement strategically and clearly understand the platforms available and their respective strengths and weaknesses. This section highlights some key considerations for brands; by being mindful and considerate, brands can better position themselves to reach and engage with their target audience, build brand awareness and loyalty, and ultimately drive business growth.

4.6.1 Managing the platform

Just because a company can have a presence on a particular platform does not necessarily mean that it is the right choice for them. It is essential for managers to carefully evaluate whether a particular platform aligns with their brand's values, goals, and target audience. Considering the resources required to manage a brand's presence on multiple platforms effectively is also imperative. Maintaining a consistent and engaging presence across multiple platforms can be challenging and time-consuming. Spreading resources too thin can lead to inconsistent and poor performance across all platforms. Instead, it may be more effective for a brand to focus its efforts on a select few platforms where it can consistently deliver value to its audience and achieve its business objectives. This approach ensures that the brand's message and identity are communicated effectively and consistently and can establish a strong presence and build meaningful relationships with its audience. Understanding the target audience is critical to choosing the right platform for a brand's digital engagement strategy.

4.6.2 Understanding the consumers on the platforms

Each platform has its unique user base and content style, and brands must choose the platforms where their target audience is most active. Additionally, brands should consider how they can effectively create content that will engage their target audience on each platform. The content should be tailored to fit the platform's format and style and align with the brand's overall messaging and values. Regarding the metaverse, there may be better fits for some brands. While it is a growing trend, it may not be a relevant platform for a brand selling vegetables on the high street. Instead, they may be better served to focus on platforms where their target audience is more likely to be found, such as social media platforms like Facebook or Instagram. Ultimately, it is essential for managers to carefully consider all of these factors when deciding on their digital engagement strategy. By doing so, they can ensure that their brand's message is communicated effectively and that they can build meaningful relationships with their target audience. You could also consider an example of a company that sells high-end luxury watches. In this case, the company's target audience will likely be affluent individuals who value luxury and quality craftsmanship. When choosing digital platforms for engagement, the company should consider platforms that cater to this demographic and align with its brand image. They may have a presence on Instagram and Facebook, where they can showcase high-quality images of their watches and connect with their audience through targeted advertising and influencer partnerships.

On the other hand, a platform like TikTok may not be the best fit for this brand, as it tends to cater to a younger audience and has a more informal content style. While there may be exceptions and opportunities for creativity, the brand needs to consider whether the platform aligns with its overall messaging and values. By carefully considering its target audience and the platforms that best align with its brand image, this company can develop a digital engagement strategy that effectively connects with its audience and helps drive business growth.

4.6.3 Digital technology dichotomies

The need to consider digital technology dichotomies aligns with the need to have a good understanding of consumers on the platform. These are critical considerations for brands when deciding the appropriate consumer platforms. These dichotomies refer to the various options available to businesses as they seek to create an effective digital presence that meets the needs and expectations of their customers. For example, many consumers prefer to transact on mobile apps instead of a website, which has implications for managers if they must invest in their mobile apps. As more and more consumers shift towards mobile devices as their primary means of accessing the Internet, there is a justification for their investment in mobile apps. Managers must also reflect on whether they would use social media to update their consumers or maintain their websites. However, there are challenges as well to see if consumers visit the websites of companies for updates or rely on their social media feeds; this can also influence a business owner to consider if they want to stay on Instagram and sell their products (shared media) or they want to open an e-commerce website (paid media). Managers would be expected to reflect on their consumers' expectations and how to meet their needs.

Likewise, many consumers will prefer to engage with brands via social media (shared media) instead of the contact form on the company's websites (owned media), which can provide faster response times and more personalised interactions than traditional customer service channels and as social media has become an increasingly important channel for brands to engage with their customers and build strong relationships with their target audience. Brands may have to invest more in training and supporting their social media staff. This may involve ongoing training and education on best practices and investing in tools and technologies that can streamline engagement and provide better insights into customer behaviour and preferences.

When it comes to developing mobile apps, one of the key decisions that brands need to make is whether to develop apps for both iOS (Apple) and Android platforms or to focus on just one platform. Both iOS and Android have large user bases, and each platform has its own unique features and capabilities that can impact the design and development of mobile apps. Managers should consider the demographics of their target audience and which platform is more prevalent among their customers. By carefully evaluating these factors and making informed decisions, brands can ensure that they are developing mobile apps that meet their customers' needs and expectations and help drive business growth. Balancing the online shopping experience with the offline shopping experience is a key consideration for brands as they look to meet the evolving expectations of today's consumers.

Many consumers now expect to be able to access products and services both online and offline, and brands need to ensure that they are providing a seamless, integrated experience across all channels; brands considering if they need to invest in their e-commerce website, their online store or redecorate their physical store on the high street, this consideration has made many brands close their physical store and move online to better engage with consumers. Other types of digital technology dichotomies are automation vs human interaction—think about self-service check-in at hotels where you engage with a machine and not a staff member at the reception, and privacy vs personalisation—where you decide on if and how to engage with the consumers personally. These dichotomies present unique challenges and opportunities for businesses to consider as they strive to create a seamless, integrated customer experience. By carefully evaluating each dichotomy and making informed decisions, brands can develop a digital presence that meets the needs and expectations of their target audience and drives business growth. Table 4.1 summarises some of these dichotomies and identifies action plans for managers.

4.6.4 Affordability

When choosing which platform to use for consumers, brands must consider their financial capabilities. Developing an owned platform or using a paid platform can be expensive, requiring a significant amount of investment. It is essential for managers to carefully evaluate their budget and resources and reflect on how many platforms they can effectively manage. Quality is often more important than quantity, and brands should prioritise creating a seamless, integrated experience for their customers across the platforms they choose to invest in.

For example, a small business that provides balloon garland decoration might focus on just Instagram or TikTok as they manage their limited finances and effectively engage with their target audience rather than trying to be present on every available platform. This allows them to focus their efforts and resources on creating high-quality content and building strong customer relationships rather than spreading themselves too thin across multiple platforms. Likewise, a large corporation like a retail store might have the financial resources to develop its custom platform or app. However, they must carefully consider the potential return on investment before committing to such a large-scale project. They might conduct market research to determine if there is sufficient demand for the platform and evaluate the costs of development and ongoing maintenance against the potential benefits of increased customer engagement and revenue. A brand like Coca-Cola, which operates in multiple countries, might need to consider the costs and complexities of managing multiple platforms across different regions. They may use a paid platform that can be customised for each region rather than trying to develop and maintain multiple owned platforms in-house. This allows them to provide a consistent user experience across all regions while minimising costs and ensuring compliance with local regulations. So it is imperative to recognise that smaller businesses may have more limited budgets and resources to invest in a large-scale digital platform and may need to prioritise which platforms to focus on based on their specific business goals and customer needs. A brand with a large customer base may need to invest in multiple platforms to reach and engage with its audience

Table 4.1 Dichotomies on digital platforms and action plans

Dichotomy	Description	Action Plan for Managers
Mobile app vs website	Consumers prefer mobile apps for transactions and access to products. Brands need to invest in mobile apps to meet consumer needs.	Evaluate if a mobile app is necessary and invest in ongoing training for social media staff.
Social media vs website	Consumers prefer social media for customer service and personalised interactions. Brands need to invest in training and supporting their social media staff.	Develop a social media strategy and invest in tools and technologies to streamline engagement and provide better insights into customer behaviour and preferences.
iOS vs android	Brands need to decide whether to develop mobile apps for both iOS and Android or focus on one platform. Demographics of the target audience can inform the decision.	Evaluate the target audience's demographics and make an informed decision about which platform to focus on.
Online vs offline	Consumers expect a seamless experience across all channels, including online and offline. Brands must ensure integration between e-commerce websites, online stores, and physical stores.	Evaluate whether to invest in e-commerce websites, online stores, physical stores, or a combination of all three to meet consumer expectations.
Virtual vs physical	Consumers are increasingly engaging in virtual experiences such as VR and metaverse. Brands must evaluate whether these platforms are relevant to their products or services.	Evaluate the relevance of virtual platforms for the products or services offered and invest in developing a strategy for engagement on those platforms.
Automation vs human interaction	Automation can provide efficient customer service, but human interaction can provide personalised experiences. Brands need to strike a balance between the two.	Evaluate the type of customer service needed for the target audience and strike a balance between automation and human interaction.
Privacy vs personalisation	Consumers expect personalised experiences but are also concerned about privacy. Brands need to balance personalisation with respect for consumer privacy.	Develop a transparent privacy policy and communicate with consumers about the collected data and how it is used. Strive to provide personalised experiences while respecting consumer privacy.

effectively. In contrast, a smaller customer base may require less investment in digital platforms. Likewise, a brand with a larger budget may be able to invest in more expensive, custom-built platforms, while a brand with a smaller budget may need to rely on pre-existing, third-party platforms that are more affordable.

4.6.5 Developers' requirement

Brands are often not responsible for developing their platforms; they rely on tech companies and developers (see Figure 1.1 on three primary stakeholders essential for digital consumption's success). When considering which digital platform to use, brands should also consider the technical requirements and capabilities of the platform. Tech companies may have specific requirements for using their platform, such as programming languages, software tools, and infrastructure. Brands should evaluate whether they have the technical expertise and resources to use the platform effectively (Mogaji & Nguyen, 2022). Additionally, brands should consider their technical requirements and needs. For example, if a brand requires a platform with robust security features, it may need to look for a platform that offers robust encryption and authentication tools. Alternatively, if a brand requires a platform with robust data analytics capabilities, it may need to look for a platform that offers advanced reporting and data visualisation tools. Ultimately, brands must carefully evaluate each platform's technical requirements and capabilities and choose a platform that best meets their needs and aligns with their technical capabilities. Though this is discussed in more detail in Chapters 5 and 6, which focus on the developers, as brands work with developers to create their digital platforms, they need to ask questions and seek clarifications about various aspects of the development process. This can include questions about regulatory requirements, intellectual property rights, and data privacy. By being proactive and asking these questions, brands can ensure that they are fully informed about the development process and that their interests are protected. Additionally, clear communication and collaboration between brands and developers can ensure that the final product meets the brand's and its customers' needs and expectations.

4.6.6 Interoperability

Interoperability refers to the ability of different software applications or systems to communicate with each other and exchange data seamlessly. When selecting a digital platform, managers should consider its interoperability with other systems and applications already used by the brand. This can help ensure that the brand's data and processes are integrated and streamlined, reducing the risk of errors and delays. For example, a retail brand may use a point-of-sale (POS) system to manage sales transactions in physical stores. When selecting an e-commerce platform, the brand should consider its interoperability with the POS system to ensure that sales data can be easily synced between both systems. This can provide a seamless experience for customers and ensure that the brand's sales data is accurate and up-to-date.

One example of a company that should have considered interoperability is Blackberry. When smartphones started gaining popularity, Blackberry continued to focus on its proprietary operating system and messaging service, which eventually led to its downfall. In contrast, companies like Apple and Google focused on interoperability, creating Software and hardware that could work with various systems and devices. This allowed them to become dominant players in the smartphone market. Another example is the healthcare industry, where interoperability is critical for patient care. Electronic health record (EHR) systems that can communicate with one another allow healthcare providers to share patient information and coordinate care more effectively. This can lead to improved health outcomes and reduced costs for patients. However, the need for interoperability between different EHR systems has been a significant barrier to achieving this goal, and efforts are underway to improve interoperability in healthcare.

4.6.7 Technical capabilities

Brands considering managing their digital platform need to consider if they have the technical capabilities to do that. For example, there are situations where the brand owner can access the back end of their Shopify e-commerce website solely because the platform has been designed to allow that. However, many brand owners will outsource this operation to a freelancer on Fiverr to help design and populate their Shopify websites. Managers need to consider whether they have the expertise and resources to manage and update their chosen platform or whether they need to outsource this task to a freelancer or a third-party service provider. In addition to considering the initial cost of setting up a platform, managers must also consider the ongoing costs associated with maintaining and updating the platform. This can include software upgrades, security patches, and server maintenance costs. By carefully evaluating these factors and developing a clear plan for managing their digital platforms, managers can ensure they make the most of their investment in digital technology and deliver a seamless, engaging experience for their customers.

Brands must decide whether to have a technical partner on retainer or to hire an in-house staff member to manage their digital platforms. Having a technical partner can be beneficial as they will have a broad range of skills and expertise that can be applied to different aspects of the brand's digital platform needs. On the other hand, hiring an in-house staff member can be beneficial in having someone dedicated to managing digital platforms and always available to address issues and concerns that may arise. For example, a small e-commerce company, called EppieLondon, is growing rapidly and wants to improve its online presence. They have a limited budget but want to invest in a platform that will allow them to manage their online store and customer data efficiently. They started with Shopify, a paid e-commerce platform that offers a content management system and a range of features that fit their needs. However, they realise they need to gain the technical expertise in-house to manage the platform and update their website regularly. To address this, they decide to hire a technical partner on retainer on Fiverr who will help them manage the platform and provide ongoing support. The technical partner will be responsible for updates, upgrades, and ensuring the platform is secure. They will also provide guidance and advice on how to make the most of the platform's features. This approach allows EppieLondon access to the technical expertise they need without the cost of hiring a full-time staff member. It also ensures they can focus on their core business while their digital platform is well-maintained and up-to-date.

Also, consider a charity organisational named Narrowgate Project that had to employ volunteers to design their website and manage their social media accounts. Here the charity can outsource its technical abilities to those who can volunteer to assist. This arrangement highlights the importance of considering the resources and capabilities available to a brand or organisation when deciding on which digital platform to use. In the case of the Narrowgate Project, they were able to leverage the skills of volunteers to help them design and manage their website and social media accounts, which may not have been possible if they had to rely solely on paid staff or outsourced professionals. This also shows that sometimes, it is about more than just financial resources but also the willingness and ability of people to volunteer their time and skills. Managers must consider all available options and find the best fit for their organisation's needs and resources.

4.6.8 Regulatory requirements

Reflecting on the role of regulators as discussed in Chapter 1 and more details to be provided in Chapter 8, managers must be mindful of the regulatory requirements that shape their digital platforms, the developers, and consumers. Different countries have different laws and regulations related to digital technology, and brands must ensure their platforms comply with those laws. For example, some countries have strict laws on data privacy, and brands must ensure that they are collecting and handling data in a compliant manner. Additionally, some countries have restrictions on certain types of content, such as political or adult content, and brands must ensure their platforms do not violate them. Failure to comply with these laws can result in legal consequences and damage the brand's reputation. Social media platforms like Facebook, Twitter, and Instagram are banned in China. Therefore, if a brand targets the Chinese market, it must rely on something other than these platforms to reach its audience. Instead, they must use local social media platforms like WeChat, Weibo, and Douyin (TikTok).

Additionally, there are strict regulations in China around what content can be posted online, particularly related to politics and sensitive topics. Brands must comply with these regulations to avoid penalties or being banned from operating in China. Seeking professional assistance or a second opinion can help brands make informed decisions about their digital platforms and ensure that they comply with relevant regulations. This can also help brands mitigate potential legal or reputational data privacy and security risks. For example, a brand may engage a cybersecurity expert's services to assess a digital platform's security features and identify any vulnerabilities that need to be addressed. Additionally, legal professionals can assist brands in navigating complex regulatory frameworks and ensure that their digital platforms comply with relevant laws and regulations.

4.6.9 Brand alignment

Brand values and philosophy are crucial when choosing a digital platform. The chosen platform must align with the brand's values, message, and objectives (Mogaji, 2021). For example, a company that prides itself on sustainability may choose a digital platform emphasising eco-friendliness and environmental responsibility. Similarly, a brand that values inclusivity and accessibility may opt for a platform that caters to diverse audiences. It is essential to ensure that the platform selected reflects the brand's core values and messaging to ensure consistency and authenticity in brand communication. In 2011, Patagonia even launched a 'Don't Buy This Jacket' campaign, encouraging consumers to buy only what they need and promoting a more environmentally conscious approach to consumerism. This type of brand philosophy and values-driven approach can impact their decision-making when selecting digital platforms for their consumers (Patagonia, 2011). The Global Anti-Social Media Policy is a trend that has emerged in recent years as concerns grow about the negative effects of social media on individuals and society. This policy seeks to regulate the use of social media by governments, organisations, and individuals, with the goal of promoting the responsible and ethical use of these platforms. As a result of this trend, some brands have decided to leave social media platforms altogether, while others have decided to use these platforms differently. For example, some brands may focus on using social media for customer service or engagement rather than for advertising or promotional purposes. In 2018, Patagonia announced that it would no longer use Facebook for advertising, citing concerns about the company's data privacy policies. Instead, the company shifted its focus to email marketing and direct-to-consumer advertising (Patagonia, 2020).

4.7 Strategic direction

As digital technology continues to evolve, brands face the challenge of selecting and implementing the right platform for their consumers. The decision-making process can be overwhelming, and managers must consider various factors described in the previous section to decide what to do. In this section, some strategic directions for brands will be presented. This direction builds on the fact that managers have reflected on the listed consideration and are now ready to act. This direction would help them make informed decisions about their digital platforms and ensure their success in the digital space.

4.7.1 Informed decision

Research is very important and essential. Managers must make an informed decision based on their evaluation of those consideration—research to know what the consumers want, the cost of designing the platforms, the developer requirement, and if there are alternatives and if it aligns with the brand's interest. Managers must be aware of the demographic information about their target audience, e.g., age, gender, location. Know your target audience and understand their preferences and behaviour. This will help select a platform that resonates well with the target audience. Your Google Analytics is an excellent place to explore. Managers should not rush into deciding the platform use, gather enough evidence, evaluate the advantages and disadvantages, and explore the technical capabilities. It is essential to research the available digital platforms and their features. Brands should compare the features and benefits of each platform and select the one that best suits their needs.

4.7.2 Business needs

Evaluate the business needs against the research. What did you learn from your research, and what can you do? Starting small and manageable can be an excellent strategy to build momentum and gain confidence. By focusing on a specific segment of your target audience, you can better understand their needs and create targeted solutions that address their pain points. Prioritise the insights that directly relate to your goals and objectives. For instance, if your objective is to increase sales, you should focus on insights that can help you understand your target audience's buying habits and preferences. Digital consumers have high needs. Can you provide 65% with full confidence instead of overpromising? Being realistic about what you can deliver to your digital consumers is essential. Overpromising and underdelivering can damage your brand reputation and erode consumer trust. Therefore, setting achievable goals and communicating them clearly to your audience is better. What do you need now—a stand-alone virtual assistant or using WhatsApp chat function on websites? Though many platforms exist, which aligns with the brand's value and business needs? Managers should stay focused on their business goals and avoid getting distracted by what other brands are doing. While it is essential to keep an eye on the competition, copying their strategies without considering their relevance to your brand and audience may not be effective. Instead, you should create a unique value proposition that sets your brand apart and resonates with your target audience.

4.7.3 Taking action

After your research and consideration of your business needs, you are ready to go and select the team, the platform, and the developers. You need to consider whether you have a subtle or full integration. For example, are you complexly changing the website and informing visitors that your site is under construction, or would you change it gradually? Practical project management skills are crucial in the development of digital technologies. Clear communication, collaboration, and planning are essential to execute the project successfully. Additionally, seeking feedback and input from technical team members can help refine ideas and identify potential roadblocks early on. It is important to continuously assess and adjust the plan as needed throughout the development process.

Being flexible and adaptable is crucial for managers in the current digital environment, especially with the unpredictability of external factors such as the COVID-19 pandemic. A contingency or 'B plan' ensures business continuity and success. Managers must also evaluate their human resources requirements and explore different options, such as partnering with technology companies, hiring freelancers, or recruiting additional staff to meet the demands of digital consumer engagement. It is essential to have a proactive approach to human resource management to ensure that the team is equipped with the necessary skills and resources to handle any challenges that may arise. Managers should know the legal, economic, and regulatory implications of their actions on their digital platforms. This includes understanding privacy laws, data protection laws, copyright laws, and other relevant regulations. Failure to comply with these regulations can result in legal and financial consequences for the brand. Managers should also consider the economic implications of their decisions, such as the cost of implementing new features or the potential revenue loss from unpopular changes.

By considering these factors, managers can make informed decisions that benefit their brand and protect their consumers' rights and interests. Managers should consider the technical requirements of the platform they intend to use. They should evaluate if they have the technical capability to manage and update the platform or if they need to outsource to a technical partner. Ensure that the selected platform complies with relevant regulations and laws, especially with regard to data protection and privacy. Brands should select a platform that aligns with their brand values and philosophy. This will ensure that the platform resonates with the brand's messaging and helps to strengthen its overall brand image.

4.7.4 Communicate

Engaging with consumers is crucial for building trust and loyalty. Brands should communicate openly and transparently about any changes or disruptions to their platforms and seek consumer feedback to improve their digital offerings continuously. This can be done through various channels such as social media, email newsletters, and customer service support. By listening to consumers and addressing their concerns, brands can foster a positive relationship with their audience and increase engagement on their platform. WhatsApp published print ads in several Indian newspapers in 2018 as part of its efforts to address concerns about its new privacy policy. The ad emphasised that WhatsApp cannot read or listen to personal conversations as they are end-to-end encrypted. The new policy only affects conversations with business accounts, allowing businesses to store and manage WhatsApp chats using Facebook's infrastructure. The ad responded to a backlash from WhatsApp users in India, concerned that their data would be shared with Facebook (Majumdar, 2018). Celebrating successes, milestones, and achievements on the platform is essential for brands to engage with consumers and build community. By acknowledging and celebrating consumer engagement, brands can foster brand loyalty and create positive associations with their products or services. An example of a brand celebrating its success on a platform is when Nike celebrated reaching 1 million followers on Instagram by posting a thank-you message to its followers and offering a discount code for its products. This showed appreciation for its followers, promoted its products, and encouraged further engagement on the platform.

4.7.5 Evaluate

Continuous evaluation and analysis of progress are essential for brands to improve their engagement strategies and stay ahead of the competition. It allows brands to identify what worked and did not and make necessary adjustments to improve their digital presence and consumer engagement. Access to analytics is vital for managers to make informed decisions about their business (Dwivedi et al., 2021). Analytics can provide valuable insights into various aspects of the business, such as customer engagement, website traffic, sales, and overall performance. By analysing this data, managers can make informed decisions about improving their products, services, and overall business strategy. Analytics can also help managers track progress towards specific goals and identify improvement areas. For example, if a manager notices a decrease in website traffic, they can use analytics to determine where the traffic is coming from and what pages are most popular. This information can be used to optimise the website for a better user experience, which could increase traffic and engagement.

Furthermore, analytics can help managers understand how stakeholders react to their progress, including investors, employees, and customers. For instance, by tracking social media engagement, managers can determine how customers respond to new products, promotions, or changes in business strategy (Gartner, 2023). This information can be used to adjust the business strategy and improve customer satisfaction. Brands must stay current and remain relevant in a rapidly changing digital landscape. By analysing analytics and making data-driven decisions, brands can continuously improve their digital presence and stay relevant to their target audience. This involves a cycle of progress where brands continually review and update their platforms based on insights from analytics data.

4.8 Conclusion

In today's digital age, brands must recognise the importance of investing in digital platforms for consumer engagement. Brands have numerous motivations for doing so, including the need to build customer loyalty and trust, the potential for cost savings and increased efficiency, and the desire to remain competitive in a rapidly evolving digital landscape. However, brands must make informed decisions when selecting a digital platform, as the wrong choice can lead to wasted resources, missed opportunities, and damage to the brand's reputation.

This chapter highlights the importance of brands investing in their digital platforms to remain competitive and relevant in the rapidly evolving digital landscape. Brands play a crucial role in creating a seamless and engaging digital experience for their customers. By investing in their digital platforms, they can differentiate themselves from their competitors, create a positive brand image, and offer a personalised experience to their customers. The chapter also identifies some critical considerations for brands when selecting platforms, such as the level of control and ownership, potential cost savings and increased efficiency, and the level of customisation and personalisation.

Additionally, the chapter provides strategic directions for brands, such as focusing on customer experience, leveraging data analytics and artificial intelligence, and collaborating with other brands and third-party providers. By critically reflecting on these insights and considerations, prospective managers, tech developers, and other stakeholders can make informed decisions and develop practical digital transformation strategies. Brands must make informed decisions when selecting a digital platform. They must consider factors such as the target audience, the content and services offered, and the level of interactivity and engagement required. Additionally, they must consider the level of control and ownership over the platform and the potential costs and benefits.

Overall, the chapter provides a comprehensive overview of the different platforms available to brands and the key considerations and strategic directions they should keep in mind as they invest in their digital platforms for consumer engagement. In conclusion, investing in digital platforms is essential for brands that want to remain competitive and relevant in today's digital landscape. However, brands must make informed decisions when selecting a platform, considering their motivations for investing, the available options, and the key considerations and challenges involved. Brands that take the time to make informed decisions and invest wisely in their digital platforms can create a positive and engaging digital experience for their customers, build strong relationships, and achieve long-term success.

4.9 Student activities

1. What key factors should brands consider when selecting a digital platform for consumer engagement?
2. How can brands ensure their digital platforms align with their values and philosophy?
3. What are the advantages and disadvantages of developing an owned platform versus using a paid platform?
4. How can brands effectively manage multiple digital platforms without sacrificing quality?
5. What role do technical partners or staff members play in managing digital platforms for a brand?
6. How can brands navigate the regulatory requirements and legal implications of providing a digital platform for their consumers?
7. Can you provide an example of a brand that went wrong with their digital platform engagement, and what lessons can be learned from their mistake?
8. What challenges do brands face when engaging with consumers on social media, and how can these challenges be addressed?
9. How can brands effectively use artificial intelligence-generated content without compromising the quality of their engagement with consumers?
10. What are some of the ethical considerations that brands should keep in mind when engaging with consumers on digital platforms?

References and further reading

Abdulquadri, A., Mogaji, E., Kieu, T. & Nguyen, P., 2021. Digital transformation in financial services provision: A Nigerian perspective to the adoption of chatbot. *Journal of Enterprising Communities: People and Places in the Global Economy*, 15(2), pp. 258–281.

Agbo, F. et al., 2020. Social media usage for computing education: The effect of tie strength and group communication on perceived learning outcome. *International Journal of Education and Development using Information and Communication Technology*, 16(1), pp. 5–26.

Balakrishnan, J., Nwoba, A. & Nguyen, N., 2021. Emerging-market consumers' interactions with banking chatbots. *Telematics and Informatics*, 65, 101711.

Campbell, I., 2021. Gucci designed virtual sneakers for hypebeasts in Roblox and VRChat [Online] Available at: https://www.theverge.com/2021/3/19/22340621/gucci-virtual-25-sneaker-ar-vrchat-roblox

Chylinski, M. et al., 2020. Augmented reality marketing: A technology-enabled approach to situated customer experience. *Australasian Marketing Journal*, 28(4), pp. 374–384.

Coca-Cola, 2021. Coca-Cola NFT Auction on OpenSea Marketplace [Online] Available at: https://www.coca-colacompany.com/news/coca-cola-nft-auction-fetches-more-than-575000#:~:text=Coca%2DCola%20NFT%20Auction%20on%20OpenSea%20Marketplace,on%20iconic%20Coca%2DCola%20merchandise

Dhaoui, C. & Webster, C., 2021. Brand and consumer engagement behaviors on Facebook brand pages: Let's have a (positive) conversation. *International Journal of Research in Marketing*, 38(1), pp. 155–175.

Dhruv, G., Hulland, J., Kopalle, P. & Karahanna, E., 2020. The future of technology and marketing: A multidisciplinary perspective. *Journal of the Academy of Marketing Science*, 48, pp. 1–8.

Djuraskovic, O., 2023. The best web analytics tools in 2023 [Online]. Available at: https://firstsiteguide.com/best-website-analytics-tools/

Dwivedi, Y. et al., 2021. Artificial Intelligence (AI): Multidisciplinary perspectives on emerging challenges, opportunities, and agenda for research, practice and policy. *International Journal of Information Management*, 57, 101994.

Dwivedi, Y. et al., 2022. Metaverse beyond the hype: Multidisciplinary perspectives on emerging challenges, opportunities, and agenda for research, practice and policy. *International Journal of Information Management*, 66, 102542.

Gartner, 2023. What is data and analytics? [Online]. Available at: https://www.gartner.com/en/topics/data-and-analytics

Giakoumaki, C. & Krepapa, A., 2020. Brand engagement in self-concept and consumer engagement in social media: The role of the source. *Psychology & Marketing*, 37(3), pp. 457–465.

Hamzah, Z., Abdul Wahab, H. & Waqas, M., 2021. Unveiling drivers and brand relationship implications of consumer engagement with social media brand posts. *Journal of Research in Interactive Marketing*, 15(2), pp. 336–358.

Hein, A. et al., 2020. Digital platform ecosystems. *Electronic Markets*, 30, pp. 87–98.

Hodapp, D. & Hanelt, A., 2022. Interoperability in the era of digital innovation: An information systems research agenda. *Journal of Information Technology*, 37(4), pp. 407–427.

Jelovac, D., Ljubojević, C. & Ljubojević, L., 2022. HPC in business: The impact of corporate digital responsibility on building digital trust and responsible corporate digital governance. *Digital Policy, Regulation and Governance*, 24(6), pp. 485–497.

Kandampully, J., Bilgihan, A. & Li, D., 2022. Unifying technology and people: Revisiting service in a digitally transformed world. *The Service Industries Journal*, 42(1–2), pp. 21–41.

Koohang, A. et al., 2023. Shaping the metaverse into reality: A holistic multidisciplinary understanding of opportunities, challenges, and avenues for future investigation. *Journal of Computer Information Systems*, pp. 1–31.

Kopalle, P., Kumar, V. & Subramaniam, M., 2020. How legacy firms can embrace the digital ecosystem via digital customer orientation. *Journal of the Academy of Marketing Science*, 48, pp. 114–131.

Kretschmer, T., Leiponen, A., Schilling, M. & Vasudeva, G., 2022. Platform ecosystems as meta-organizations: Implications for platform strategies. *Strategic Management Journal*, 43(3), pp. 405–424.

Labrecque, L., Swani, K. & Stephen, A., 2020. The impact of pronoun choices on consumer engagement actions: Exploring top global brands' social media communications. *Psychology & Marketing*, 37(6), pp. 796–814.

Majumdar, K., 2018. WhatsApp takes to print ads to curb fake news in India [Online] Available at: https://www.businessinsider.in/whatsapp-takes-to-print-ads-to-curb-fake-news-in-india/articleshow/64934810.cms

McKinsey, 2022. Marketing in the metaverse: An opportunity for innovation and experimentation [Online] Available at: https://www.mckinsey.com/capabilities/growth-marketing-and-sales/our-insights/marketing-in-the-metaverse-an-opportunity-for-innovation-and-experimentation

Miric, M., Boudreau, K. & Jeppesen, L., 2019. Protecting their digital assets: The use of formal & informal appropriability strategies by app developers. *Research Policy*, 48(8), 103738.

Mogaji, E. & Erkan, I., 2019. Insight into consumer experience on UK train transportation services. *Travel Behaviour and Society*, 14, pp. 21–33.

Mogaji, E., 2021. *Brand Management*. Cham: Springer.

Mogaji, E. & Nguyen, N., 2022. Managers' understanding of artificial intelligence in relation to marketing financial services: Insights from a cross-country study. *International Journal of Bank Marketing*, 40(6), pp. 1272–1298.

Mogaji, E., Soetan, T. & Kieu, T., 2020. The implications of artificial intelligence on the digital marketing of financial services to vulnerable customers. *Australasian Marketing Journal*, 29(3), pp. 235–242.

Morgan-Thomas, A., Dessart, L. & Veloutsou, C., 2020. Digital ecosystem and consumer engagement: A socio-technical perspective. *Journal of Business Research*, 121, pp. 713–723..

Olson, E., Olson, K., Czaplewski, A. & Key, T., 2021. Business strategy and the management of digital marketing. *Business Horizons*, 64(2), pp. 285–293.

Oosthuizen, K., Botha, E., Robertson, J. & Montecchi, M., 2021. Artificial intelligence in retail: The AI-enabled value chain. *Australasian Marketing Journal*, 29(3), pp. 264–273.

Patagonia, 2011. Don't buy this jacket, Black Friday and the New York Times [Online] Available at: https://eu.patagonia.com/gb/en/stories/dont-buy-this-jacket-black-friday-and-the-new -york-times/story-18615.html

Patagonia, 2020. CEO's statement: Why we stand by our continued Facebook ban [Online] Available at: https://eu.patagonia.com/gb/en/facebook-boycott.html#:~:text=We%20believe%20Facebook %20has%20a,continue%20to%20withhold%20our%20advertising

Ponzoa, J. & Erdmann, A., 2021. E-commerce customer attraction: Digital marketing techniques, evolution and dynamics across firms. *Journal of Promotion Management*, 27(5), pp. 697–715.

Sağkaya Güngö, A. & Ozansoy Çadırcı, T., 2022. Understanding digital consumer: A review, synthesis, and future research agenda. *International Journal of Consumer Studies*, 46(5), pp. 1829–1858.

Santos, Z., Cheung, C., Coelho, P. & Rita, P., 2022. Consumer engagement in social media brand communities: A literature review. *International Journal of Information Management*, 63, 102457.

Sheth, J., 2020. Impact of Covid-19 on consumer behavior: Will the old habits return or die? *Journal of Business Research*, 117, pp. 280–283.

Soetan, T., Mogaji, E. & Nguyen, N., 2021. Financial services experience and consumption in Nigeria. *Journal of Services Marketing*, 35(7), pp. 947–961.

Vander Schee, B., Peltier, J. & Dahl, A., 2020. Antecedent consumer factors, consequential branding outcomes and measures of online consumer engagement: Current research and future directions. *Journal of Research in Interactive Marketing*, 14(2), pp. 239–268.

CHAPTER 5

Dominant platform developers

5.1 Background

Previous chapters have discussed the need for consumers to engage on digital platforms and the need for brands to provide and use the platform to engage with their consumers, and different types of platforms has also been discussed, but the question remains who is responsible for developing these platforms? If you are not a tech company developing platforms, you would surely need someone to develop your platform. An advertising agency will require someone to develop their website, a university will require an organisation to provide their email services and virtual learning environment, and likewise a government parastatal will need the services of platform developers to develop their apps. This chapter focuses on the role of these platform developers to enable digital consumption, recognising how to work with these developers as this will ensure a better experience for consumers being invited to the platforms. This understanding is needed for managers who will be providing digital platforms for their consumers and also for students who will be exploring the different platforms to use for their client or their own business.

5.2 Learning outcomes

By the end of this chapter, you should be able to:

- Understand the roles of platform developers in digital consumptions.
- Recognise different strategies to keep brands and consumers engaged on the platforms.
- Identify the challenges in keeping brands and consumers engaged on the platforms.
- Explain the responsibilities of platform developers.
- Understand the key considerations for brands.
- Understand the key considerations for students.

DOI: 10.4324/9781003389842-5

5.3 Introduction

Linking this chapter back to the story about the party on Friday night, the brands have their own VIP sections in the clubs, they invite their friends, clients, and customers to come into their VIP section to party and enjoy themselves, but you need to understand their VIP section may not exist if there is no club or if their club is shut. The club owner here is the digital platform provider who is ensuring that brands have enough platforms (with the needed security and infrastructures) to ensure that consumers engage and enjoy themselves. This chapter focuses on the platform developers to recognise their role, contribution, and responsibilities in enhancing digital consumption.

Specifically, this chapter focuses on the dominant platform developers—the large technology companies that have established dominant positions in their respective markets. These companies often have significant market power and influence over the digital platforms and ecosystems they create, which can impact competition and innovation in the broader technology industry (Rikap & Lundvall, 2022). Examples of dominant platform developers may include companies like Google (Alphabet), Apple, Facebook (Meta), Amazon, and Microsoft (GAFAM), among others. These companies develop and maintain large-scale platforms that are used by millions of users and developers worldwide. Consider them to be developers of paid and shared platforms (see Chapter 4). Though these are not the only platform providers, it is intended at this stage for you to have a better understanding and contextualised this topic (additional platform developers—called third-party developers are discussed in Chapter 6). These big tech companies have provided numerous platforms like the App stores, social media, e-commerce, and collaborative tools like Teams, emails, and cloud storage that have shaped digital consumption and digital consumers' experiences.

The platform developers are responsible for ensuring the availability of these platforms, they are expected to continually innovate to meet the growing needs of digital consumers, and they are expected to keep creating more platforms and even acquiring different platforms to enhance consumer engagement (Klinge et al., 2023). Google and Microsoft are working on developing generative AI; Google acquired YouTube to provide video services; and Meta (Facebook) acquired WhatsApp. The digital platform providers serve as gatekeepers, ensuring the security of the platforms (like the club owners who have recruited bouncers and security and provided CCTV in the club); these dominant platform developers have significant responsibilities, and they do their best to make sure that brand and consumers remain actively engaging on their platforms.

To further understand the responsibilities of the platform developers, you need to reflect on the PESCO platforms as previously discussed in Chapter 4, you see brands choosing to use platforms that are being provided by these big tech companies (either as paid platforms or shared platforms) instead of investing money to build their own platforms. Small business owners choose to sell on Instagram instead of having their own website, brands choose to use WhatsApp for their chat services instead of investing in a new chatbot, or brands allow consumers access to their platforms through existing accounts with these dominant platform developers (e.g. signing in through Gmail or Apple ID). You see organisation relying on the infrastructure that has been provided by these dominant platform developers. More reason many people will choose to have their party in a club, with security, sound systems, and the right atmosphere instead of hosting the party in their house. Though big techs are working on providing platforms, it is imperative to know that they may not be able to meet the needs of different brands that require platforms. This therefore opens opportunities for many third-party developers (to be discussed in Chapter 6).

The remainder of this chapter will focus on the business operations of these platform developers, to understand how they work: How business managers can engage with them and for students to understand these operations to enhance their chances of securing employment with the company or still develop a better alternative. This chapter will also discuss the growth strategies being adopted by these developers, the challenges they face, and key considerations for brands and students. It is anticipated that at the completion of this chapter, you will have a better understanding of digital platforms and how to many a working relationship in ensuring a suitable digital environment for your brands and consumers.

Reflective question

What should tech developers do to ensure consumers stay on their platforms?

5.4 Business operations

Platform providers recognise their responsibilities to provide the needed infrastructure for digital consumers. Irrespective of the size of the developer—either a big tech company or an emerging tech start-up, there are expected responsibilities on their part to ensure their growth and sustainability. This section discusses some of these business operations which would shape digital consumption and digital consumers' experiences.

5.4.1 Developing the platform

Developing the platform can be considered the most important job of the platform developers, to make sure the platforms are readily available to enable digital consumption (Birch & Bronson, 2022). Platform development involves designing, building, and maintaining a set of software components that provide a foundation for building more complex applications or services. You would expect platforms developers to support brands' digital transformation drive. For businesses looking at automating their email marketing, they would be expecting platform developers to make a provision; for companies thinking of integrating chatbot into their websites, they would be expecting some solutions from these developers; and for brands considering going into the metaverse, they need platform developers that would make this happen. The platform developers are in the business of innovating to meet the growing needs of the business and brands. So, if you are a prospective tech start-up founder, thinking of developing a digital platform, you need to be mindful of these expectations. Consumers are interested in a platform that will enhance their digital consumption experiences (Chylinski et al., 2020; Sağkaya Güngö & Ozansoy Çadırcı, 2022) and brands (including private and public organisations) are also interested in digital platforms that will enhance digital consumers' experiences for their target market (Dwivedi et al., 2022; Koohang et al., 2023). There is a need to meet the demands in the market—to bridge the gap between the needs of the consumers and that of the brands.

5.4.2 Bringing users to the platform

Developing the platform is not enough, digital consumption is about engaging on the platforms; therefore, it is very imperative to get people on board with what has been developed. Imagine having a club and you are not having revellers and partygoers on Friday nights, you would need to start questioning the value of your club. Digital platform providers need to make sure the platform is inviting, making sure it is user-friendly and meeting a need in the market. Imagine having Uber for Tractors, where farmers go to website to borrow tractors and farm equipment, do you think that will work? Even though you might think it's tricky, it can be a success if you are able to bring the brands (those who have tractors) and consumers (farmers who need tractors) into the app (the platform). It is not enough to bring users to the platform, but to ensure that they keep using it and stay engaged—to ensure that more people are bringing tractors and more people are renting tractors. This is the responsibility of the developers to work on growth strategy and ensure that people don't just download the app, but they use it, and they keep using it. Consumers and brands must be supported and encouraged to stay on the platforms.

5.4.3 Marketing the platform

Getting people to stay on the platform can be enhanced by marketing and advertising, provided there is a need and value for the platforms. You need to be sure of what you are marketing. It's not just about the metrics, number of visitors or downloads but long-term sustainability and viability strategy (Hendrikse et al., 2022). The developers must make sure that people are aware of the platforms and are willing to try them out and recommend them to others. Sending motivation and reminders to consumers about the platform is also a good way of marketing the platform. See Figure 5.1 showing different notifications on a mobile phone. The more people are aware, the more likely they will use it and change their business operations. Apple started as an outsider to Nokia and Blackberry, but with their innovative products and marketing strategies, they have become a top brand. You see companies changing their business operations to align with the new platforms and different apps solely designed for the Apple app store. Now with smart speakers, many businesses are developing their products and services to be more pronounceable and searchable. There are many platforms supporting the integration of smart speakers because they are being marketed as a platform to revolutionise digital consumption.

Likewise, it is imperative to recognise the amount of money being spent on advertising and marketing, to make sure that people still know these platforms, willing to download, and engage with it (Braun & Eklund, 2019; Abdulquadri et al., 2021). TikTok for example has been sponsoring various sporting events from football to rugby and even hockey—in 2021, they signed a deal to become Wrexham AFC's sponsor for the next two seasons, and they became a global sponsor of UEFA Euro 2020 and partnered with Confederation of African Football to sponsor the 2022 Africa Cup of Nations (AFCON) competition. They are the sponsor and title partner for the 2023 Women's Rugby Six Nations and also signed a new integrated partnership with Maple Leaf Sports & Entertainment Ltd, a professional sports club in the National Hockey League based in Ontario, Canada. This platform is investing a lot of money in marketing their platform to both the consumers and the brands. Brands must see that

Figure 5.1 Push notifications on a mobile phone.

consumers are on the platform as this will motivate them to join to support the digital consumption. So, think about it, why do people choose to go to a particular club on the high street, even though there are many clubs out there? It's about the vibe, value, and fun on that platform.

5.4.4 Allowing brands on platform

Developing the platform to allow brands is an essential business operation for the developers. The platform will succeed more if there are general acceptances, where brands are able to take ownership of the platform and introduce it to their stakeholders. Why is your university using Teams for online learning instead of Google Meet, Zoom, or Webex? Why is your university using Moodle as a virtual learning environment instead of Blackboard or Canvas? Ensuring business adopts the digital platforms contributes to the long-term viability of the company. You can imagine what happens to a platform that no one is willing to use. Google+ was a social media platform developed by Google that was launched in 2011, but due to low user engagement and security concerns, it was shut down in April 2019. Likewise, Apple Music Connect was a social media platform for musicians that was launched in 2015. However, it did not gain traction due to limited features, lack of engagement from artists, and competition from other music social networks. It was eventually shut down in 2018. The platform developers need to create different gateways and opportunities to allow brands to engage. This may include allowing company pages, content creation, page management, links with third party, and analytical insights like Google Analytics and Facebook pixel. Twitter is even offering a different type of verification for brands. Getting brands unto the platform also allows for sharing and selling of data; this however should be ethically done. Though consumers may have signed and accepted the terms and conditions for data to be shared, brands' engagement on the platform needs to align with ethical values.

5.4.5 Protecting the platform

As discussed in Chapter 4 and earlier in the introduction, brands choose paid and shared platforms to benefit from the security infrastructure of these dominant platform developers. Brands want to believe that their digital environment is safe as they are covered by the effort of its digital platform developers. Consumers want to be safe using these dominant platforms, they want to know that their data (and secret) are safe, and consumers want to feel they are not being exploited, abused, or unnecessarily targeted when they use the digital platform, to be reassured that data are being properly and ethically collected. Likewise, brands want to be sure that their data is safe; they don't want to be exposed to cyberattack, and they rely on the dominant platform developers to guarantee this protection. The platform provider is also tasked with providing policies to reassure people of their safety, to give people the ability to control their activities and engagement on the platform (Jelovac et al., 2022). For example you can block people who you don't want to engage with, block some keywords, and take some form of responsibilities for your well-being on the platforms. Consumers can sign in using their password, PIN, or even biometrics. Platform providers are providing two-factor authentication to further demonstrate their effort to protect users on the platforms. Platform providers are expected to protect people from abuses, trolls, and negativities. Globally, YouTube has approximately 10,000 employees dedicated to monitoring and removing content, as well as policy development. On the other hand, Facebook has a much larger team with over 35,000 people working on safety and security around the world. These teams are responsible for a variety of tasks, such as content moderation, reviewing reports of abusive content, and developing policies to ensure user safety on their platforms.

5.4.6 Innovating the platform

There is a need for continuous innovation of the platforms (Nuccio & Guerzoni, 2019). We will always share the examples of Nokia and Blackberry mobile phones which were the forerunners of platform developments but are now considered obsolete because they were not very innovative. The demands of digital consumers are ever-increasing; there is a growing quest for more innovative platforms, and this desire should keep platform developers on their toes. There is a need to provide more user-friendly interface, making sure people are able to use the platforms, and making sure people don't have to get extra lessons or tutorials on how to use the platforms. The subtle changes to the platform and upgrades are also important, where consumers are able to recognise the innovations and appreciate them. You see Instagram introduces Reel, YouTube has short videos, and even Teams upgrading their interface and functionalities. Apple will always be a good example of innovative platform developers, while it has not always been about success (MobileMe, a cloud-based platform, Apple Music Connect, a social media platform for musicians, and Ad, a mobile advertising platform, were examples of their failed innovations), they have continually innovated to keep digital consumers in their ecosystem.

5.4.7 Interoperability

As you innovate, you want to be mindful of the prospects of interoperability—ability of different systems or products to work together seamlessly and efficiently. This interoperability can be achieved using open tech standards (like USB or C port charging), common protocols, and interfaces that allow different systems to exchange data and communicate with each other (De Hert et al., 2018; Hodapp & Hanelt, 2022). This helps to reduce barriers to entry for new products and services, encourages competition, and fosters innovation. Platform developers need to ensure that their platforms can work with other systems and infrastructure. This understanding is important because many digital consumers and brands are using many other platforms, and therefore if a digital platform is different from norms, it might be difficult to integrate it. That's why you see those using Teams for the meetings will use the Microsoft Office packages and likewise those using Google Meet might be using Google Workspace. Zoom, a video-conferencing platform that has become increasingly popular in recent years, especially during the COVID-19 pandemic, has made significant efforts to integrate with existing infrastructures, providing a seamless user experience and reducing barriers to entry for its users. For example, Zoom has developed integrations with popular software applications such as Microsoft Outlook, Google Calendar, and Slack, allowing users to easily schedule and join meetings directly from these platforms. Additionally, Zoom has developed integrations with hardware systems such as conference room cameras and microphones, making it easier for users to join meetings from different locations.

The ability to sign into other platforms using a Facebook or Google account can also be an advantage for easy adoption for brands and consumers. For example, to sign into Adobe (a digital platform) consumers can either use their Google, Facebook, or even Apple account. This ensures that consumers have a seamless experience when signing into the platforms, Likewise, think about how you use your university email and how that has been connected to your students; record account, library, and virtual learning environment. The interoperability could also be around the design of the hardware (and devices). For example, the USB port is standard for many computers, and the QWERTY keyboard is also standard, while Apple will have to ditch the Lightning connector on its iPhones and use the USB-C connector for their charging ports as the European regulators decided all smartphones sold after autumn 2024 to use the USB charging as standard. The goal of this initiative is to reduce electronic waste and make it easier for consumers to use their devices with different chargers and cables.

It is however imperative to recognise the possibilities of moving away from interoperability to ensure the sustenance of the company and revolutionise the market. Apple is a good example of this, as the company has a history of moving away from industry standards and norms to create its own proprietary technologies that have become wildly successful. For example, Apple moved away from the traditional QWERTY keyboard with the launch of the iPhone in 2007, introducing a new touchscreen interface that quickly became the industry standard for smartphones. Apple also moved away from interoperability by developing its own proprietary Lightning connector, which replaced the standard 30-pin connector on its devices, and later by removing the headphone jack on the iPhone 7, pushing users towards wireless and Lightning-connected headphones. While these moves away from interoperability can create challenges for users who are used to industry standards, they can also lead to innovation and new ways of using technology. Apple's innovations with touchscreen interfaces, wireless headphones, and proprietary connectors have helped to shape the way we use technology today and have contributed to the company's success in the market. It is important to note, however, that not all moves away from interoperability are successful. Some companies have attempted to create their own proprietary technologies that have failed to gain traction in the market due to consumer preferences for interoperability and compatibility with existing systems. Ultimately, the success of a move away from interoperability depends on a variety of factors, including market demand, user preferences, and the ability of the company to create a compelling new technology that meets those needs.

5.4.8 Engaging with regulators

Digital platforms are not operating in isolation, we must recognise the socio-political environment in which they are being used. There are different examples of situations where some platforms are not allowed in some countries, this is to further recognise the need for platform developers to engage with regulators to ensure their platforms are available to brands and consumers. Regulatory engagement has become an increasingly important part of business operations for platform developers. As digital platforms continue to grow in importance and influence, governments around the world are paying closer attention to how they operate and how they impact society. This has led to the development of new regulations and laws that platforms must comply with. For example, in the case of Mark Zuckerberg appearing before the House of Parliament, this was in response to the Cambridge Analytica scandal and the misuse of user data. This demonstrates that platforms must be held accountable for how they handle user data and must comply with regulations designed to protect users' privacy. Similarly, Uber's case in London highlights the importance of complying with local regulations and laws. Uber had its license to operate in London revoked due to concerns around passenger safety and other regulatory issues. This shows that platforms must be aware of and comply with local regulations in the regions they operate in. Likewise, Twitter's ban in Nigeria demonstrates the challenges that platforms face when dealing with governments and regulators in different regions. Platforms must navigate a complex regulatory environment and must be prepared to engage with governments and regulators to address any concerns or issues that arise. Regulatory engagement is a critical part of platform development, and platforms must be prepared to engage with governments and regulators in order to comply with laws and regulations and to build trust with their users and the broader public.

As part of ensuring national security, the government may have to work with platform developers and to ensure citizens' well-being (Bonina & Eaton, 2020). The ban on TikTok on UK government phones was reportedly due to concerns about data security and privacy. While this decision may have been necessary to protect government information and systems, it also highlights the importance of ensuring that platforms are secure and that user data is protected. Similarly, requests for access to WhatsApp messages must be balanced with users' rights to privacy and the protection of their personal information. WhatsApp's encryption technology is designed to protect users' messages from unauthorised access, and the company has been vocal in defending users' privacy and resisting government attempts to access user data.

What do you think will happen if a government requests to read WhatsApp messages of those plotting terrorist attacks against the state? There is often tension between platform developers and governments over the regulation of their operations. On the one hand, platform developers may resist government involvement in their operations as they seek to maintain control over their platforms and protect user privacy. On the other hand, governments have a responsibility to protect citizens and ensure that platforms are not being used to spread harmful content or violate the law. One approach that has been suggested is self-governance, where platform developers take responsibility for ensuring the well-being of users on their platforms. This involves implementing policies and practices that promote user safety and address harmful content or behaviour, without relying solely on government regulations (Mogaji & Nguyen, 2022). Self-governance can help reassure regulators that platform developers are taking user safety seriously, while also allowing for greater flexibility and innovation in the development of digital platforms (see more in Chapter 8 on regulating digital consumption). However, it is important to ensure that self-governance is accompanied by transparency and accountability and that users have a say in the policies and practices that are being implemented. Ultimately, the relationship between platform developers and governments is a complex one and requires ongoing dialogue and collaboration in order to strike the right balance between protecting user privacy, promoting innovation, and ensuring public safety. Notwithstanding, if you are a prospective tech developer, you should start considering the regulatory requirements within your business operations (Khalil et al., 2022).

Reflective question

How have platform developers responded to the increasing regulatory scrutiny of the tech industry?

5.5 Growth strategies

Having a platform that people are using is not enough, developers need to be mindful and reflect on their growth strategy, especially for emerging tech start-ups, you need to start evaluating the competition in the digital consumption marketplace, reflecting on strategic direction and desire to grow. This section highlights some growth strategies that are important for digital platform developers as they consider consumer engagement in the digital environment.

5.5.1 Marketing

Aligning with earlier points around marketing the platforms, platform developers need to be strategic about their marketing. Prospective digital platform developers can learn from what other brands have been doing. There are bundle offers where consumers can get more benefits by buying and using more platforms. There are pricing strategies to appeal to different target audiences. There is Amazon Prime for students and likewise YouTube music for students. Sponsorship is also a great opportunity to market the digital platforms and get more people to know about it. Providing free starter plans (or trial versions) can also be used to introduce people to the platforms in the anticipation that they would enjoy it and want to stay. You may have seen Apple TV or Disney Plus providing a 7 day free trial session to encourage people to have a feel of the platform and hopefully they can stay back. I remembered signing up for Netflix using their free 30 days trial version because I wanted to watch *Narcos* in 2015. Since then, I have been on it. These platforms may however request prospective consumers to share their card detail. Concerns regarding consumers sharing their credit card information with a platform can arise due to issues related to trust, convenience, and privacy. Platform owners can build trust with their users by implementing strong security measures, clearly communicating their privacy policies, offering alternative payment methods, and delivering high-quality services and excellent customer support over time. By taking these steps, platform owners can mitigate consumer concerns and promote a more seamless and secure payment process for their users.

Reflective question

Would you share your bank details or credit card details with a platform so that you can use their seven days free trial offer?

5.5.2 Acquisition

Platform developers need to be aware of the prospect of acquisition and mergers because this is very common within the digital platform ecosystems (Affeldt & Kesler, 2021). Many platforms are being developed with the hope that they would be acquired someday by a bigger brand. There are possibilities that platform developers may have to merge with another company to ensure their financial viability. Especially if they are struggling and they are operating within the same space. Also, many developers may get acquired by another company or acquire another company that aligns with their business values. Platform developers need to be aware of the competition in the market and position themselves for the possible growth strategy. There are possibilities of acquiring companies that will enhance your present offerings in the market—Facebook acquired WhatsApp even though they have messengers; they needed a better platform that appeals to their target audience. Likewise, platform developers can acquire a company that offers what their competitors are offering—so instead of going ahead to develop a new platform, Google acquired Fitbit to compete with Apple and Samsung smartwatches. Likewise, even though Google has Google Video, which operated between 2005 and 2009, they bought YouTube in 2006 to fast track their access to video-sharing platforms. Digital platforms must be on the lookout for these opportunities and be mindful of the implications of these merges. It is important to always seek professional advice as the success of mergers and acquisitions may not always be guaranteed. In 2005, eBay acquired Skype Technologies, a European VOIP provider for USD 2.6 billion with the anticipation that sellers and buyers on eBay can communicate over Skype but that didn't work out as consumers found it not necessary to communicate over the phone, and in 2011, eBay sold its Skype to Microsoft, and Skype is now integrated with Microsoft Teams. Similarly, in 2013, Microsoft acquired Nokia's Devices & Services business, the license of Nokia's patents, and the license and use of Nokia's mapping services.

5.5.3 Funding

Platform developers need funds to keep developing the innovative platforms that consumers want. It is not surprising to see companies get acquired and merged. Platform developers need funds for expansion, and there will be a growing need to see investment into the platforms. There are many platforms that have not got funds, and they have to stop trading because they can sustain the need of the consumers. Many platform developers and tech founders are always on the lookout for venture capitalists (VC) to back their start-ups, and this can be a very daunting task. Many people will believe that getting VC is a prerequisite for success, but this can't always be true as you can be strategic with your funding approach. This is because having funds is not always enough to sustain the company. You will not be surprised to see many starts-up celebrating their latest rounds of funding and investment. It's something to celebrate and a sense of trust and ability to deliver. However, there are many companies that have failed even despite having funds. Fast, the easy checkout start-up which expedites online purchases, attracted more than $120 million in investment but had to shut down, despite the huge investment, as their platform was generating less revenue. Reali, a real estate tech start-up, also shut down after raising $100M. So, raising money is not enough, but how to bootstrap, effectively manage resources, and develop innovative products that can keep brands and consumers continually engaging.

5.5.4 Upgrades

Providing upgrades to the digital platform is also an important growth strategy to consider—what are you doing now and what can you be doing tomorrow? These upgrades could either be through innovative products like Apple extending their ecosystem to have additional products like Apple TV or acquiring another company like Microsoft acquiring LinkedIn to come into the social media space. Ultimately this is about improving the services and improving the experiences of the consumers. Digital consumers need to see that there is always something new for them on digital platforms. While this can benefit the consumers, it's also another stream of income for the platform developers. Zoom had to introduce Zoom phone during the hypes of online meetings during the COVID-19 pandemic, Google had to upgrade from just a platform to having Google Pixel which is a mobile phone, and likewise Microsoft had to extend into Surface laptops. Here we see platform developers moving from being just a platform and software to devices and hardware, taking control and managing their ecosystem. Recognising these upgrades as an opportunity for strategy growth is important in managing consumer engagement in the digital environment.

5.6 Getting people to stay

Remember the story of the club owner? They want to have revellers and partygoers stay all night in their club—because the longer they stay, the more money the club is going to make, the more drinks that will be sold, and possibly more food. Likewise, platform owners have the responsibility to ensure that consumers and brands stay on their platform. This ongoing engagement is important because the longer the brands and consumers stay, they are able to gain more insight through data analytics, they get addicted and more interested in the platforms, and they open that stream of income for platform developers where they have more data to sell and share.

5.6.1 Integration with other systems

Platform owners know that they can't always survive on their own, and there is a need to integrate with other platforms and systems. Aligning with the idea of interoperability, people are able to stay on their platform and engage with other content from different platforms (Hodapp & Hanelt, 2022). You can be on Instagram and still see many TikTok videos, and you can be on Teams and still be able to open your calendar and access your Word documents. You can be on Google Workspaces and access your files and emails. The ability to connect different platforms together on the same devices allows digital platform developers to ensure many people stay on their platform. Beyond the big tech companies, there are opportunities to ensure that people stay longer on your e-commerce websites, giving them the information they want, making sure the payment system is well integrated, and possibly ensuring they do not log out or open another browse or tab before they pay, ensuring that the payment is well integrated. Also, you could have your chatbot integrated into your website, where consumers do not have to leave the website to access the chatbot or you could transfer it to their WhatsApp where you can chat with the business official WhatsApp account; with this integration, the brand is able to gain deeper insight into the customers (through the WhatsApp) and also provide a seamless service (addressing their concerns promptly on WhatsApp). So, possibly by a social media post, to the company's website, to the chatbot, and then to WhatsApp—different platforms have been integrated to meet the need of the digital consumers. Here you recognise the characteristics of digital consumers, who may not always be patient and would need answers to their concerns immediately.

5.6.2 Pre-installation on devices

As previously discussed in Chapter 4 (under devices and platforms), the devices are the hardware, and the platforms are the software. To make people stay longer on the platform, there are possibilities of installing these platforms on the devices. For example when you buy your PC (your device), you are likely to have Microsoft Edge (platform) pre-installed on it and that means you are more likely to keep using it instead of taking time to download Chrome or other browsers (platforms). Likewise on your mobile phones you may have already installed apps like Facebook which automatically ensures that you continually stay on the platform by the virtue that it has been installed. For example, many smartphones in Africa come with Facebook pre-installed, which means that users do not need to download the app or create an account to start using it (Barrett & Matthee, 2019). This can be particularly beneficial in areas with limited Internet connectivity or low levels of digital literacy, as it simplifies the process of accessing social media. Facebook has also initiated the pre-installation of Facebook and WhatsApp on the latest KaiOS-operated mobile devices in India. This has enabled millions of individuals in India to access these services, possibly for the first time, due to their pre-installation on the devices. Facebook works with partners to pre-install apps on devices to help people get the most up-to-date version of their apps and ultimately get them to spend more time on the platform (Varela, 2019). Similarly, Netflix has a deal with Samsung where the platform (Netflix) is pre-installed as a system app on the phone (devices) and cannot be uninstalled (Samsung Community, 2021). Likewise, you have some smart TVs that have Netflix pre-installed; there are select models from TV brands like Panasonic, Samsung, and Sony that have met the criteria and can carry the Netflix Recommended TV logo (Netflix, 2020). These pre-instalments are all business arrangements between the platform developers (Microsoft, Facebook, and Netflix) and the device manufacturers (Dell, HP, Samsung, Panasonic, and Sony), to make sure that many people stay with the platform.

The ethical consideration of this business arrangement is however important. For example, on some of these devices, you are not able to uninstall the app, but you can only disable it if you don't want to use it (Samsung Community, 2021). Likewise, the United States Department of Justice (DOJ) sued Microsoft over its anticompetitive behaviour, mostly that it was forcing PC manufacturers to include Microsoft Internet (Department of Justice, 1998; Aten, 2023), eventually, Microsoft and the DOJ reached a settlement, wherein Microsoft consented to facilitate the utilisation of Application Programming Interface (APIs) on Windows by third-party developers. Moreover, pre-installed apps like Facebook can also contribute to the digital divide between developed and developing countries (Lai & Widmar, 2021; Abdulquadri et al., 2021). While many users in Africa may have access to smartphones, they may not have access to the same range of apps and services as users in more developed regions. This can limit their ability to engage with the wider digital economy and may reinforce existing inequalities between different parts of the world.

5.6.3 Creating own devices and platforms

To encourage people to stay on the platforms, we are seeing many tech developers ensuring that they have control over the devices and the platforms (Fortino et al., 2020). Many of these dominant platform developers are now working on developing their own decisions, even for those who can't make theirs, they are building partnerships, as seen with Netflix and recommended TVs (Netflix, 2020). These are strategies employed by dominant tech companies such as Facebook, Amazon, and Microsoft to expand their market reach and maintain control over their respective ecosystems. By developing their own hardware devices and platforms, these companies can create an integrated user experience that encourages users to remain within their ecosystem, thereby increasing the likelihood of user retention and loyalty.

Google, like other dominant tech companies, has also expanded into the hardware space. The company started as a platform provider with its popular search engine and later developed the Android operating system for smartphones and other mobile devices. However, Google has since expanded its hardware offerings with the introduction of the Pixel smartphone and other hardware devices such as the Google Home smart speaker and the Nest line of smart home devices.

Facebook started as a social media platform but has developed hardware devices such as the Portal and Oculus VR headset, which integrate with its social media platform and offer a unique user experience. By doing so, Facebook is not only able to expand its market reach but also maintain control over the user data and content generated through its devices and platform.

Amazon also moved from just providing a platform to sell books to creating devices such as Ring, Amazon Kindle, and Echo. These devices have helped the company expand its market reach beyond e-commerce and into the smart home space. By creating an integrated user experience that combines its voice assistant with various smart home devices, Amazon has been able to build a loyal user base and maintain control over the data generated by these devices.

In the case of Microsoft, its Surface line of devices has helped the company expand its market reach beyond software and into hardware. By developing its own hardware devices, Microsoft can offer a unique user experience that integrates with its software products, such as Windows and Office. This not only increases the likelihood of user retention but also helps Microsoft maintain control over the user data generated through its devices and platform.

When dominant platform developers create their own hardware devices and platforms, they are able to control the user experience, integrate their software products more seamlessly, and retain users within their ecosystem. By doing so, they can expand their market reach and maintain control over the data generated by their devices and platform.

However, the expansion of these tech ecosystems also raises concerns about data privacy and security (Bandara et al., 2021). With more users staying within a particular ecosystem, there is a risk that user data could be exploited or misused by the dominant tech companies. Additionally, the creation of these ecosystems could limit competition and innovation in the tech industry, as users are incentivised to remain within a particular ecosystem rather than exploring alternative options. Facebook introduced their Meta Portal devices, an alternative to Amazon Echo and Google Home, but they are no longer selling Meta Portal devices (Notopoulos, 2023). Google also had Daydream, which was a virtual reality platform; it could have been rivalling Facebook Quest, but it was discontinued in 2019 (Failory, 2023). For those who have got the device and platform combination right, it's always an important growth strategy for the developers.

5.6.4 Creating an ecosystem

Following on from the discussion of dominant tech developers creating their devices and platforms, there is an effort towards integrating these devices and platforms into a large tech ecosystem (Kopalle et al., 2020). Tech companies are constantly striving to expand their ecosystems and retain users on their platforms. They do this by investing in the development of new devices and platforms, as well as improving their existing ones. For example, Google is expanding its Google Workspace to offer a suite of services including email, calls, and cloud storage. Similarly, Microsoft offers Teams for communication and collaboration, email services, and cloud storage. Amazon also offers cloud storage for pictures through its Amazon Photos service. By providing a suite of services, tech companies are able to create a more integrated user experience and retain users within their ecosystem. Additionally, these services can generate revenue through subscriptions or advertising, allowing companies to further invest in the development of their platforms and devices.

These tech developers recognise that when people stay within the ecosystems and get comfortable, it might be difficult for them to switch, so would you switch your Gmail account making use of Android and then start using Apple iPhone? The stress of these changes makes many people stay within these ecosystems. Moving away from the big tech companies, Uber for example is also trying to create its ecosystem where you are able to do many things on their app. You are able to book a taxi (instead of using Bolt or Lyft), you are able to book food (instead of using Just Eat or Deliveroo), and you are able to rent a card (instead of using Hertz or Enterprise) and also able to book train tickets (instead of using Trainline or the train company's app). Uber is trying to ensure that they have many people on their platform for as long time as possible. This is a strategic move that could help to strengthen the company's market position and potentially generate additional revenue streams. However, it remains to be seen how successful this approach will be in the long run, and whether it will face any regulatory challenges as it competes with established players in these industries.

Despite these moves to create and expand tech ecosystem, the continuous stay in the ecosystem has significant implication.

First, the limited ability to switch and benefit from other platforms, consumers who stay within a single tech ecosystem may miss out on better deals or services offered by competing platforms. For example, if a user exclusively uses Uber to book rides, they may not be aware of better deals available on Bolt or Lyft. This limits the consumer's ability to make informed decisions and obtain the best value for their money.

Second, difficulty breaking through ecosystems will continue to grow. It can be challenging for new players to enter the market and compete with established tech ecosystems. New smartphones, for example, may not want to create a new operating system and instead align with existing dominant platforms like Android or iOS. This makes it difficult for consumers to switch to new or niche platforms, as there may not be enough support from device manufacturers or developers.

Third, there would be limited options for consumers. As dominant tech companies continue to expand their ecosystems, the list of possible platforms for consumers to choose from becomes smaller. This can reduce competition, limit innovation, and potentially lead to monopolisation of the tech industry.

Fourth, there are concerns about monopolisation and impact on competition and innovation. As tech ecosystems expand, there are concerns about the potential monopolisation of the industry and the impact on competition and innovation. This can lead to reduced consumer choice, higher prices, and a lack of innovation in the industry. It is important for regulators and consumers to carefully consider these risks and benefits and take steps to ensure that competition and innovation are not stifled.

Fifth, conflict of interest can also be a concern when tech companies develop their own devices and platform to monopolise digital consumption. For example, if a company like Amazon owns a popular e-commerce platform and also produces its own products, there is a risk that the company will give preference to its own products on the platform over those of its competitors. This can limit consumer choice and negatively impact competition in the market. Similarly, if Facebook creates its own virtual reality hardware and software, there is a risk that it will prioritise its own content and services over those of its competitors. It is important for regulators and consumers to remain vigilant and address any potential conflicts of interest that may arise as tech companies expand their ecosystems.

Reflective question

Do you envisage any other potential concerns for dominant tech companies developing and expanding their ecosystem?

Table 5.1 presents a summary of the growing ecosystem of the GAFAM big tech companies. Note that this is not an exhaustive list of all the products and services offered by these companies, but rather a summary of their major offerings. Additionally, these companies are constantly expanding and evolving their offerings, so this table may not reflect the most current state of their product portfolios.

5.6.5 Collaboration

Building a collaboration with other brands and platforms can also get people to remain on the platforms. With the growing prospects of metaverses, there are ongoing collaboration between brands and musicians, to host concerts and events (Dwiledi et al., 2022). Brands like Barclays and Curry's can also offer their customers three-month access to Apple TV; there is the collaboration to ensure that consumers feel an integral part of the community. Platforms can offer incentives for people to stay on their platforms by collaborating with other partners. This could mean having a reduced rate for some times or offering discounts on some selected products. There is also a possible collaboration between platforms like Google suggesting Bolt (instead of Uber) as an alternative taxi on their map (Tucker, 2020), Facebook has also worked with Ray-Ban to have smart glasses which allow consumers to use voice control to take photos and videos (Meta, 2021). It is, however, important to recognise Google Glass who made an initial attempt at these smart glasses, but it was not a collaboration; perhaps glasses were not their forte and they got it wrong. Facebook however has been strategic in their effort to collaborate with the glasses company instead of making it on their own. Platform developers need to be very strategic about who they partner with, another brand that will complete their effort and ensure consumer engagement on their platforms.

5.7 Challenges

Developing and managing a digital platform is not an easy task. These dominant platform developers have many failed products and services, an indication that success is not always guaranteed. Consumer engagement in the digital environment is critical to the success of a digital platform, and these challenges can have a significant impact on the ability to attract and retain users. This section of the chapter highlights some of these challenges as developers try to present platforms for digital consumption. By being aware of the challenges, developers and managers can take a proactive approach to addressing them and managing their expectations. However, it's also important to note that the challenges associated with developing a digital platform are constantly evolving, and developers and managers need to be agile and adaptable in their approach. The challenges discussed in this section are not an exhaustive list, but rather an overview of some of the key challenges that developers and managers may face when developing and managing a digital platform, especially as these challenges can be complex and multifaceted, and require ongoing attention and adaptation to ensure the success of the platform.

5.7.1 Innovative ideas

What really defines innovative ideas? This is the billion-pound question many platform developers are thinking about. What is the guarantee that the product you are

Table 5.1 A summary of the growing ecosystem of the GAFAM big tech companies

Company	Google	Apple	Facebook	Amazon	Microsoft
Search	Google Search	—	—	—	Bing
Email	Gmail	—	—	—	Outlook.com
Cloud	Google Drive, Google Cloud Platform	iCloud, iCloud Drive, Apple Cloud Services, Apple CloudKit, Apple TV+	—	Amazon Web Services (AWS), Amazon Drive, Prime Now	Azure
Mobile OS	Android	iOS, iPadOS	—	Fire OS	Windows
Web	Google Chrome	Safari	—	Amazon Silk	Microsoft Edge
Video	YouTube	Apple TV+, iTunes, Apple Music	Instagram, Oculus, Facebook Watch, Portal	Amazon Prime Video, Amazon Studios, Twitch	Xbox
Devices	Google Home, Google Nest, Pixel	iPhone, iPad, Apple Watch	Oculus, Portal, WhatsApp	Amazon Echo, Fire TV, Fire Tablet	Surface
Social	—	—	Facebook, Instagram, Messenger	—	LinkedIn
Payments	Google Pay	Apple Pay	—	Amazon Pay	Microsoft Pay
AI	Google Assistant, Google AI Platform, TensorFlow	Siri, Core ML, Apple Neural Engine	Facebook AI Research	Amazon Alexa, Amazon Machine Learning	Microsoft Cognitive Services, Cortana
Ads	Google Ads, AdSense, AdMob, DoubleClick	—	Facebook Ads, Instagram Ads	Amazon Advertising, IMDb Ads	Microsoft Advertising, LinkedIn Ads

developing will be considered innovative and revolutionary? Defining innovative ideas is indeed a challenging task. An innovative idea is generally one that brings a new perspective or approach to an existing problem or introduces a completely new concept that has the potential to disrupt an industry or market (Johannessen et al., 2001). It's important to note that innovation is not just about creating something entirely new, but also about improving upon existing products, services, or processes in a meaningful way. In terms of guaranteeing that a product will be considered innovative and revolutionary, there are no guarantees in this regard. Innovation is inherently risky, as it involves taking chances and exploring new territories that may or may not be successful. However, there are certain factors that can increase the likelihood of a product being considered innovative and successful. Platform developers must be aware there are no guarantees when it comes to developing innovative products and therefore need to manage their expectations. There are instances where these dominant platform developers have tried to do something innovative, and it has not always panned out. Like the Google+ example, who would have thought that Google will struggle to maintain a digital platform? This is a challenge that the brands need to address amidst the impeding challenges and competition from other developers. Platform developers need to find a way to keep disrupting the ecosystem and challenge the expectations of the consumers.

5.7.2 Competition from other developers

Technology developers should not become complacent and must keep in mind that there is a significant number of developers also striving to create innovative products and services. Platform developers must continually innovate and improve their products and services to stay ahead of the competition. This can be challenging as technologies and consumer preferences evolve rapidly and the ecosystem is becoming very competitive; there are many social media platforms that are coming out and more consumers are spending time on those platforms. It is not surprising to see that the number of users on Facebook is reducing, and people are exploring other alternatives. There is the world of short videos and reels with TikTok, YouTube Shorts, and Instagram reels all craving for consumers' attention. Developers need to always find a niche when developing their product. As the technology-organization-environment (TOE) framework suggests (see Chapter 1 on theoretical framework for digital consumption), the technology solution may be there, and the organisation has got the resources but how about the environment? Is the world ready for another Facebook 2.0 or do we need to start looking for alternatives?

Looking at the streaming platforms, Netflix is facing intense competition in the streaming market from a number of other platforms, including Amazon Prime Video, Apple TV+, Disney+, and Paramount+. These platforms are all vying for subscribers and investing heavily in creating high-quality original content and acquiring popular titles to attract viewers. This competition has led to a rapidly evolving market, with new players entering the market and existing platforms adapting their strategies to stay ahead of the curve. For Netflix to remain competitive, it must continue to innovate and invest in original content and technology, while also offering a user-friendly and engaging platform experience for viewers. Warner Bros. Discovery decided to shut down CNN+, a new streaming service from CNN just one month after its launch (Fitzgerald,

2022), suggesting how competitive it is to create and manage a digital platform. The needs of consumers are continuously evolving, and their attention spans are becoming shorter, leading to intensified competition within the industry (Zhao et al., 2020). Brands must respond to this competition by adapting to the changing landscape and finding innovative ways to capture the attention and loyalty of their target audience. This may involve investing in new technologies and platforms, developing personalised and engaging content, and creating seamless and convenient user experiences. By staying ahead in the competition and meeting the evolving needs of consumers, brands can position themselves for long-term success in the industry.

5.7.3 Keeping customers to stay

As alluded earlier, this is a challenge that needs to be addressed on an ongoing basis. As platform developers making this effort as suggested in the previous section, it is not a guarantee that brands and consumers will stay, even with the innovative idea of Google Daydream, Google could not get many people to adopt the technology, and there are fewer consumers engaging on the platform, and it was not surprising to see HBO and Hulu discontinuing the Daydream apps on their platform. Retaining users on a digital platform is an ongoing challenge for developers. Without sufficient brand and consumer usage, investing in a platform becomes unjustifiable. To keep users engaged, digital platform developers must consistently exceed their expectations, provide incentives, and support engaging activities that align with the platform's goals. This may involve investing in cutting-edge technologies, enhancing the user experience, creating relevant and compelling content, and fostering a strong sense of community among users. By continuously striving to improve and offering a value proposition that meets the needs of both brands and consumers, digital platforms can improve user retention and remain competitive in the market. When Instagram was first launched, it was a simple photo-sharing app, but over time it has evolved into a major social media platform that allows users to share photos and videos, interact with others, and discover new content.

To keep users engaged, Instagram has continuously updated its platform with new features such as Stories, Reels, and IGTV, which have all proved popular among users. Instagram also offers incentives to users through its algorithm, which promotes content that is relevant to their interests, and through partnerships with influencers and brands, which help to keep the platform fresh and engaging. As a result of these efforts, Instagram has become one of the most popular social media platforms in the world, with over 1 billion monthly active users. More so, to maintain consumer engagement and loyalty in a highly competitive streaming market, major players like Netflix, Apple TV, and Amazon are taking various strategic steps. For instance, Netflix has experimented with different pricing structures, such as offering lower-cost mobile-only plans in certain markets, to attract new users and retain existing ones. Netflix's mobile-only plan is available in select markets like India, Malaysia, and Indonesia. This plan is designed for users who primarily watch Netflix on their mobile devices and offers a lower cost option compared to their standard plans. The mobile-only plan restricts access to the service on tablets, computers, and TVs and allows streaming on only one mobile device at a time. This pricing structure helps to attract and retain users who prefer to watch content on their smartphones and tablets, while also providing a more affordable option for those who may be cost-sensitive or price-conscious. Meanwhile, Apple TV has been heavily investing in producing original content, including acclaimed series like 'The Morning Show' and 'Ted Lasso', to keep audiences engaged and interested in their platform. In addition to this, Amazon is expanding beyond just movies and TV shows, and investing in other areas like sports, music, and gaming to provide a more well-rounded entertainment experience to users, which can help to retain them on the platform. These strategies demonstrate how companies are adapting to the evolving needs and preferences of consumers and finding new ways to differentiate themselves in a highly competitive market.

5.7.4 Human resources

To develop these platforms and ensure ongoing engagements, human resources are very important. Platform development requires a range of skills, including software engineering, systems design, database management, and security. It also requires an understanding of how developers and users will interact with the platform and how to provide documentation, support, and tools to facilitate their work. In addition, these developers compete for top talent in a highly competitive job market. Attracting and retaining skilled developers and engineers can be a challenge, particularly in areas such as artificial intelligence and machine learning. As you would need people to work on these innovative ideas. You want to be sure that you have the needed manpower to deliver. Possibly you are a small start-up founder, you need to be looking at recruiting staff and retaining your best staff before they are poached by bigger companies with bigger budgets. Would you be working with freelancers to help develop your platforms? How long would you be doing this? Would you want to go and learn how to code? Going back to the TOE framework, you need to be sure that the organisational issues are addressed as you think of your offers to the digital consumers.

As dominant platform developers like Facebook and Google continue to face financial pressures, there is a growing concern about the need for large staff numbers in the future. With the increasing prospects of Artificial Intelligence and ChatGPT, there is a possibility that companies may need to start considering alternatives to traditional staffing models (Jain et al., 2023). AI and chatbots can be used to automate many routine tasks, such as customer service and data entry, freeing up human employees to focus on more complex and strategic tasks that require a human touch. This could lead to a shift in the types of jobs that are available in the tech industry, as well as the skills that are required to succeed in these jobs. Companies may need to invest in training their workforce to adapt to these changes, or even consider partnering with AI and automation companies to ensure that their workforce remains competitive in the industry. While the use of AI and chatbots may not completely replace the need for human employees, it may provide an opportunity for companies to rethink their staffing models and find ways to remain competitive in a rapidly changing industry.

As a student, it is important to start thinking about developing skills that will make you stand out and less prone to being laid off (Chattopadhyay et al., 2022). With the rise of automation and AI, certain jobs and industries may be more vulnerable to being automated in the future. To remain competitive, students should consider developing skills that are in high demand and are less likely to be automated, such as critical thinking, problem-solving, creativity, and emotional intelligence. They can also consider pursuing careers in emerging fields that are less likely to be impacted by automation, such as healthcare, renewable energy, and cybersecurity. Similarly, as a start-up founder, it is important to start thinking about how to automate business processes to remain competitive and increase efficiency. By adopting technologies like AI and automation, start-ups can reduce costs, improve customer service, and streamline their operations. For example, AI-powered chatbots can be used to handle customer inquiries and provide support, while automation can be used to streamline supply chain and inventory management. This can help start-ups to scale their businesses faster and compete with larger, more established companies in their industry.

5.7.5 Ethical considerations

Platform developers need to always reflect on their ethical stance—how far can they push their luck? For example, the use of algorithms and artificial intelligence to make decisions that affect people's lives, such as hiring, lending, and criminal justice, needs to be unbiased, non-discriminating, fair, transparent, and accountable. Likewise, as these platform developers collect and store vast amounts of data, which can be used for targeted advertising and other purposes, they must ensure that this data is secure and protected from unauthorised access or misuse, ensuring that they comply with relevant data protection laws and respect users' privacy (Mogaji et al., 2020). There were concerns raised about the privacy issues surrounding Facebook smart glasses with Ray-Ban, as the cameras on the glasses can be used to take photos and videos without the knowledge or consent of those around the wearer. Protecting the environment is also an integral ethical challenge; with platform developers consuming significant amounts of energy and resources, they must begin to consider the environmental impact of their operations. This includes reducing carbon emissions, using renewable energy sources, and minimising waste and pollution.

In alignment with the triple bottom line, which seeks to protect the people, profit, and planet, platform developers need to be mindful of the ethical implications of their actions (Khan et al., 2021). Protecting the people, whether it's by preventing online harassment and hate speech, or ensuring ethical human resources practices, particularly around the treatment of gig workers and the use of contract staff, should be a key consideration for platform developers. There needs to be a balance between prioritising the well-being of people and generating profits. Platforms have a responsibility to ensure that their users are safe from harassment and hate speech, which can cause real harm and contribute to a toxic online environment. Platform developers can implement measures such as content moderation and user reporting systems to ensure that their platforms are safe and welcoming for all users. Additionally, platform developers need to be mindful of their treatment of gig workers and contract staff, who often have limited job security and lack access to benefits such as healthcare and paid time off. By implementing fair labour practices and providing support to these workers, platform developers can improve the well-being of their employees and contribute to a more ethical and sustainable business model.

> **Reflective question**
>
> How do platform developers ensure that their products and services are accessible to users with disabilities or other special needs?

5.7.6 Regulatory requirements

Platform developers are subject to numerous regulations, such as data protection and privacy laws governing how data are collected, used, and stored. For example, in the European Union, the General Data Protection Regulation (GDPR) sets strict requirements for how companies handle personal data. Antitrust laws are designed to prevent monopolies and promote fair competition, to ensure that the developers are not benefiting from monopoly and undue market dominance. Intellectual property laws protect inventions, designs, and other forms of creative work (Holgersson & Aaboen, 2019). Consumer protection laws are designed to protect consumers from fraudulent or deceptive business practices. Content moderation regulations are to ensure that hate speech, fake news, and terrorist content are moderated though this can be challenging and controversial. Cybersecurity regulations require companies to take steps to protect their networks and systems from cyber threats. Platform developers need to provide infrastructures that can protect stakeholders from cyberattacks. Compliance with these regulations can be complex and expensive. Platform developers need to be aware of the legal framework that binds their operations. Would you be able to attend the House of Common to explain about your products? Would you be able to lobby with the government to allow your business to thrive. What compromise are you willing to reach? These are some of the challenging questions that brand developers need to reflect on as they anticipate growth and adoption of their platforms.

5.7.7 Managing the operations

Unlike the smaller, independent, and third-party developers (to be discussed in the next chapter), the platform developers have a lot on their plate. They often have complex organisational structures, with multiple products, teams, and stakeholders. Managing this complexity can be challenging and requires effective communication, collaboration, and decision-making. Imagine laying off 10,000 staff at once, that's a huge human resources issue, imagine providing support to different people around the world in different languages. Imagine the resources invested in building security infrastructures. Platform developers will often find challenges with their big sizes and not surprising to see them try managing their operations by redefining their brand architecture—Google upgraded to Alphabet and likewise Facebook upgraded to Meta.

Addressing these challenges requires a willingness to continuously monitor and evaluate the platform, gather feedback from users, and make necessary changes and updates to address emerging issues and meet changing user needs (Mogaji et al., 2023). Overall, by critically reflecting on the challenges associated with developing a digital platform, prospective developers and managers can gain a deeper understanding of the complexities involved and develop strategies to effectively manage these challenges and ensure the success of their platform. This can include developing strategies to address issues related to user privacy and security, ensuring that the platform is user-friendly and accessible to a diverse range of users, and developing effective marketing and communication strategies to promote the platform.

Reflective questions

How should a manager choose the platform developer they want to work with? What would you consider as key criteria?

5.8 Key consideration

With the understanding of digital platform providers, it is imperative to reflect on key considerations for brands. This is an attempt to connect the responsibility of *platform developers* with the desire of *brands* to provide an engaging platform for their *digital consumers* to facilitate digital consumption. There are some key considerations for brands (and prospective start-up founders) and students.

5.8.1 For brands

Brands are at liberty to choose whose platform they want to use—You can choose Google Meet, Webex, Zoom, or Teams. When brands are looking for a digital platform to use, it is important for them to research and understand what each platform offers. For example, they should look at the features available, the level of support provided, the available security infrastructure, and the platform's flexibility. In addition to these technical considerations, brands should also consider the values and principles of the platform developers. For instance, if a brand is concerned about ethical practices, they should look for a platform that has a track record of responsible and ethical behaviour (Mogaji, 2021). If a brand is focused on sustainability, they may want to seek out platforms that prioritise environmentally friendly practices. Ultimately, the choice of platform should align with the brand's goals, values, and needs. It is also important for brands to be aware of the potential risks associated with each platform and to take steps to mitigate those risks. This can include implementing strong security protocols, regularly monitoring the platform for potential issues, and staying up-to-date with platform updates and best practices.

The context of B2B (business-to-business) versus B2C (business-to-consumer) is important to consider when evaluating digital platforms. B2B platforms typically have different requirements and expectations compared to B2C platforms. For example, B2B platforms may need to prioritise security and confidentiality, as they may be handling sensitive business information. They may also require more customisation and integration with existing systems, such as customer relationship management (CRM) or enterprise resource planning (ERP) software. On the other hand, B2C platforms may need to focus more on user experience, accessibility, and scalability to handle large volumes of users. They may also need to prioritise features such as social media integration, mobile compatibility, and personalised recommendations to engage consumers and keep them coming back. In either case, it's important for brands to research and understand the industry standard and best practices for their specific context, as well as evaluate the platform's features, support system, security infrastructure, and flexibility before making a decision.

As discussed in previous chapters, brands need to know their financial, technical, and human resources before adopting and selecting platforms. It's important for brands to conduct a thorough assessment of their resources and needs before selecting a digital platform. This includes evaluating their financial capacity to invest in a platform, their technical capabilities to effectively utilise it, and their human resources to manage and maintain it. Moreover, managers should carefully consider the features, functionality, and compatibility of the platform they choose with their specific business needs and goals. This will help ensure that the platform aligns with their overall digital strategy and enables them to effectively engage with their target audience. By making informed decisions about the platform and provider they choose, managers can maximise their chances of success and enhance their overall digital presence and engagement with consumers. Just like brands who want to host their customer at a party, they need to be sure that the venue is safe, and their customers will have fun.

5.8.2 Students

Staying informed about the latest technologies and platforms can definitely improve one's employability and career prospects, especially in the tech industry. It is important for individuals to continuously develop their skills and knowledge and stay up-to-date with industry trends and advancements (Chattopadhyay et al., 2022). This can involve taking courses, attending conferences, reading industry publications, and networking with professionals in the field. Additionally, having a strong understanding of the needs and expectations of both consumers and brands can help in developing and selecting effective platforms.

Here are a few points for your consideration.

1. Be aware of the devices and platforms. It's important to stay up-to-date on emerging technologies and how they could potentially impact the digital landscape. Metaverse, virtual reality, and cryptocurrency are just a few examples of rapidly evolving technologies that could have significant implications for digital consumption. By staying informed, you can position yourself to take advantage of new opportunities and stay ahead of the curve in your industry. Additionally, being knowledgeable about these technologies can help you make informed decisions about which platforms or tools to use for your business or personal use.
2. Be ready to explore. The best way to keep yourself informed about new technologies is to explore and try them out yourself. Attend industry events, read technology news and articles, and even take online courses or tutorials to learn more about specific technologies. This will give you a deeper understanding of how these technologies work and how they can be applied in different contexts. Additionally, it will help you stay ahead of the curve and be better equipped to adapt to changes and new developments in the digital world.
3. Be versatile. Digital consumption goes beyond social media and retail. It is important to recognise the potential for digital consumption in various industries and human activities. For instance, digital consumption can occur in the education

sector through e-learning platforms, in the healthcare sector through telemedicine and health apps, in the entertainment industry through streaming platforms and gaming, in the financial sector through online banking and fintech, and in the transportation industry through ride-sharing and delivery apps. It is important to keep an open mind and explore the potential for digital consumption in various industries and activities. This can help individuals and businesses identify new opportunities and stay ahead of the curve in the ever-evolving digital landscape—visit to Gym (Peloton), visit to GP (online consultation with doctor), visit to Greenland (Virtual reality).

4. Be innovative. Think about the next platform. Think about what you can create. Explore what digital consumers will need on that digital platform and see if you can meet their needs. How about the idea of Uber for tractors or Tinder for vegetarians or Instagram for dogs. Network with people, and you can be a co-founder of an innovative idea. Remember you may have the idea; you need many other people to support you as you spur your entrepreneurship prospects. Be aware of different support for entrepreneurs that is available at your university.

5. Be aware of the dark sides. You need to know that as we have the good sides of these digital platforms, there are also the dark sides (more in Chapter 9). It is important to be aware of the negative aspects and potential risks associated with digital platforms and to take measures to address them. Being alert, observant, and critical can help you identify and avoid potential threats such as phishing emails, fake news, and cyberbullying. It is also important to educate others about these issues and encourage safe and responsible use of digital platforms. You can be a digital role model for your friends and family, helping them navigate the online world with confidence and security. By taking these steps, you can help create a safer and more positive digital environment for everyone.

5.9 Conclusion

This chapter has explored the role of dominant platform developers in enhancing digital consumption. These are organisations that are responsible for providing digital platforms that bring consumers and brands together. This chapter has highlighted their business operations and their growth strategies as they try to meet the ever-growing needs of consumers. The chapter reiterated the need to always have consumers engaging on the platform. This is important because the more we have consumers, the more brands are willing to invest and engage with the consumers (Balakrishnan et al., 2021). Platform developers must also continuously innovate and improve their platform to keep up with evolving consumer needs and industry trends. They need to be responsive to feedback and concerns raised by users and be able to quickly address any technical issues or security breaches. Platform developers also need to build strong relationships with brands and developers and provide them with the necessary tools and resources to create engaging experiences on their platform. Ultimately, the success of a platform developer relies on their ability to create a sustainable ecosystem that benefits all stakeholders involved.

The platform developers also have huge responsibilities to make sure that everyone on the platform is safe. It is imperative to recognise that platform developers are not limited to the big tech companies—GAFAM. There are many other companies like Uber, Netflix, and Trainline that are developing platforms that will allow consumers to engage. The chapter also highlights some challenges that need to be addressed. These platform developers face a range of complex and interrelated challenges that require a deep understanding of technology, business, and society (Abdulquadri et al., 2021; Agbo et al., 2020). Addressing these challenges requires a proactive approach, a commitment to ethical principles, and a willingness to adapt and evolve over time. The chapter concludes with some key considerations for brands and students.

5.10 Student activities

1. List different platform developers and identify the platforms they have developed. Try and think beyond social media and e-commerce/retail stores.
2. How do platform developers balance the needs of different stakeholders, such as users, developers, and regulators?
3. What are some of the ethical considerations that platform developers must consider when designing and deploying their products and services?
4. Can you give an example of a platform developer that has faced significant ethical or regulatory challenges in recent years? How did they respond to these challenges?
5. How would you describe the responsibility of the government and regulators in developing and maintaining platforms?
6. Why is it important for platform developers to market and showcase their achievements and milestones?
7. How else do you think developers can ensure digital consumers stay on their platform?
8. How do platform developers incorporate user feedback into their product design and development processes?
9. What skills and knowledge do you think are most important for a platform developer to have in order to succeed in today's tech industry?
10. Can you identify any emerging trends or technologies that you think will have a significant impact on platform development in the near future?

References and further reading

Abdulquadri, A., Mogaji, E., Kieu, T. & Nguyen, P., 2021. Digital transformation in financial services provision: A Nigerian perspective to the adoption of chatbot. *Journal of Enterprising Communities: People and Places in the Global Economy*, 15(2), pp. 258–281.

Affeldt, P. & Kesler, R., 2021. Big tech acquisitions—Towards empirical evidence. *Journal of European Competition Law & Practice*, 12(6), pp. 471–478.

Agbo, F. et al., 2020. Social media usage for computing education: The effect of tie strength and group communication on perceived learning outcome. *Journal of Education and Development Using Information and Communication Technology*, 16(1), pp. 5–26.

Aten, J., 2023. Microsoft is trying to force you to use its software like it's 1998 all over again, Microsoft really wants you to use edge and teams [Online] Available at: https://www.inc.com/jason-aten/microsoft-is-trying-to-force-you-to-use-its-software-like-its-1998-all-over-again.html

Balakrishnan, J., Nwoba, A. & Nguyen, N., 2021. Emerging-market consumers' interactions with banking chatbots. *Telematics and Informatics*, 65, 101711.

Bandara, R., Fernando, M. & Akter, S., 2021. Managing consumer privacy concerns and defensive behaviours in the digital marketplace. *European Journal of Marketing*, 55(1), pp. 219–246.

Barrett, A. & Matthee, M., 2019. Context-aware technology public discourses and (un)-informed use: The case of users in a developing country. *South African Computer Journal*, 31(2), pp. 1–33.

Birch, K. & Bronson, K., 2022. Big tech. *Science as Culture*, 31(1), pp. 1–4.

Bonina, C. & Eaton, B., 2020. Cultivating open government data platform ecosystems through governance: Lessons from Buenos Aires, Mexico City and Montevideo. *Government Information Quarterly*, 37(3), 101479.

Braun, J. & Eklund, J., 2019. Fake news, real money: Ad tech platforms, profit-driven hoaxes, and the business of journalism. *Digital Journalism*, 7(1), pp. 1–21.

Chattopadhyay, A., Kupe, T., Schatzer, N. & Mogaji, E., 2022. Fireside chat with three vice chancellors from three continents. In: E. Mogaji, V. Jain, F. Maringe & R. Hinson, eds. *Re-imagining Higher Education in Emerging Economies*. Cham: Palgrave Macmillan, pp. 85–96.

Chylinski, M. et al., 2020. Augmented reality marketing: A technology-enabled approach to situated customer experience. *Australasian Marketing Journal*, 28(4), pp. 374–384.

De Hert, P. et al., 2018. The right to data portability in the GDPR: Towards user-centric interoperability of digital services. *Computer Law & Security Review*, 34(2), pp. 193–203.

Department of Justice, 1998. Justice department files antitrust suit against Microsoft for unlawfully monopolizing computer software markets [Online] Available at: https://www.justice.gov/archive/atr/public/press_releases/1998/1764.htm

Dhruv, G., Hulland, J., Kopalle, P. & Karahanna, E., 2020. The future of technology and marketing: A multidisciplinary perspective. *Journal of the Academy of Marketing Science*, 48, pp. 1–8.

Dwivedi, Y. et al., 2022. Metaverse beyond the hype: Multidisciplinary perspectives on emerging challenges, opportunities, and agenda for research, practice and policy. *International Journal of Information Management*, 66, 102542.

Failory, 2023. Google daydream [Online] Available at: https://www.failory.com/google/daydream

Fitzgerald, T., 2022. 5 valuable lessons from the abrupt failure of CNN+ [Online] Available at: https://www.forbes.com/sites/tonifitzgerald/2022/04/30/5-valuable-lessons-from-the-abrupt-failure-of-cnn/?sh=169b335a28ce

Flew, T., Martin, F. & Suzor, N., 2019. Internet regulation as media policy: Rethinking the question of digital communication platform governance. *Journal of Digital Media & Policy*, 10(1), pp. 33–50.

Fortino, G., Savaglio, C., Spezzano, G. & Zhou, M., 2020. Internet of things as system of systems: A review of methodologies, frameworks, platforms, and tools. *IEEE Transactions on Systems, Man, and Cybernetics: Systems*, 51(1), pp. 223–236.

Hein, A. et al., 2020. Digital platform ecosystems. *Electronic Markets*, 30, pp. 87–98.

Hendrikse, R., Adriaans, I., Klinge, T. & Fernandez, R., 2022. The big techification of everything. *Science as Culture*, 31(1), pp. 59–71.

Hodapp, D. & Hanelt, A., 2022. Interoperability in the era of digital innovation: An information systems research agenda. *Journal of Information Technology*, 37(4), pp. 407–427.

Holgersson, M. & Aaboen, L., 2019. A literature review of intellectual property management in technology transfer offices: From appropriation to utilization. *Technology in Society*, 59(1), 101132.

Jain, V., Rai, H., Subash, P. & Mogaji, E., 2023. The prospects and challenges of ChatGPT on marketing research and practices. *SSRN Electronic Journal*, pp. 1–16. http://dx.doi.org/10.2139/ssrn.4398033.

Jelovac, D., Ljubojević, C. & Ljubojević, L., 2022. HPC in business: The impact of corporate digital responsibility on building digital trust and responsible corporate digital governance. *Digital Policy, Regulation and Governance*, 24(6), pp. 485–497.

Johannessen, J., Olsen, B. & Lumpkin, G., 2001. Innovation as newness: What is new, how new, and new to whom? *European Journal of Innovation Management*, 4(1), pp. 20–31.

Kandampully, J., Bilgihan, A. & Li, D., 2022. Unifying technology and people: Revisiting service in a digitally transformed world. *The Service Industries Journal*, 42(1–2), pp. 21–41.

Khalil, A., Abdelli, M. & Mogaji, E., 2022. Do digital technologies influence the relationship between the COVID-19 crisis and SMEs' resilience in developing countries? *Journal of Open Innovation: Technology, Market, and Complexity*, 8(2), pp. 100–109.

Khan, I., Ahmad, M. & Majava, J., 2021. Industry 4.0 and sustainable development: A systematic mapping of triple bottom line, circular economy and sustainable business models perspectives. *Journal of Cleaner Production*, 297, 126655.

Klinge, T., Hendrikse, R., Fernandez, R. & Andriaans, I., 2023. Augmenting digital monopolies: A corporate financialization perspective on the rise of Big Tech. *Competition & Change*, 27(2), pp. 332–353.

Koohang, A. et al., 2023. Shaping the metaverse into reality: A holistic multidisciplinary understanding of opportunities, challenges, and avenues for future investigation. *Journal of Computer Information Systems*, 63 (3), pp. 735–765.

Kopalle, P., Kumar, V. & Subramaniam, M., 2020. How legacy firms can embrace the digital ecosystem via digital customer orientation. *Journal of the Academy of Marketing Science*, 48, pp. 114–131.

Lai, J. & Widmar, N. O., 2021. Revisiting the digital divide in the COVID-19 era. *Applied Economic Perspectives and Policy*, 43(1), pp. 458–464.

McKinsey, 2022. Marketing in the metaverse: An opportunity for innovation and experimentation [Online] Available at: https://www.mckinsey.com/capabilities/growth-marketing-and-sales/our-insights/marketing-in-the-metaverse-an-opportunity-for-innovation-and-experimentation

Meta, 2021. Ray-Ban and Facebook introduce Ray-Ban stories, first-generation smart glasses [Online] Available at: https://tech.facebook.com/reality-labs/2021/9/ray-ban-and-facebook-introduce-ray-ban-stories-first-generation-smart-glasses/

Miric, M., Boudreau, K. & Jeppesen, L., 2019. Protecting their digital assets: The use of formal & informal appropriability strategies by app developers. *Research Policy*, 48(8), 103738.

Mogaji, E., 2021. *Brand Management*. Cham: Springer.

Mogaji, E. & Nguyen, N., 2022. Managers' understanding of artificial intelligence in relation to marketing financial services: insights from a cross-country study. *International Journal of Bank Marketing*, 40(6), pp. 1272–1298.

Mogaji, E. & Nguyen, N., 2022. The dark side of mobile money: Perspectives from an emerging economy. *Technological Forecasting and Social Change*, 185, 122045.

Mogaji, E., Restuccia, M., Lee, Z. & Nguyen, N., 2023. B2B brand positioning in emerging markets: Exploring positioning signals via websites and managerial tensions in top-performing African B2B service brands. *Industrial Marketing Management*, 108, pp. 237–250.

Mogaji, E., Soetan, T. & Kieu, T., 2020. The implications of artificial intelligence on the digital marketing of financial services to vulnerable customers. *Australasian Marketing Journal*, 29(3), pp. 235–242.

Morgan-Thomas, A., Dessart, L. & Veloutsou, C., 2020. Digital ecosystem and consumer engagement: A socio-technical perspective. *Journal of Business Research*, 121, pp. 713–723.

Netflix, 2020. Netflix recommended TV [Online]. Available at: https://devices.netflix.com/en/recommendedtv/2020/

Notopoulos, K., 2023. The Facebook portal died. This is how it almost lived [Online] Available at: https://www.buzzfeednews.com/article/katienotopoulos/facebook-portal-rip-amazon

Nuccio, M. & Guerzoni, M., 2019. Big data: Hell or heaven? Digital platforms and market power in the data-driven economy. *Competition & Change*, 23(3), pp. 312–328.

Olson, E., Olson, K., Czaplewski, A. & Key, T., 2021. Business strategy and the management of digital marketing. *Business Horizons*, 64(2), pp. 285–293.

Oosthuizen, K., Botha, E., Robertson, J. & Montecchi, M., 2021. Artificial intelligence in retail: The AI-enabled value chain. *Australasian Marketing Journal*, 29(3), pp. 264–273.

Ponzoa, J. & Erdmann, A., 2021. E-commerce customer attraction: Digital marketing techniques, evolution and dynamics across firms. *Journal of Promotion Management*, 27(5), pp. 697–715.

Rikap, C. & Lundvall, B., 2022. Big tech, knowledge predation and the implications for development. *Innovation and Development*, 12(3), pp. 389–416.

Sağkaya Güngö, A. & Ozansoy Çadırcı, T., 2022. Understanding digital consumer: A review, synthesis, and future research agenda. *International Journal of Consumer Studies*, 46(5), pp. 1829–1858.

Samsung Community, 2021. I cannot delete the Netflix app from my phone [Online] Available at: https://eu.community.samsung.com/t5/galaxy-s20-series/i-cannot-delete-the-netflix-app-from-my-phone/td-p/3369979

Sheth, J., 2020. Impact of Covid-19 on consumer behavior: Will the old habits return or die? *Journal of Business Research*, 117, pp. 280–283.

Soetan, T., Mogaji, E. & Nguyen, N., 2021. Financial services experience and consumption in Nigeria. *Journal of Services Marketing*, 35(7), pp. 947–961.

Tucker, C., 2020. Estonian taxi app Bolt integrates with Google Maps to appear in the 'journey planner' [Online] Available at: https://www.eu-startups.com/2020/02/estonian-taxi-app-bolt-integrates-with-google-maps-to-appear-in-the-journey-planner/

Varela, F., 2019. Facebook expands preinstall partnerships [Online] Available at: https://tech.facebook.com/artificial-intelligence/2019/9/preinstall-partnerships/

Zhao, Y., Von Delft, S., Morgan-Thomas, A. & Buck, T., 2020. The evolution of platform business models: Exploring competitive battles in the world of platforms. *Long Range Planning*, 53(4), 101892.

CHAPTER 6

Third-party platform developers

6.1 Background

The previous chapter has extensively discussed the platform developers, and this chapter aims at extending that discussion to other types of platform developers. You should know that sometimes you might not like the big dancehall and club music, you want something small and intimate with your friends, and you have decided to host the party in your house. So likewise, there are many other platform developers that are not developing paid platforms for brands but developing owned and co-created platforms. These platform developers are the focus of this chapter. The previous chapter focuses on dominant platform developers working on bigger platforms that can accommodate other brands—like Google developing apps stores, Facebook developing social media pages, and Shopify developing e-commerce websites. This chapter focuses on those who develop websites for companies, develop apps for organisation, and serve the immediate needs of brands who want bespoke offers. This chapter introduces you to third-party developers, highlighting the values they offer and their advantages and challenges.

6.2 Learning outcomes

By the end of this chapter, you should be able to:

- Build on your understanding of the roles of platform developers in digital consumptions.
- Identify the prospects and challenges in working with third-party developers.
- Recognise the possibilities of white labelling and Software as a Service (SaaS) digital platforms.
- Understand the importance of API in connecting different platforms.
- Understand the key considerations for brands.

DOI: 10.4324/9781003389842-6

6.3 Introduction

We have recognised the dominant platform developers—GAFAM—Google, Amazon, Facebook, Apple, and Microsoft, creating and maintaining a platform for global audiences and business enterprises (Birch & Bronson, 2022). These dominant developers develop a platform that allows many brands and consumers to engage. These dominant platform developers have large teams working around the chocks on existing platforms and developing new ones. It is however imperative to recognise that these brands may sometimes be too big to meet the needs of small business that wants something customised, bespoke, and manageable. Often, they are not able to use the platform Google (and other dominant platform developers) has provided or they wanted something on a short time basis to meet their immediate needs.

Brands are aware of the growing prospect of digital platforms and for managers interested in understanding and managing digital consumers; they are bound to look for different alternative to meet their needs. They may consider moving beyond dominant platform developers to establish an in-house team that may help them achieve their goals. This business decision has created need for smaller digital platform developers—which may be an individual or a small company that can engage with the brand, understand their needs, and provide solutions to the business pain point (Mogaji et al., 2023). These smaller companies and platform developers are called third-party developers and they will be discussed in this chapter. Specifically, we would be trying to answer the following questions: What defines a third-party developer? Why are they relevant? What options do they offer? What are their benefits? and What are their challenges?

The subsequent section highlights the value and advantages of working with these third-party developers, to recognise the enormous benefits of having a small team to work on your project, and likewise the inherent challenges are discussed, especially with regard to the limited security infrastructure and the human resources. Alternative options like white labelling are also discussed. At the end of this chapter, you should have a better understanding of third-party developers, to recognise how to build a working relationship and get the best out of their involvement in your project. The understanding of third-party developers is important for perspective digital platform developers who may be working as freelancers working with other smaller companies and for businesses who may require the services of these developers.

> **Reflective question**
>
> As brands and digital consumers, should we be worried about the GAFAM's dominance?

6.4 Third-party developers

Addressing GAFAM's dominance has provided opportunities for third-party developers to meet a need in the market for brands who need bespoke and customised platforms. Think of yourself as a small business owner looking to design a website—who would you contact? Think of a football club considering having an app to monitor players' progress—who would they contact? Think of a restaurant that wants to develop a self-service kiosk in store for customers—who would they contact? Would you expect these businesses and brands to reach out to Google to develop their apps and their websites? Or they could benefit from having a local service provider? That's the concept of a third-party developer.

Third-party developers can be described as an individual, freelancer, or organisation that designs, builds, and maintains a customised and bespoke owned and/or co-created platform to enhance digital consumption between brands and digital consumers. These third-party developers can work on a range of technologies, from traditional software applications to cloud-based platforms and mobile operating systems. Their work involves not only the development of the platform itself but also the documentation and support necessary to attract and enable digital consumption.

They can also be referred to as external developers, independent developers, or non-affiliated developers. Your cousin, niece, or nephew who is versatile in computer programming can be considered a third-party developer because they are able to create a website for you. The freelancer on Fiverr or Upwork, working from India, can be considered a third-party developer as they have created a mobile app for your business, even though you have not seen them before. The website design company on the high street that has worked on your website can be considered a third-party developer.

6.5 Features of third-party developers

From the offered definition of third-party platform developers, there are unique characteristics and features that set them apart from the dominant platform developers discussed in the previous chapter.

6.5.1 Size

These third parties can range from small to mid-sized agencies. Their size is one of the significant features of the third-party developers, they are not as big as the big tech companies, they may not have head offices in Silicon Valley, and they may not have thousands of staff or have platforms that are accessible to the global audience. Larger third-party developers may have more resources, such as a larger workforce and more experience, which can enable them to develop more complex and sophisticated platforms. On the other hand, smaller third-party developers may offer more personalised attention and flexibility, allowing them to be more responsive to the needs of their clients. These third-party developers are often individuals, starting up their own businesses and managing one platform at a time. They seldom have their own ecosystem. Third-party developers can be a cost-effective option for organisations, as they can often provide services at a lower cost.

6.5.2 Speed

Considering the small sizes of these third-party developers, they are able to jump on projects and get things done in time. The bureaucracy and bottlenecks may be removed as they work directly with the client, often able to streamline the development process and create efficient workflows. You can imagine putting your brief on Upwork at 9 pm your local time and you see different freelancers from different parts of the world, in different time zones contacting you and pitching that they can do the job. You can actually decide by 11 pm on who to work with. There are people working round the clock and you have speed of response to your advantage as a brand. However, it's important to note that the speed of development may come at the expense of quality, so it's crucial to find a balance between speed and quality to ensure a successful project outcome. Importantly, the third-party developers can often offer more flexible engagement models than the established platform; they can offer on-demand services, short-term contracts, or project-based work.

6.5.3 Symbiotic

Third-party developers have a symbiotic relationship with their clients, and there is a mutually beneficial relationship between both the developer and the brand (Azeem et al., 2022). The developer is not fully obligated to the brand, and they can choose to work with different brands. For example, you have a freelancer on Fiverr who is able to develop different apps and websites for different businesses. These third-party developers are very mindful of their business operations, working simultaneously with different clients and just trying to complete the project and get to the next. It is important to reiterate that since they are often self-employed and therefore, they may always take up more clients than they can handle, they want to maximise their profit opportunities.

6.5.4 Strategic

The third party will not always go all the way to reinvent the wheel, and they are not the main platform developers as described in the previous chapter. These developers are strategic in how they develop and manage the platforms; they are able to use open-source technologies, templates, and other available library. They work and engage with other platforms, including the established platforms. They rely on the platform provided by another entity, such as a software company or a cloud computing provider, to host, distribute, and operate the applications or services on behalf of the brand. Third-party developers are often early adopters of new technologies, which can provide organisations with access to new and innovative solutions.

6.5.5 Specialisation

Third-party developers often specialise in certain areas of platform development, such as web development, mobile app development, or cloud computing. They have considerable high level of technical expertise in their field, which can be beneficial for organisations that do not have the in-house resources or skills to develop certain software applications. They can customise different platforms for the brand's needs. Managers however may need to verify this specialisation before engaging their services. These developers may have different certifications to establish their credibility. These third-party developers may be previous staff of the big tech companies, who are now working as a freelancer where they can now share their expertise with other clients. Managers interested in managing consumer engagement in the digital environment should be aware of the possibilities of working with different developers based on their level of expertise and specialisation.

> **Reflective question**
>
> Why should you use a third-party platform developer for your project?

6.6 Types of third-party developers

This section aims to identify a generalised type of third-party developers. This is important for a student thinking of which type of platform developer they want to become, the type of developer they want to work with as a staff or the type of developer their company wants to work with. Each of these types of third-party developers has its own strengths and weaknesses and may be better suited for certain types of projects or clients. Choosing the right type of developer for a particular project depends on factors such as budget, timeline, and project requirements.

6.6.1 Freelance developer

Self-employed, offering digital platform design services such as website design, mobile app design, or software design. They could be working in the gig economy as well, operating on sites like Fiverr and Upwork, pitching for businesses. They are individuals who could work from a remote location, often communicating with clients and team members online rather than in person. This is where the example of your cousin comes in—a one man battalion who is able to develop digital platforms. They could also be considered an independent developer as they are not affiliated with any particular company or organisation. They work for themselves and are responsible for managing their own business and clients. Freelancing suggests that the individual works alone and does not have a team or employees but after taking on many clients and employing more staff, it is anticipated that a freelance developer would expand to become an agency developer.

6.6.2 Contract developer

They could also be considered a self-employed but can be employed on a contract basis to work on a particular project. They work as an independent contractor, typically on a project-by-project basis. Contract developers may be hired directly by companies or may work through staffing agencies or consulting firms. They are typically hired to provide specific technical expertise, to help augment an existing team, or to help meet short-term project needs. Maybe a company wants to have a website design and they prefer to have someone in-house but can't employ them on a permanent basis, so the developer comes in to do the job as they are hired for a specific project or time period rather than being employed full-time. Contract developers are often responsible for developing, testing, and deploying code, as well as collaborating with other developers, project managers, and stakeholders. They also need to be able to work independently and manage their own workflow effectively, as they may not have direct supervision or guidance from a dedicated team lead. Contract developers may need to navigate legal and financial considerations related to their work, such as contracts, taxes, and insurance.

6.6.3 Agency developer

They are companies, albeit of different sizes, providing a wide range of digital services, including website design and development, e-commerce solutions, search engine optimisation, and digital marketing. This developer shares a similar working arrangement with advertising or marketing communications agencies, where you have a partner/co-founder working together to grow their business. This could be two freelancer developers merging and coming together to start an agency. They go out to pitch for businesses, and they could also have an account on Fiverr and Upwork to attract prospective clients who need some bespoke service an individual freelancer can't provide. They may work on a range of technologies and platforms, including content management systems (CMS), e-commerce platforms, and custom web applications. They often work closely with clients to understand their business needs and goals, and design solutions that meet those needs. In addition to technical skills, agency developers require strong communication and project management skills to effectively collaborate with clients and deliver projects on time and within budget. They also need to keep up with the latest trends and best practices in web development to ensure that their clients' websites and applications are both functional and visually appealing. Depending on the size of the agency, there could be those offering more specialised and more focused personalised service, while there could be larger, more versatile agencies that are more focused on scalability and efficiency (Mogaji et al., 2023).

6.6.4 Boutique developer

This can be considered an extension of agency developer in the sense that they have a specialised offer and ability to develop their own technology solutions and platforms in-house, rather than relying on existing off-the-shelf software or third-party platforms. They may also have a particular expertise in a specific technology or platform and may be sought out for their unique skills and knowledge in that area. They are often responsible for the entire development lifecycle, from concept and design to testing and deployment, and may use a variety of programming languages, frameworks, and tools to build their solutions. They may also need to navigate legal and regulatory requirements related to their technology solutions, such as data privacy and security regulations. In addition to technical skills, boutique developers require strong project management and business strategy skills to ensure that their solutions meet their clients' needs and align with their overall business goals. They may need to invest in ongoing maintenance and support of their technology solutions to ensure they remain functional and up-to-date over time. These companies typically have a specific business need or market opportunity that requires a unique solution, and they have the technical expertise to develop that solution themselves (Abuhassna et al., 2020). They may be involved in developing their own app ecosystem and AI algorithm that they can sell to other companies. They often have a business-to-business (B2B) arrangement. They have a strong focus on delivering exceptional customer service and personalised attention to their clients. Due to their specialised focus and attention to detail, boutique developers may command higher rates than more generalist developers or development firms (Sharma et al., 2022). However, their clients may be willing to pay more for the high-quality, tailored solutions they provide.

Overall, boutique developers offer a unique blend of technical expertise, personalised service, and specialised focus that can be valuable to clients with specific needs and requirements and with the anticipation that they could merge, acquire, or be acquired by a bigger platform developer. Runtastic GmbH is a digital health and fitness company from Austria that was acquired by Adidas in 2015 for €220 million. Likewise, in 2015, Under Armour acquired two popular fitness tracking apps, MyFitnessPal and Endomondo, for a total of $560 million. In 2020, Firstbeat Analytics Oy was acquired by Garmin Ltd. These are boutique developers creating platforms that later got acquired and integrated into a bigger platform providers' ecosystem. These acquisitions typically help larger companies expand their digital offerings and capabilities by acquiring smaller, more specialised start-ups. They can also provide access to new customer bases and data analytics capabilities.

Table 6.1 presents a summary of these different types of third-party developers. It is however imperative to know that these are generalisations and there may be overlap or exceptions within each category. Additionally, there are many other types of third-party developers beyond those listed here, and the advantages and disadvantages can vary depending on the specific company and project.

6.7 Advantages of working with third-party developers

Working with third-party developers can provide a range of benefits that allow companies to focus on their core business while getting quality platforms for consumer engagement at an affordable cost rather than getting bogged down in technical details. It is imperative for managers to explore these advantages before making decision on the type of third party to use and the type of projects they will execute.

6.7.1 Suitable platforms

Getting a suitable platform for initiating digital consumption with your digital consumers might not be possible with the big platform developers; there are cases where the paid platforms are not suitable for your business needs. For example, Google Sites offers website design for companies but if you are a large company, employing over 300 staff, would you want to go to Google to design your website? You would more likely get a better service from an agency developer. These developers will meet with you, discuss your business needs, and offer you digital solutions. When you work with third-party developers, you are able to get a suitable platform that can enhance consumer engagement in your digital environment. This can help to ensure that clients are able to get the most value from their platform investment and can continue to use it as an effective tool for achieving their business goals. They can ramp up resources quickly, work on multiple projects at the same time, and use their experience to streamline the development process.

6.7.2 Customised platform

You are not only getting a suitable platform, but you can get a customised platform for your brand. For example, you won't expect Apple to design a mobile app for your bank. The bank is most likely going to have an in-house team working on this type of project

Table 6.1 A summary of different types of third-party developers

Features	Boutique Developers	Agency Developers	Contract Developers	Freelance Developers
Size	Small	Medium to Large	Variable, may be an individual	Individual, but may also be a sole-proprietor company
Specialisation	Niche areas	Wide range of technologies	Variable	Variable
Service model	Customised solutions	Standardised processes	Project-based	Ad-hoc projects
Expertise	Personalised service	Scalability and efficiency	Technical expertise	Flexibility and autonomy
Communication	Close collaboration with clients	Structured communication channels	Limited direct communication. Simply work on their allocated project	Direct communication with clients, can be so direct via text messages and phone calls at different times of the day
Pricing	High-end, premium pricing	Competitive, variable pricing	Hourly or project-based rates	Flexible rates, negotiable
Project management	Direct involvement, hands-on management	Formal project management processes	Collaborative approach with client or project manager	Self-directed, individual project management
Advantages	Highly personalised solutions, deep expertise in niche areas	Scalable services, access to wide range of technical expertise	Efficient use of resources, cost-effective solutions	High flexibility, direct communication with clients
Disadvantages	Higher costs, limited scalability	Potential for impersonal service, lack of niche expertise	Limited long-term commitment, lack of personal involvement	Potential for inconsistency, lack of project management oversight, inability to manage risk and security infrastructures

or employ a contract developer. Likewise in cases when there is no existing digital platform to meet your business needs, you would need to contact third-party developers to work on your idea. IKEA's Place app uses AR to let users see what furniture would look like in their own home; with plans for virtual warehouses and AI assistants, it was developed by Dutch augmented reality agency TWNKLS. Third-party platform providers can offer customised solutions that are tailored to meet the specific needs of each client, rather than providing a one-size-fits-all approach. This can include features such as customisable themes, plugins, and integrations, as well as the ability to add or remove functionality as needed.

6.7.3 Personalised platform

Working with third-party developers comes with the advantage of having a personalised service. The brand is not lost in the crowd with the big tech platform developers but can benefit from a developer who tries to understand their unique needs and requirements. The third-party developers can offer customised solutions and tailor the platform to fit the client's specific business processes and workflows, they can develop the platform using appropriate technology stacks and frameworks, ensuring that it meets the client's specifications. The developers have the technical knowledge and experience to build complex systems quickly and efficiently. The third-party developers can also provide a personalised support system where a manager can have direct access to the platform developers to address their technical needs, providing ongoing maintenance and support to ensure its smooth functioning.

6.7.4 Affordable platform

For many businesses, they don't have the resources to develop their platforms, they are trying to bootstrap and explore opportunities, and they may find freelancers affordable to build their platform. This may be a young freelancer who is trying to gather experience by working on a smaller project or a small agency that is trying to build its client base. Third-party developers have the ability to provide cost-effective solutions that are tailored to their clients' needs, by using existing software libraries and tools, which can reduce development time and costs, use of open-source software, which is often free and can be customised to meet specific needs and can offer flexible pricing options based on the scope and complexity of the project, which can make it easier for clients to budget and manage costs. Third-party developers can provide services at a lower cost due to economies of scale and lower overhead costs. These platform providers can also continue to offer affordable platforms that remain up-to-date and continue to meet the changing needs of their clients over time.

6.7.5 Flexible platform

In addition to the provision of personalised offers and affordable platforms comes the advantage of flexibility. Brands are able to take control of their owned platform, and they don't need to rely on the availability of the paid or shared platform owners. The flexibility allows brands to work on their platforms at their own pace. They can employ a contractor to come and do some things at a time. They can make changes to their platform anytime they want, and they can pay for the type of services they have used. The flexibility can also come with the payment plan where brands are not stuck with the big platform developers, and they can make payment arrangements with third-party developers. This payment arrangement provides businesses with the flexibility to pay for the services they need on a monthly or annual basis. This can help businesses manage their cash flow more effectively. The flexibility can also come with scalability where the brand starts with something small and they increase it with time, adding more features as they grow. You can negotiate with the developer on what to include in the platform at different stages of the project.

6.8 Disadvantages of working with third-party developers

Working with third-party developers can be a good way to access specialised expertise and resources, but it is important to recognise some inherent challenges in this business arrangement. This section highlights some of these challenges and it's expected that managers will carefully consider the potential disadvantages and risks before deciding.

6.8.1 Competencies and expertise

Verifying the competencies and expertise of third-party developers can be a challenge. You have just met someone on Fiverr who said they can do the job; they showed you their portfolio and you were convinced but how can you be so sure that's their portfolio. It can be challenging to establish that trust and that's why managers need to be very careful and selective when working with third-party developers. You want to be sure you can verify their claims. Like Mogaji et al. (2023) found in the analysis of B2B firms in Africa, these companies use clients' feedback, testimonial, certification, and accreditation to establish their credibility. Fiver has their 'Top Rated freelancers' who have a consistent and successful work history, and this is an attempt to reassure the brand manager looking for a freelancer.

6.8.2 Commitment

Third-party developers have many businesses relationship they are maintaining simultaneously. That freelancer has many other gigs they are working on. The contractor developing may be employed and working virtually with another company while working on your project. Commitments on their part could be an issue, where they are not very much committed to the project, they might get a better offer and move on to another project, or they might see a better contract and choose to ignore yours. The boutique developer working on your project can get acquired and your project is abandoned. Managers need to manage their expectations while working with these developers. You may have become dependent on their services, which can make it difficult to switch to another provider if needed. This can also limit your ability to make changes or improvements to your project in the future (Dunn, 2020). Managers should put measures in place to manage this disruption and over-reliant on uncommitted developers. There should be terms and conditions of services, contracts should be signed, and a level of commitment should be expected. There should be alternative options for managers, reflection on what they will do, and putting contingency plans in place in case the developers disappoint them.

6.8.3 Control

Following up with the concerns about the third-party developers' commitment, there are significant concerns about the control the manager has over the project (Nemkova et al., 2019). You may have limited control over the development process, which can lead to miscommunications and unexpected changes that may negatively impact the project. There are concerns about quality control to ensure that things are done very well. Third-party developers may not adhere to the same quality control standards as your company, which can lead to code that is difficult to maintain or that doesn't meet your requirements. Often these developers are working with managers who may not have the technical skills to check if the platforms have been designed, making it difficult to establish the quality of the platforms. The inability to carry out enough quality control can jeopardise the credibility of the company, especially when digital consumers on these platforms are not enjoying their time on the platform. Managers need to put quality control measures in the project execution, to see professional help check and review the platforms, and to be sure there are no hidden costs associated with coordinating, project management, or communication.

6.8.4 Communication challenges

Technology has broken geographical barriers and brands are able to work with different developers from different parts of the world. While they may be coding in a similar language, they may not be able to converse and engage in similar languages. Since third-party developers are not part of your team, communication can be difficult, which can lead to misunderstandings and delays. Differences in time zones, languages, and cultures can make it harder to collaborate effectively and efficiently. However, though there are translators that are integrated into communication platforms like Google Meet and Zoom, this language barrier may be addressed. Notwithstanding, managers need to be aware of these limitations and ensure it does not affect the project.

6.8.5 Cybersecurity risks

Engaging with third-party developers can pose security risks, particularly if sensitive data or intellectual property is being shared. It is important for organisations to have proper security protocols in place to mitigate these risks. You can imagine you are working with a freelancer who has access to all your files to develop your website, and they can use that same information for someone else, another company, and you may not know. By working with freelancers and third parties, you may not be able to control how and where your data is being shared and this can pose a security breach. These third-party developers may also use insecure development practices that could introduce vulnerabilities to your systems. Managers need to be mindful of how they share data with the third party, and there should be information shared on 'need to know' basis. Managers should put measures to address this security threat, do their own risk assessment, and continually evaluate their business relationships with third-party developers.

> **Reflective question**
>
> **What are other alternatives for possibly overcoming the challenges of working with a third-party developer?**

6.9 White labelling

For many brands who are considering taking ownership of their platforms and may not want to engage the services of third-party developers, they may be considering white labelling. White labelling is a business strategy where a product or service is created by one company but is sold and marketed under the brand of another company (Mariani & Nambisan, 2021). In this case for platform, you could have a boutique developer working on a platform for your company and sell it. White label it for your company. This could be a virtual learning environment (VLE) for a university, mobile app for a food delivery company, or a software for a training company.

White labelling is often used by businesses that lack the resources or expertise to create their own platform, but still want to offer it to their customers. It allows them to take advantage of existing products and services, possibly from boutique developers without investing in the development and production process. White labelling can also be used to increase brand recognition and customer loyalty, as the product or service can be marketed under the company's own brand. The platforms may have the same features and functionality as the original, but digital consumers perceive it as being created and owned by the company that has branded it.

There are advantages to using white labelling as a solution to platform provision. White labelling allows businesses to offer products and services without investing in the development and production process. This can be a cost-effective way to expand the range of products and services offered by a business without significant investment. White labelling also saves time making it easier for brands to release their platform to the market quickly, they don't need to develop it from scratch, and they just buy what's readily available. Businesses can save time and resources that would have been used to develop their own product. White labelling can also offer businesses flexibility to adapt to changing market conditions, as they can quickly add or remove products and services from their offerings based on demand.

Despite these advantages, managers must be aware of the disadvantages, and managers must be sure they are making a good decision and carefully consider the potential drawbacks and ensure that they are not sacrificing their own brand credibility or reputation in the process. Managers must recognise that not all platforms can be white labelled, and therefore they have to manage their expectations with regard to what they can get. The quality control measures can also be a disadvantage for a white-labelled platform, especially if the original platform that is being white-labelled is not of high quality, the company may suffer as a result. This can lead to negative customer experiences and harm the company's reputation. In addition, while white labelling can save time and money, it also limits the company's ability to customise the platform to its own specific needs, the brand may not be able to use the platform as they want, and they may be restricted by what the boutique developer has provided for everyone to use. The limited opportunity to customise their platforms can lead to a lack of differentiation from other companies using the same white label product.

Another disadvantage is lack of control, very similar to the idea of a paid platform where the brands will have to rely on the existing infrastructure of the boutique developer, when using a white label product or service, the company is dependent on the provider to maintain and update it. This can lead to delays and limitations in product updates and fixes. Ethical and legal implication also poses a significant disadvantage—as often there is no indication to say a brand developed an app in-house or they bought it and white labelled it. Would you expect the brand to declare to their customers that they are using a white labelled platform? Using a white label product or service can lead to legal issues if the provider does not have proper licensing or intellectual property rights. This can result in legal action against the company and damage to its reputation.

Managers responsible for managing consumer engagement in the digital environment should carefully evaluate the potential benefits and drawbacks of white labelling before deciding whether to pursue this strategy and should take steps to ensure that they are able to successfully integrate the white label product or service into their overall business strategy.

Reflective questions

Think about a mobile banking app? Who developed it? The bank (they provide banking services) or a third party (app developers) or it's a white label (from a boutique developer).

6.10 Consideration for brands

Brands now have options with regard to their platform. There is little to no excuse for not having a platform, and brands can use either a freelance developer or white labelling. Brands need to ask and reflect on their options and make an informed decision. This section highlights some relevant questions for brand's consideration.

6.10.1 Consumers' needs

Digital consumption is all about satisfying the desires of digital consumers and providing platforms that allow consumers to effectively engage. If the brand is developing a new platform, they must be sure and certain that their consumers will find it useful. Brands need to evaluate if their consumers will prefer a white label option, which is common and easier to use or to go for a bespoke design from a boutique agency which consumers might find difficult to use. The digital platform should be designed to provide a seamless and intuitive user experience. This means the platform should be easy to navigate, load quickly, and be visually appealing. Brands should ensure that their digital platforms meet the specific needs and preferences of their targeted digital customers. This will help to ensure that the platform resonates with their audience and adds value to their brand. Importantly, digital consumers expect personalised experiences, and brands should use platforms that can collect data and analytics to deliver customised content and recommendations to users. The digital platform should be integrated with other digital channels such as social media, email marketing, and mobile apps. This allows for a cohesive and consistent user experience across all channels, and consumers should not struggle to use your platform because it has been designed by a third-party developer.

6.10.2 Inclusive design

Brands should not take inclusive design for granted. Even though they may be working with a third party, they should make an effort to integrate inclusive design into their platform development—asking their platform developing questions to ensure things are done properly. For example, the height of a self-service kiosk should be considered as part of inclusive design. The digital platform should be accessible to everyone, regardless of their abilities. Brands should prioritise accessibility features such as alt text for images, captions for videos, and keyboard navigation for users who may have visual or motor impairments.

6.10.3 Quality control

What are the quality control measures in place? Haven decided on which approach to take, brands need to reflect the quality of the platform they are getting. Brands should make their due diligence to carefully evaluate their options (Williams et al., 2021). They need to know the developers they are dealing with, their expectation, and to ensure that the platform meets their standards and aligns with their brand values. This will help to ensure that the brand's reputation is not negatively impacted by any issues with the digital platforms.

6.10.4 Cost implications

Brands need to consider the cost implications of using third-party developers. Managers need to reflect on the cost of getting their platforms, exploring if they could be better off using paid or shared platforms (having your e-commerce website on Shopify) or engaging the service of an agency developer to work on a customised e-commerce website. Brands need to consider potential costs associated with owning the platform, the ongoing maintenance, and updates. This will help them decide on the most financially viable option.

6.10.5 Legal implications

What are the legal implications of our platform developers' choice? Do they have the proper licensing and intellectual property rights to the platform? The freelancer developing the website should not be using another client's copyrighted materials for their platform. Brands would be expected to reflect on these questions before engaging the services of a third-party developer. You don't want to work with someone who will jeopardise your company. If in doubt, you may seek a second opinion, read more about it, and ask friends and colleagues.

6.10.6 Security implications

Using third-party developers comes with its security concerns as often the companies are not versatile enough to provide security infrastructure and not surprising to see many people go for the more established platform developers. Managers need to carry out their own risk assessment and exposure to cyber risk by virtue of working with third-party developers. Digital consumers expect their personal information to be protected when using online platforms. Brands should prioritise security measures such as SSL certificates, two-factor authentication, and regular security audits to ensure the safety of their users' data.

6.10.7 Long-term strategy

Brands need to reflect on if they want to keep using third-party developer or have an in-house team working on the platforms. Do they want to outsource their app development and maintenance or employ someone in-house to keep managing it? Brands should consider how using third-party developers fits into their long-term business strategy, including how it may impact their ability to grow, take control of their platform, and enhance digital consumption on their platforms. Using third-party developers can be a valuable option for businesses looking to create digital platforms. By carefully weighing the pros and cons and taking appropriate precautions, businesses can successfully outsource their development work and create effective and engaging digital platforms that meet the needs of their users.

6.11 Conclusion

Third-party developers are an important part of the technology ecosystem, as they bring innovation and diversity to the platform by building on top of it. This chapter has described the concept of third-party developers and has highlighted the key features, especially as it differs from the platform developer that was discussed in the previous chapter. Third-party developer could be an individual, a small company, or a bespoke developer. Using third-party developers can be a great way for businesses to save time and resources while creating their digital platforms. However, it is important for businesses to carefully evaluate the advantages and disadvantages and make an informed decision about the approach to take.

Brands would be expected to prioritise the user experience, mobile optimisation, security, personalisation, accessibility, integration, analytics, and content strategy when developing their digital platform for digital consumers. When working with a third-party developer, businesses should ensure that they have a clear and comprehensive contract in place that outlines the scope of work, deadlines, and payment terms. They should also thoroughly research the developer's experience, reputation, and track record before hiring them. Managers should ensure they maintain open and frequent communication with their third-party developers, closely monitor the development process, and ensure that all parties involved understand their roles and responsibilities.

6.12 Student activities

1. Research and identify three examples of companies that have successfully outsourced development work to third-party developers. What factors contributed to their success, and what lessons can be learned from their experiences?

2. Identify and evaluate three different third-party developers that specialise in developing digital platforms. What are their areas of expertise, and what services do they offer? What are their rates, and how do they compare to other developers in the market?

3. Evaluate the pros and cons of outsourcing development work to a third-party developer versus hiring an in-house development team. What are the advantages and disadvantages of each approach, and under what circumstances is one approach preferable to the other?

4. What is the role of communication and collaboration in outsourcing development work to a third-party developer? How can businesses ensure effective communication and collaboration with the developer, and what tools and methods are available to facilitate this?

5. Create a checklist of best practices for businesses considering outsourcing development work to a third-party developer. What factors should they consider when selecting a developer, and what provisions should be included in the contract? How can they ensure effective communication and collaboration with the developer, and how can they mitigate the risks associated with outsourcing?

6. What are the potential implications of outsourcing development work to a third-party developer for the business's bottom line, such as cost savings, productivity, and revenue growth? How can businesses measure and evaluate these impacts?

7. What are the key lessons learned from businesses that have successfully outsourced development work to a third-party developer? How can these lessons be applied to other businesses considering outsourcing?

8. What are the trends and developments in the third-party development industry, such as new technologies, business models, and competition? How can businesses stay up-to-date with these developments and ensure that they are working with the best possible developers?

9. How do third-party developers manage the development process, such as project management, quality assurance, and testing? What tools and methods are available, and how do they ensure that the platform meets the needs of the client?

10. What are the ethical considerations associated with outsourcing development work to a third-party developer, such as labour practices and environmental impact? How can businesses ensure that the developer operates in an ethical and responsible manner?

References and further reading

Abdulquadri, A., Mogaji, E., Kieu, T. & Nguyen, P., 2021. Digital transformation in financial services provision: A Nigerian perspective to the adoption of chatbot. *Journal of Enterprising Communities: People and Places in the Global Economy*, 15(2), pp. 258–281.

Abuhassna, H., Al-Rahmi, W., Yahya, N. & Zakaria, S., 2020. Development of a new model on utilizing online learning platforms to improve students' academic achievements and satisfaction. *International Journal of Educational Technology in Higher Education*, 17(1), pp. 1–23.

Agbo, F. et al., 2020. Social media usage for computing education: The effect of tie strength and group communication on perceived learning outcome. *Journal of Education and Development Using Information and Communication Technology*, 16(1), pp. 5–26.

Azeem, M., Haleem, A. & Javaid, M., 2022. Symbiotic relationship between machine learning and Industry 4.0: A review. *Journal of Industrial Integration and Management*, 7(3), pp. 401–433.

Balakrishnan, J., Nwoba, A. & Nguyen, N., 2021. Emerging-market consumers' interactions with banking chatbots. *Telematics and Informatics*, 65, 101711.

Birch, K. & Bronson, K., 2022. Big tech. *Science as Culture*, 31(1), pp. 1–4.

Chattopadhyay, A., Kupe, T., Schatzer, N. & Mogaji, E., 2022. Fireside chat with three vice chancellors from three continents. In: E. Mogaji, V. Jain, F. Maringe & R. Hinson, eds. *Re-imagining Higher Education in Emerging Economies*. Cham: Palgrave Macmillan, pp. 85–96.

Chylinski, M. et al., 2020. Augmented reality marketing: A technology-enabled approach to situated customer experience. *Australasian Marketing Journal*, 28(4), pp. 374–384.

Dhruv, G., Hulland, J., Kopalle, P. & Karahanna, E., 2020. The future of technology and marketing: A multidisciplinary perspective. *Journal of the Academy of Marketing Science*, 48, pp. 1–8.

Dunn, M., 2020. Making gigs work: Digital platforms, job quality and worker motivations. *New Technology, Work and Employment*, 35(2), pp. 232–249.

Dwivedi, Y. et al., 2022. Metaverse beyond the hype: Multidisciplinary perspectives on emerging challenges, opportunities, and agenda for research, practice and policy. *International Journal of Information Management*, 66, 102542.

Flew , T., Martin, F. & Suzor, N., 2019. Internet regulation as media policy: Rethinking the question of digital communication platform governance. *Journal of Digital Media & Policy*, 10(1), pp. 33–50.

Hein, A. et al., 2020. Digital platform ecosystems. *Electronic Markets*, 30, pp. 87–98.

Hodapp, D. & Hanelt, A., 2022. Interoperability in the era of digital innovation: An information systems research agenda. *Journal of Information Technology*, 37(4), pp. 407–427.

Jelovac, D., Ljubojević, C. & Ljubojević, L., 2022. HPC in business: The impact of corporate digital responsibility on building digital trust and responsible corporate digital governance. *Digital Policy, Regulation and Governance*, 24(6), pp. 485–497.

Kandampully, J., Bilgihan, A. & Li, D., 2022. Unifying technology and people: Revisiting service in a digitally transformed world. *The Service Industries Journal*, 42(1–2), pp. 21–41.

Kopalle, P., Kumar, V. & Subramaniam, M., 2020. How legacy firms can embrace the digital ecosystem via digital customer orientation. *Journal of the Academy of Marketing Science*, 48, pp. 114–131.

Mariani, M. & Nambisan, S., 2021. Innovation analytics and digital innovation experimentation: The rise of research-driven online review platforms. *Technological Forecasting and Social Change*, 172, 121009.

McKinsey, 2022. Marketing in the metaverse: An opportunity for innovation and experimentation [Online] Available at: https://www.mckinsey.com/capabilities/growth-marketing-and-sales/our-insights/marketing-in-the-metaverse-an-opportunity-for-innovation-and-experimentation

Miric, M., Boudreau, K. & Jeppesen, L., 2019. Protecting their digital assets: The use of formal & informal appropriability strategies by App developers. *Research Policy*, 48(8), 103738.

Mogaji, E., 2021. *Brand Management*. Cham: Springer.

Mogaji, E. & Nguyen, N., 2022. Managers' understanding of artificial intelligence in relation to marketing financial services: Insights from a cross-country study. *International Journal of Bank Marketing*, 40(6), pp. 1272–1298.

Mogaji, E., Restuccia, M., Lee, Z. & Nguyen, N., 2023. B2B brand positioning in emerging markets: Exploring positioning signals via websites and managerial tensions in top-performing African B2B service brands. *Industrial Marketing Management*, 108, pp. 237–250.

Mogaji, E., Soetan, T. & Kieu, T., 2020. The implications of artificial intelligence on the digital marketing of financial services to vulnerable customers. *Australasian Marketing Journal*, 29(3), pp. 235–242.

Morgan-Thomas, A., Dessart, L. & Veloutsou, C., 2020. Digital ecosystem and consumer engagement: A socio-technical perspective. *Journal of Business Research*, 121, pp. 713–723.

Nemkova, E., Demirel, P. & Baines, L., 2019. In search of meaningful work on digital freelancing platforms: The case of design professionals. *New Technology, Work and Employment*, 34(3), pp. 226–243.

Olson, E., Olson, K., Czaplewski, A. & Key, T., 2021. Business strategy and the management of digital marketing. *Business Horizons*, 64(2), pp. 285–293.

Oosthuizen, K., Botha, E., Robertson, J. & Montecchi, M., 2021. Artificial intelligence in retail: The AI-enabled value chain. *Australasian Marketing Journal*, 29(3), pp. 264–273.

Ponzoa, J. & Erdmann, A., 2021. E-commerce customer attraction: Digital marketing techniques, evolution and dynamics across firms. *Journal of Promotion Management*, 27(5), pp. 697–715.

Sağkaya Güngö, A. & Ozansoy Çadırcı, T., 2022. Understanding digital consumer: A review, synthesis, and future research agenda. *International Journal of Consumer Studies*, 46(5), pp. 1829–1858.

Sharma, H., Soetan, T., Farinloye, T. & Noite, M., 2022. AI adoption in universities in emerging economies: Prospects, challenges and recommendations. In: Emmanuel Mogaji, Varsha Jain, Felix Maringe, Robert Ebo Hinson, eds. *Re-imagining Educational Futures in Developing Countries: Lessons from Global Health Crises*. Cham: Springers, pp. 159–174.

Sheth, J., 2020. Impact of Covid-19 on consumer behavior: Will the old habits return or die?. *Journal of Business Research*, 117, pp. 280–283.

Soetan, T., Mogaji, E. & Nguyen, N., 2021. Financial services experience and consumption in Nigeria. *Journal of Services Marketing*, 35(7), pp. 947–961.

Williams, P., McDonald, P. & Mayes, R., 2021. Recruitment in the gig economy: Attraction and selection on digital platforms. *The International Journal of Human Resource Management*, 32(19), pp. 4136–4162.

CHAPTER 7

Data analytics on digital platforms

7.1 Background

The use of digital platforms has significantly increased in recent years, resulting in a massive accumulation of data. However, having large amounts of data is not enough; the ability to extract meaningful insights from this data is critical. This is where data analytics comes in—the process of examining data to extract insights and make data-driven decisions. Data analytics is increasingly becoming important in digital platforms, enabling organisations to make better decisions and gain a competitive advantage. In this chapter, we will explore the four types of data analytics: Descriptive, predictive, prescriptive, and diagnostic, and the techniques used in data analytics, including data mining, machine learning (ML), text analytics, social network analysis, and web analytics. We will also examine the applications of data analytics in digital platforms, including e-commerce, social media, healthcare, finance, manufacturing, and transportation. Finally, we will discuss the challenges that come with data analytics on digital platforms, such as data quality, privacy, security, and the need for a skilled workforce.

7.2 Learning outcomes

By the end of this chapter, you should be able to:

- Describe descriptive analytics techniques to a given dataset to summarise and understand its key characteristics.
- Evaluate the effectiveness of different predictive analytics techniques in making accurate forecasts of future trends or events.
- Analyse a real-world case study of prescriptive analytics in action to identify the optimal course of action for a given business problem.
- Critically compare and contrast different data analytics on digital platforms and determine their relative strengths and weaknesses in different scenarios.
- Recognise the inherent challenges to data analytics on digital platforms and how to address these challenges.

DOI: 10.4324/9781003389842-7

7.3 Introduction

As you work your shift at the bustling bar, you notice the familiar sight of a regular customer entering the bar. This particular customer visits the bar every Friday, without fail, and confidently orders the same drink each time. This weekly routine has been a constant for the past two years you have been working at the bar. As the customer takes their usual seat at the bar, you begin to feel a sense of familiarity and have decided to take a risk and prepare the customer's drink without receiving an order. As you set the drink down in front of them, the customer's eyes widen in surprise but quickly soften into a warm smile. They pause for a moment, taking in the unexpected gesture, and then express their gratitude with a heartfelt 'thank you'.

Now let's link this to data analytics and business decisions on digital platforms and the importance of customer knowledge in the story. As you work at the bar, you realise that the regular customer's consistent visits and orders offer valuable insights into their preferences and behaviours. By leveraging the digital analytics tools at your disposal, you can analyse the customer's order history and identify patterns and trends in their behaviour. Using this information, you decide to take a data-driven approach to surprise and delight the customer. You make the calculated decision to prepare their drink without an order, based on your understanding of their preferences and habits. This small act of personalised service demonstrates the power of customer knowledge and the importance of utilising digital analytics tools to create meaningful interactions. By leveraging the data at your fingertips, you were able to strengthen the bond between the customer and the bar, ultimately creating a positive experience that will keep them coming back for more.

In today's digital age, consumers are engaging with brands on digital platforms, big data are being generated through engagement on these platforms, and the ability to collect and analyse customer data is a powerful tool for businesses to enhance their customer experience and build long-term loyalty. By utilising digital analytics tools, businesses can gain a deeper understanding of their customers' needs and preferences and use that knowledge to create tailored experiences that surprise and delight them. This chapter aims to explore the huge prospects of being able to collect and analyse consumers' data to make an informed decision, to understand how brands can enhance their business operations through data analytics. It is imperative to recognise that these are not easy task, depending on the size of the company, their capabilities, and human resources, notwithstanding, students and prospective managers need to understand analytics, to know what to do and when to do it.

According to Wazurkar et al. (2017), organisations are adjusting to the modern computing era by enhancing the efficient utilisation of technology to meet global business demand. Such technological interventions include using data analytics to draw patterns from large datasets and work towards maximising efficiency. The increasing importance of data analytics has been necessitated by a shift from the traditional approaches to big data computing to develop better predictive models for organisations (Mazumder et al., 2017). Data analytics, specifically predictive modelling is an emerging application transforming products and services availed by corporate entities.

Moving on, it is imperative to set some background and manage your expectations with regard to this particular chapter. It is important to note that this chapter will not teach you how to do analytics, this will not teach you how to develop and design algorithms that will influence business decision, but you will gain the much-needed theoretical understanding of data analytics, and this will serve as a foundation for you to build on and develop some practical knowledge. The insights provided in this chapter will help you join the right conversation at your place of work, share your thought, and make significant contribution when discussing analytics with your developers. At the end of this chapter, you should be able to make an informed decision about analytics, describe your action point, and address any challenges that may inhibit your data analytics strategies.

7.4 Contextualisation of data analytics

Data analytics involves analysing data that has been collected from consumers and making an informed business decision.

On a much larger scale, data analytics involves examining, cleaning, transforming, and modelling data in order to extract meaningful insights and information that can be used to inform business decisions. Data analytics creates a unique customer experience to suit particular individuals by assessing customer behaviour and developing profiles with specific preferences (Thyago et al., 2019). Gartner (2023) describes data analytics as the ways data is managed to support all uses of data, and the analysis of data to drive improved decisions, business processes, and outcomes, such as discovering new business risks, challenges, and opportunities. Data analytics involves using various statistical and computational techniques to analyse data, uncover patterns and correlations, and make predictions about future trends. It encompasses the use of various statistical techniques such as ML, modelling, and data mining to analyse current and historical data for predicting future events or behaviours. Data analytics is implemented through AI algorithms and big data to facilitate the advancement of predictive analytics (PA) in different applications. Data analytics is used in a wide range of fields, including marketing, finance, healthcare, and social sciences, among others. The goal of data analytics is to help organisations and individuals make better decisions by providing them with accurate and relevant information.

Lee et al. (2019) also investigated the application of predictive maintenance using AI techniques. The key focus is on extracting useful data that can help in decision-making and enable the implementation of transformative changes. Predictive maintenance is deployed as a quality control initiative by ensuring that the tools always maintain top-notch performance. It is also a suitable technique for breaking the trade-off by enhancing the useful life of a component and increasing uptime (Lee et al., 2019). Predictive maintenance is also a crucial intervention in the competitive environment as it helps monitor the equipment's condition and predict its failure. PI can also be harnessed in the development of condition monitoring by extracting meaningful information from raw analog signals, extracting features from the signal, and using these features to train AI algorithms. AI techniques in this exercise include supervised, unsupervised, and reinforcement learning (Hiran et al 2021). Supervised learning techniques include artificial neural networks (ANN), support vector machines (SVM), regression models, and decision trees, among others. Its other applications include monitoring using two AI algorithms: Recurrent neural networks (RNN) and convolutional neural networks (CNN). These techniques are applied alongside different extraction techniques.

According to Mohapatra et al. (2021), data analytics can be used to analyse energy consumption and utilisation. This application incorporates ML models and deep neural network (NN) learning models and attributes optimisation models. ML combines statistical algorithms and can be deployed in the statistical, engineering, and hybrid approaches. Deep NN learning models are applied when ML fails in making forecasts due to large volumes for data analysis. It is an efficient strategy because it is efficient when executing internal hidden layers. This technique has also been effectively applied in energy retention analysis and forecasting by combining the use of Recurrent Neural Networks (RNN), Convolutional Neural Networks (CNN), and Long Short Term Memory (LSTM). Attribute optimisation models use various techniques such as Particle Swarm Optimisation (PSO), Genetic Algorithm (GA), and Evolution Strategies (ES). An assessment of these models shows that LSTM is more consistent and has high precision. Deep learning (DL) performs better in predictive intelligence (PI) because it is efficient at learning hidden patterns.

According to Lowe (2017), data analytics can be applied to implement anti-money laundering (AML) programs in the financial sector. PI is essential in implementing know your customer (KYC) checks, sanctions, and the identification of politically exposed persons (PEP). KYC is implemented by checking personal details against a list of electronic registers and other known information. Identifying PEPs is also important to apply due diligence to prevent corruption and money laundering. Sanctions form part of national strategies and international relations (IR) and target transnational organised crime groups and key individual terrorists. Financial service companies also perform other checks against publicly available information in an exercise known as adverse media checking (Lowe, 2017). This information encompasses the historical activity that is vital in customer risk assessment. It's majorly applied as a risk mitigation activity by assessing previous suspicious activity reporting. Many players in the financial service sector have implemented safeguards such as financial intelligence units in a combination with external information for threat detection and prevention.

Data analytics is also applied through approximate collaborative context reasoning through IoT devices. It is applied in two contexts: Centralised context reasoning and collaborative context reasoning. In centralised context reasoning, data processing occurs in the concentrator that collects node measurements and uses the intelligence to infer events. Under collaborative context reasoning, data processing occurs locally in the nodes alongside knowledge inference and intelligence acquisition for collaborative event reasoning. Collaborative context reasoning combined the current fused context, outliers' context, and predicted context to make inferences. Context fusion involves the evaluation of the event inference rule from the current context vector, and context prediction uses a trend of historical context vectors for short-term context forecast. Context outliers incrementally evaluate and revise their belief that there is a significant deviation in the context vectors from the statistical patterns. According to Anagnostopoulos and Kolomvatsos (2018), data analytics in IoT applications can be realised through event reasoning schemes. This scheme incorporates real-time event reasoning mechanisms through devices equipped with sensing and computing capabilities. Collaborative reasoning and edge predictive intelligence are realised through autonomous nodes that perform local data processing to convey inferred knowledge.

Data analytics is extensively applied in employee performance and engagement management by incorporating data from shopping history and social media activity. The recommendations are forwarded to sales personnel for appropriate action (Daugherty & Wilson, 2018). AI is also used in predicting the messaging that will increase the possibility of customer responses. The same applies to learning salespeople and estimating their repetitive business patterns. This data is used to predict sales and performance by combining it with correlations and patterns from the management systems. Data analytics is applied in talent acquisition and onboarding using various predictive tools such as programmatic recruitment advertising. This integration extensively relies on algorithms to sort applicants and implement automatic screening using ML. The approach is faster, delivers greater precision, and is fairer because of the limited degree of bias (Taska, 2018). Data analytics in hiring has reduced the hiring period from months to a few weeks, alongside significant reductions in the recruiter screening time (Daugherty & Wilson, 2018). According to Harth et al (2018), PI is also applicable in the onboarding process as the algorithms use data collected from the hiring process to predict the team fit and learning needs and allow managers to craft tailored onboarding plans.

Data analytics has found useful applications in employee retention through predictive retention analysis to implement predictive workforce analysis (Westfall, 2017). Algorithms can predict the employees more likely to exit the organisation by analysing everyday behaviour and other signals that allow employees to develop predictive statistical models that can comprehend and predict turnover. Such data is vital in the retention of promising talent through the use of tailored incentives and other interventions. PI platforms also use ML to analyse employee social media activities and assess job-seeking behaviour. This data is vital in assessing the possibility of an employee leaving within the following few months. It is also essential in implementing learning programs at the workplace by creating engaging and personalised instruction. This solution is implemented through AI-enabled intelligent tutoring systems (ITS) that adapt the course content to each learner's needs.

Mellers et al. (2015) consider the aspect of prediction accuracy in the global political sphere through the psychology of intelligence analysis. Generally, making future predictions is integral to human cognition, and the accuracy of cognitive predictions is of special importance. This aspect can be measured by assessing theories of intelligence, including the single-factor model, seven basic abilities, the two-factor fluid intelligence framework, and the 120-factor cube (Mellers et al 2015)). In geopolitical forecasting, inductive reasoning, numerical reasoning, and cognitive control are intelligence's three most important aspects. Real-world applications of predictive analytics utilise data from different sources.

Decision science can be applied in the enhancement of intelligence analysis. According to Dhami et al. (2015), intelligence analysis involves the process of data collection, selection, processing, and interpretation to obtain insights into current situations and make forecasts about future developments. Its policy implications include improving the forecast accuracy and communicating uncertainty. Forecast accuracy is attained by collecting probabilistic forecasts, outcomes, and putative moderators (Friedman & Zeckhauser, 2012). There is also a need to leverage decision research, theories, and methods to enhance the forecasting abilities. Communicating uncertainty involves exploiting the means of improving communication using verbal probabilities and monitoring inconsistencies. The other solution involves using numerical probabilities instead of verbal probabilities.

Data analytics can be applied in precision immuno-profiling using AI. It is a clinical immunotherapy approach that is applied to improving prognostic and predictive patient stratification (Koelzer et al., 2018). The approach relies on multiplexing for powerful stratification and characterisation through histological analysis. ML and AI have found extensive applications in this field by driving a paradigm shift that will transform data collection and analysis. ML is a data-driven approach that enables the derivation of unbiased statistics from available datasets. It can also harvest meaningless and un-interpretable features from data that has not been carefully pre-processed. The application of ML and AI in computational pathology will also help to derive complete, standardised, and individualised predictions (Sampat et al 2023). This application in the medical field can be extended to other areas in the corporate sector to achieve varied results. It can be used in the prognosis and stratification of various corporate variables for effective decision-making. ML can also be used to eliminate unnecessary data from available datasets to eliminate noise that can hinder effective decision-making. Lastly, it can be harnessed in process automation to maximise productivity through accurate histological analysis.

Data analytics is important in data-driven management because of its numerous advantages, including producing better business forecasts (Seebacher, 2021). It also enables organisations to stay ahead of the competition through better lead conversion rates, shorter sales, and order intakes. Significant advantages of data analytics-based marketing include revenue increments, increased email click-through rates, optimal email conversion rates, and increased sales (Seebacher, 2021). Data analytics has become essential in marketing industrial goods through the storage, management, and evaluation of customer data. It has become integral in marketing and sales through automated generation, evaluation, and implementation. Data analytics has developed from its origins as business intelligence (BI) and found extensive applications in dynamic optimisation, speech recognition, signal recognition, and autonomous systems.

7.5 Types of data analytics

Considering the significant opportunities presented by data analytics, there are several types of data analytics that can be performed depending on the nature of the data and the specific objectives of the analysis. According to Gartner, analytics can be categorised into four segments: Descriptive, Diagnostic, Predictive, and Prescriptive.

7.5.1 Descriptive analytics—What happened?

Descriptive analytics, as its name implies, provides a basic summary of what has happened in the past. Descriptive analytics is used to analyse historical data to gain insights into past events and trends. This type of analytics is useful for summarising and presenting data in a meaningful way. For example, a retailer might use descriptive analytics to analyse sales data and identify which products are most popular in different regions. By using descriptive analytics, the retailer can make informed decisions about which products to stock in different stores and how to price them. Additionally, descriptive analytics can help the retailer identify potential growth opportunities in new markets.

While descriptive analytics can provide a basic summary of past events and trends, its limitations are becoming increasingly apparent in today's rapidly evolving business landscape. By relying solely on descriptive analytics, businesses risk missing out on critical insights that could help them stay ahead of the competition and make informed decisions that drive growth. For example, consider a retailer that uses descriptive analytics to analyse sales data and identify popular products in different regions. While this may be useful in informing decisions about stocking and pricing, it fails to provide deeper insights into the underlying factors that drive sales. Without a more nuanced understanding of sales performance, the retailer may miss out on critical opportunities to optimise their operations and gain a competitive advantage. Moreover, descriptive analytics can be time-consuming and resource-intensive, making it difficult for businesses to respond quickly to changes in the market. In today's fast-paced business environment, the ability to make quick, data-driven decisions is essential for staying competitive.

So, while descriptive analytics has its uses, it is no longer sufficient for businesses to rely solely on this technique to gain insights into their data. To stay competitive in today's data-driven business landscape, companies must adopt a more sophisticated approach to analytics that leverages the full range of techniques available. By doing so, they can gain a more comprehensive understanding of their data, make informed decisions, and stay ahead of the competition.

7.5.2 Diagnostic analytics—Why did it happen?

According to Gartner, diagnostic analytics is the second stage of the analytics process, which focuses on identifying the root causes of problems or occurrences in the data. This stage is critical for businesses looking to gain a deeper understanding of their data and make informed decisions based on those insights. By analysing historical data, diagnostic analytics can help businesses identify patterns and trends that may have contributed to a specific outcome or event. For example, a company may use diagnostic analytics to understand why sales of a particular product have declined in a specific market. By examining factors like pricing, marketing, and consumer behaviour, the company can identify the root cause of the decline and take corrective action to improve sales. Types of diagnostic analysis are the root cause analysis that involves identifying the underlying cause of a problem or issue. It can be used to determine why certain events or outcomes occurred and to identify potential solutions to prevent them from happening in the future. There is the trend analysis which involves examining historical data to identify patterns or trends. It can be used to identify changes in performance over time and to understand the factors that may have contributed to those changes.

However, it is worth noting that diagnostic analytics is not a panacea for all business problems. While it can help businesses diagnose specific issues and develop targeted solutions, it can also be time-consuming and resource-intensive. Moreover, relying too heavily on diagnostic analytics can lead to a narrow focus on specific problems, potentially leading businesses to miss out on broader opportunities for growth and innovation.

While diagnostic analytics can be a powerful tool for uncovering the root cause of a problem and developing targeted solutions, its limitations must also be acknowledged.

One of the key challenges of diagnostic analytics is the need for extensive data preparation and cleaning, which can be time-consuming and resource-intensive. Without a thorough understanding of the data being analysed, diagnostic analytics can also be prone to errors and misinterpretation. Furthermore, the process of hypothesis testing and refinement can be subjective, influenced by the biases and assumptions of the analysts involved. This can lead to a narrow focus on specific hypotheses, potentially missing out on broader opportunities for growth and innovation. Additionally, by focusing solely on past data, diagnostic analytics may not be able to account for changes in the business environment or new opportunities that may arise.

7.5.3 Predictive analytics—What will happen?

Predictive analytics is the process of using historical data, statistical algorithms, and machine learning techniques to make predictions about future events or trends. It involves analysing data sets to identify patterns and relationships, and then using those insights to make predictions about future outcomes. By analysing patterns and trends in the data, predictive analytics can help businesses make more informed decisions, anticipate future trends and changes, and identify potential opportunities for growth and innovation. Predictive intelligence can indeed be a powerful tool for businesses seeking to gain insights into consumer behaviour and optimise their digital marketing and content strategies. By leveraging advanced analytics techniques, including machine learning and artificial intelligence (AI), businesses can analyse vast amounts of data to identify patterns, trends, and correlations in consumer behaviour. This, in turn, can help businesses to predict future consumer behaviour and preferences, enabling them to tailor their marketing and content strategies to better meet the needs and preferences of their target audience.

Predictive analytics focuses on predicting future customer behaviour by deriving patterns from the available data by applying different algorithms. Organisations can maximise the effectiveness of PI by identifying their business goals, collecting data from different sources, effective data preparation, and developing valid predictive models (Brown et al., 2015). Since predictive analytics majorly concerns probabilistic results, the models can be compared to quantify outcomes and evaluate their efficiency. Consequently, analysts can identify suitable predictive models and apply them effectively to meet organisational goals. Subsequent recommendations in the use of predictive modelling include assessing the model's effectiveness and its results to maintain a firm stance in the competitive market.

Sudhir and Sundaram (2017) investigated the possibility of PI becoming the 5th P of marketing through insights into the future of marketing. PI employs an intellectual framework combining thought leadership, extensive experience, and an understanding of business, scientific, and behavioural issues with predictive modelling. Important tools used in PI include ML, AI, intelligent apps, and chatbots (Oracle, 2015). The advent of PI is a relief to address the increasing demand for real-time data analysis. PI may become the 5th P of marketing by promoting the statistical analysis and management of the businesses to enhance profit. It will also improve the efficiency of marketing initiatives through effective.

However, it is worth noting that predictive analytics is not a perfect science. While statistical models and algorithms can help predict likely outcomes, they cannot account for all possible variables and factors that may impact the outcome. Moreover, relying too heavily on predictive analytics can lead to a false sense of certainty. It is also important to note that predictive intelligence relies on the availability of high-quality data, which must be collected, stored, and processed in a responsible and ethical manner. Inaccurate or incomplete data can lead to faulty predictions and misguided marketing strategies, which can ultimately harm a business's bottom line.

While predictive intelligence can help businesses identify broad patterns and trends in consumer behaviour, it may not be able to account for individual consumer preferences or nuances. As such, it is important for businesses to supplement their predictive intelligence with more targeted and personalised marketing and content strategies, which consider the unique needs and preferences of individual consumers. Managers must note that predictive intelligence is not a substitute for good judgement and human insight. While predictive analytics can help businesses identify patterns and predict future outcomes, it is ultimately up to human marketers and content creators to interpret these insights and develop effective strategies that resonate with their target audience. By combining the power of predictive intelligence with human creativity and intuition, businesses can develop truly impactful marketing and content strategies that drive engagement, loyalty, and revenue growth.

7.5.4 Prescriptive analytics—What should we do?

Prescriptive analytics is the process of using advanced data analysis techniques and algorithms to recommend specific actions that will optimise business outcomes. It involves combining insights from descriptive and predictive analytics with optimisation algorithms to identify the best course of action to take. Applications of prescriptive analytics in business involve lead scoring whereby the business determines the prospects customers are in their journey. Predictive lead scoring uses a customer's past behaviour and purchase history to establish their prospective purchases and the possibility of purchase (Strohmeier, 2020). It uses big data to establish the leads with the highest conversion probability. This approach helps the salespersons to focus on the most valuable leads so that the company can attain maximum value. Prescriptive analytics is applied with AI to collect information such as marketing channels used, hiring trends, and the technologies in use. PI also helps marketers gain better insights into customer behaviour. The evolution of big data has enabled marketers to effectively harness prescriptive analytics by managing extremely large datasets beyond the human scope.

> **Reflective question**
>
> **What are some potential drawbacks or limitations of relying too heavily on data analytics, and how can businesses mitigate these risks?**

7.6 Value for data analytics

Have you considered why brands need to analyse data that are emerging on digital platforms? Managing consumer engagement in the digital environment involves collecting the data, but more importantly, managers must see reasons to do something with the data they are collecting. They must see value in the data and what they can do with it. This section highlights some key benefits, values, and justifications for data analytics.

7.6.1 Better understanding of customer behaviour

Like the illustration shared in the introduction of this chapter, the staff working at the bar has understood the ordering pattern of the customers and is able to serve them their drink even before asking. With data analytics, brands are able to gain a deep understanding of their customers and their behaviour. The brand is able to know how well consumers are engaging on their platform, the types of products and services they are buying, and the location in which these sales are coming from. Understanding the consumer behaviour can be done by analysing customer data, such as their browsing history, purchase history, and social media activity, to gain insights into their preferences and interests. For example, Amazon uses data analytics to personalise product recommendations for each customer based on their purchase history and browsing behaviour. This has helped Amazon to increase customer loyalty and drive sales. Even your university can see how well you engage with the library, lectures, and virtual learning environment (VLE) like Moodle through data analytics. They can track how often you tap in your card to access the library, how often you sign your attendance in class, and how often you log on to the VLE and how long you stay there. This information can be modelled to gain an understanding of student behaviour.

7.6.2 Improved decision-making

Data analytics provides businesses with data-driven insights that can inform better decision-making. For example, Netflix uses data analytics to understand which shows and movies are most popular among its subscribers, and this data is used to inform its content creation and acquisition strategy. By using data analytics to make informed decisions, businesses can reduce the risk of making costly mistakes and improve their chances of success. In addition, linking this back to the University, they may need to increase or reduce the number of staff at the library at a particular time based on the analytics of student engagement. Maybe the data shows that students go to the library after 6 pm compared to 12 pm, the university may decide to reduce staffing level at 12 pm because not many people are coming to use the library and increase staffing at 6 pm when more people are coming. With these data on student engagement with library, the student can change their staffing needs.

7.6.3 Optimised business processes

Data analytics can be used to identify inefficiencies in business processes, enabling businesses to streamline their operations and reduce costs. For example, United Parcel Service (UPS) uses data analytics to optimise its delivery routes and reduce fuel consumption, resulting in significant cost savings. By using data analytics to identify and address inefficiencies, businesses can improve their operational efficiency and reduce costs. Again, linking this to the University, the model and algorithm that has connected students' attendance at library, lectures, and VLE could be used to optimise business operations by identifying students who are likely to fail, and they are supported in time. So, the algorithm may have seen that students who don't go to lecture and library are likely to fail, and the University may put more resources for staff to reach out to these students on a personal level, asking them if they need additional support in accessing the library.

7.6.4 Enhanced product development

Data analytics can provide valuable insights into how customers are using products and what features they find most valuable. Brands can analyse data to see the trends of their customers, to see what interests them and what they are likely to buy. For example, Fitbit uses data analytics to understand how its customers are using its products and which features are most popular. This data is used to inform the development of new products and features that meet the needs and preferences of its customers. By using data analytics to inform product development, businesses can stay competitive and meet the evolving needs of their customers. Looking at the University for example, the data has shown that many students are struggling with a particular course, and they may have to introduce additional resources, learning apps, and support systems to support the students.

7.6.5 Competitive advantage

With the analytics the university has been collecting from student engagement on different platforms as alluded in the examples above, universities have that competitive advantage because most of their students are graduating on time, and most of their students are supported in time before it is too late, and because of this support structure informed by data analytics, the students are leaving positive reviews and inviting others to join them at the University. Data analytics can provide businesses with a competitive advantage by ensuring that their customers stand out, are well supported, and are provided with personalised offers. Data analytics also enables brands to identify new market opportunities, stay ahead of trends, and respond quickly to changing market conditions. For example, Airbnb uses data analytics to identify new market opportunities and tailor its offerings to meet the needs of different customer segments. By using data analytics to stay ahead of the curve, businesses can maintain their competitive edge and capitalise on emerging trends and opportunities.

Data analytics is critical for businesses operating in digital platforms, as it enables them to gain a deep understanding of their customers, make informed decisions, optimise their operations, and stay competitive in a rapidly evolving market. However, in order to realise these benefits, managers must be able to see the potential of the data they are collecting and be willing to invest in the tools and resources needed to analyse and interpret that data effectively. This may involve developing new skills and expertise within the organisation, as well as investing in new technologies and software.

Reflective question

In what ways can data analytics help businesses address social and environmental issues?

7.7 Techniques used in data analytics on digital platforms

As alluded to in the beginning, this chapter will not teach you about carrying out data analytics, but it will introduce you to possible different techniques, you have some insight to build on and expand your practical knowledge. Rather than providing a step-by-step guide to carrying out data analytics, this section will focus on providing an overview of different techniques and tools that can be used to analyse data. By doing so, it aims to help you build a foundation of knowledge and understanding that you can then apply to your own data analysis projects. This approach will allow you to gain a broad understanding of different types of data analysis techniques, which can be useful in a variety of contexts. Additionally, by introducing you to a variety of tools and techniques, it may inspire you to explore new approaches to data analysis that they may not have otherwise considered. It is important to keep in mind that learning about data analytics requires a combination of theoretical knowledge and practical experience and that this section (and chapter) should be seen as just one piece of a larger puzzle.

Some common techniques used in data analytics on digital platforms are discussed below.

7.7.1 Data mining

The process of extracting useful patterns and insights from large datasets. It is often used to identify trends and patterns in customer behaviour, such as purchase history or browsing behaviour on a website. For example, e-commerce companies may use data mining to analyse customer purchase history to recommend products that are likely to be of interest to them.

7.7.2 Machine learning

The use of algorithms and statistical models to identify patterns and make predictions based on data. It can be used to analyse large datasets and to identify patterns and trends that would be difficult or impossible for humans to identify on their own. For example, machine learning algorithms can be used to analyse customer browsing behaviour on a website to predict which products they are most likely to purchase. Artificial intelligence (AI) and machine learning (ML) are suitable solutions to data analytics challenges involving large datasets, different data types and sources, and many predictors. Despite its suitability, concerns are indicating that some AI applications in data analytics are overhyped and may be subject to methodological shortcomings alongside transparency and reproducibility issues if not used with precaution (Collins & Moons, 2019). Methodological concerns include limited assessment of the predictive accuracy, insufficient transparency in the AI and ML algorithms, incorrect focus on classification than a prediction, and weak and unbiased comparisons, which limit independent evaluation. ML techniques also need to adhere to established methodological standards that have already been defined in the research of prediction models. ML-based prediction models are extremely computer reliant in implementing underlying models and are often labelled as a black box. It is characterised by an inherent complexity that hinders the interpretation of the prediction model algorithm. This feature hampers the implementation and independent validation of ML algorithms.

7.7.3 Text analytics

The process of analysing unstructured data such as text documents, emails, and social media posts. It can be used to identify patterns in customer feedback and to monitor brand sentiment on social media. For example, businesses can use text analytics to analyse customer reviews to identify common complaints or issues with their products or services.

7.7.4 Social network analysis

The process of analysing social networks to identify patterns of connections between individuals or groups. It can be used to understand the relationships between customers and to identify potential influencers or advocates for a brand. For example, businesses can use social network analysis to identify individuals who have a large following on social media and are likely to be influential in promoting their products or services.

7.7.5 Web analytics

The process of analysing website traffic to identify patterns and trends in customer behaviour. It can be used to identify which pages on a website are most popular, which products are most frequently purchased, and which marketing campaigns are most effective. For example, businesses can use web analytics to identify which products are most frequently abandoned in shopping carts and to optimise the checkout process to reduce abandonment rates. Google Analytics will come in handy here, likewise Hotjar and other analytics tools. You may also want to check the analytics tool provided by the paid platform (see Section 4.5 on typology of digital platform for brands) such as Shopify or Squarespace.

7.7.6 Bibliometric analytics

Klongthong et al. (2020) proposed a data mining model based on the bibliometric PI that harnesses emergent technologies (ET) in biomedical applications. ETs are at the centre of disruptive transformations in human-centric fields. Attributes of emergence include societal impacts, newness or innovativeness and transformational potential, growth prospects, and community involvement in practice. Such technologies include text mining and Natural Language Processing (NLP). NLP is essential in extracting key phrases from different sources, including keywords, articles, and abstracts (Koohang et al., 2023). These techniques incorporate AI, computational linguistics, mathematics, and information science. It enables the computer to understand the natural language and perform specified tasks. This integration has been extensively deployed in business through various products such as AI customer support assistants, Chatbots, and the current Siri, Cortana and Google Assistant integrations. NLP methods have been applied to analyse semantic and grammatical structures (Kole et al., 2019). These methods include tokenisation, part-of-speech tagging, text chunking, parsing, and splitting. Therefore, the disruptive nature of PI using data mining models can be harnessed in different business areas to maximise productivity.

> **Reflective questions**
>
> How do you see data analytics evolving in the future, and how might it impact businesses and industries?

7.8 Challenges in data analytics on digital platforms

The use of data analytics has become increasingly popular in today's business landscape. Companies are leveraging digital platforms to gather and analyse large amounts of data in order to gain insights that can help them make better-informed decisions. However, data analytics is not without its challenges. Many organisations assume that having a digital platform is enough to ensure that their data analytics processes are effective, but this is far from the truth. In fact, data analytics can be a very complex and challenging business strategy that requires careful planning, implementation, and ongoing maintenance. This section lists some of these challenges for your consideration.

7.8.1 Data quality

Data quality is critical to accurate analytics. Poor data quality can lead to incorrect insights, and this can negatively impact business decisions. One example of this is the Wells Fargo scandal, where the bank created millions of fake customer accounts to meet sales quotas (Meagher, 2023). The bank used the data from these fake accounts to make business decisions, leading to incorrect insights and negative consequences for the bank. The source and quality of the data used to feed algorithms are critical to the success of any data analytics project. Organisations need to continually monitor and evaluate the data being used to ensure that it is reliable, accurate, and relevant to business needs. Data quality is essential for making informed business decisions, and poor-quality data can lead to flawed insights and inaccurate conclusions. In order to ensure the accuracy and relevance of the data, organisations need to have effective data governance policies and procedures in place. This includes regularly checking and verifying the accuracy of data, as well as ensuring that the data is relevant to the business needs. Additionally, organisations should also be mindful of the ethical implications of using data. As data analytics becomes more widespread, there are growing concerns about the potential for bias and discrimination in the use of data. Organisations need to be transparent about their data sources and methods and ensure that they are not perpetuating any unfair biases or stereotypes.

> **Reflective question**
>
> How might biases in data collection and analysis impact the outcomes of data analytics strategies, and how can these biases be addressed?

7.8.2 Data privacy

Data privacy is a major concern in the era of big data. Companies must ensure that they collect and use customer data in a way that respects individual privacy. For example,

Facebook's Cambridge Analytica scandal involved the unauthorised use of user data by a third-party analytics firm for political purposes. The scandal led to widespread backlash and calls for increased privacy regulations. Once a company has obtained high-quality data, it is important to ensure that they have the legal right to use it. Organisations must be aware of the laws and regulations governing data privacy and intellectual property rights and ensure that they are not infringing on any rights or violating any laws. The use of data without proper consent or authorisation can have serious legal and ethical implications. In addition, managers must be able to challenge their developers about the data being used for their analytics. This means asking questions about the sources of the data, how it was obtained, and whether it was obtained in an ethical and legal manner. This can help ensure that the organisation is using data responsibly and in a way that aligns with its values and principles. Managers should also be aware of the potential ethical implications of using data for analytics. Data analytics can be used to discriminate against certain groups or individuals, perpetuate harmful stereotypes, or invade people's privacy. Organisations need to be transparent about their use of data and ensure that they are not engaging in any unethical or discriminatory practices. Obtaining quality data is just the first step in the data analytics process. Organisations must also ensure that they have the legal right to use the data and that they are using it in an ethical and responsible manner. By doing so, companies can avoid legal and ethical risks and build a reputation for responsible data use.

7.8.3 Data security

Data storage is a critical component of any data analytics strategy. Organisations must be able to store and manage data in a way that is secure, reliable, and scalable. This requires having the right technology infrastructure, such as servers, databases, and data centres, to handle large volumes of data. Organisations must also ensure that they are complying with data privacy regulations and that the data is stored in a way that protects individual privacy. This includes implementing appropriate access controls, encryption, and other security measures to protect against data breaches or unauthorised access. In addition, organisations must also consider the costs associated with storing and managing data. The cost of data storage can be significant, especially as the volume of data grows. Organisations must be able to balance the cost of data storage with the potential benefits of using data analytics to drive business decisions. Data security is essential to prevent data breaches and protect sensitive information. In 2013, Target suffered a massive data breach in which the personal and financial data of millions of customers were compromised. The breach was caused by a vulnerability in the company's payment system, which allowed hackers to steal the data. Organisations must be strategic and thoughtful about how they store and manage their data. They must be able to balance the need for security and privacy with the benefits of data analytics, and they must be prepared to invest in the technology and infrastructure necessary to support their data analytics strategy.

7.8.4 Lack of skilled workforce

Data analytics is a complex task that requires human resources with a range of skills and expertise. These skills can include data collection, data structuring, data analysis, and business decision-making. There is a shortage of skilled workers in the field of data analytics. This can make it challenging for companies to find and retain qualified staff to analyse their data. For example, in 2018, the US Bureau of Labour Statistics projected a shortage of over 250,000 data scientists by 2024. Many companies do not have the in-house expertise to conduct complex data analyses and may need to invest in training or hiring specialised data analysts to support their analytics projects. Effective data analytics starts with quality data, which requires a team of people to collect, clean, and structure the data in a way that is usable for analysis. This can involve using tools such as data scraping, data cleaning, and data transformation to ensure that the data is accurate, complete, and consistent. Once the data has been collected and structured, it must be analysed by a team of data analysts who have the skills to extract insights and patterns from the data. This can involve using statistical analysis, data visualisation, and machine learning techniques to uncover insights and trends in the data. The insights derived from the data must be translated into actionable business decisions, which requires a team of business analysts and decision-makers who can use the insights to make informed decisions. Effective data analytics requires a diverse team of people with a range of skills and expertise. From data collection to business decision-making, every step of the data analytics process requires human resources to ensure that the data is of high quality, the insights are accurate, and the business decisions are informed.

Reflective question

What skills do you think are most important for professionals in the field of data analytics, and how can you develop these skills?

7.8.5 Regulatory compliance

The role of regulators in managing digital consumption is critical to ensure that data collected by digital platforms and brands are used properly and ethically. However, for brands, this creates an additional challenge to ensure that their data analytics strategies align with regulatory requirements and ethical standards. Brands must ensure that the data they collect is aligned with data privacy regulations and ethical standards. They must also ensure that the data is accurate, reliable, and of high quality. However, as regulations change and evolve, brands must continually adapt their data analytics strategies to remain compliant with the latest regulatory requirements. Moreover, regulatory compliance alone is not enough to ensure that data analytics is being used ethically. Brands must also consider the ethical implications of their data analytics strategies and ensure that they are not engaging in practices that could harm consumers or compromise their privacy. Furthermore, transparency and accountability are important factors in building trust with consumers. Brands must be transparent about the data they collect and how it is being used to build trust with their consumers. However, this transparency can also be a challenge, as brands must balance the need for transparency with the need to protect sensitive business information.

Companies must comply with various regulations and laws that govern the collection, use, and protection of customer data. For example, the General Data Protection

Regulation (GDPR) requires companies to obtain explicit consent from individuals before collecting and using their data. Failure to comply with these regulations can result in significant fines and reputational damage. The challenge for brands in data analytics is to ensure that their data analytics strategies align with regulatory requirements and ethical standards, while also considering the ethical implications of their strategies. They must balance the need for transparency with the need to protect sensitive business information to build trust with their consumers.

7.9 Conclusion

Data analytics has become an increasingly important tool for businesses of all sizes, as they seek to gain insights into consumer behaviour, identify trends, and make data-driven decisions. There are different types of analytics, including descriptive, diagnostic, predictive, and prescriptive analytics, each providing different levels of insight and value to businesses. Descriptive analytics helps businesses understand what has happened in the past, while diagnostic analytics helps them understand why it happened. Predictive analytics allows businesses to anticipate what may happen in the future, while prescriptive analytics provides recommendations on what actions should be taken.

According to Dwivedi et al. (2021), brands can use data analytics to implement personalised experiences by incorporating the extensive capabilities of Big Data Analytics (BDA). Generally, technological transformations have promoted the development of better ways to provide value to clients. The increasing proliferation of mobile devices and IoT devices will increase the role of PI and BDA in business by supporting large-scale correlational techniques. Many brands target to provide personalised customer experiences that will enable them to gain new customers while retaining existing ones. Therefore, PI is an essential solution to personalised experience marketing (PEM) initiatives by enabling businesses to obtain insights that will enable them to achieve their marketing objectives. It is harnessed in data mining to derive interesting patterns and techniques that can be later applied in market segmentation, direct marketing, interactive marketing, and fraud detection. PI using BDA can be incorporated into developing a product recommender system and effective online marketing by maximising conversion and enabling product sales with minimal exposure.

Data analytics has found other great applications in proactive situational business analytics as one of its data-driven business management applications. Its key focus is on the market and economic data for sensitive assessment of market and industrial data (Halb & Seebacher, 2020). Data analytics extensively uses customer data in various capacities, including marketing automation, whereby the organisation runs focused product promotion campaigns. It is also essential in interactive-dynamic business intelligence, whereby the main objective is implementing data-driven corporate management and development frameworks. The integration of this functionality requires the development of a Key User Network (KUN), Integration of Project Data, and expansion of activities to incorporate tertiary analyses (Xu et al 2016). Developing a KUN is essential for promoting the independence of internal customers because valuable data is available. Other data required for the effective implementation of the PI model includes the digital footprints of the customers and prospects. This data helps reduce lead times for major projects in organisations.

The value of data analytics for brands cannot be overstated. Data analytics can help brands identify new opportunities for growth, optimise their marketing strategies, and make more informed decisions. By leveraging data analytics, brands can gain a competitive advantage, improve customer experiences, and increase revenue. However, data analytics is not without its challenges. Brands must ensure that the data they collect is accurate, reliable, and of high quality. They must also ensure that they are using the data in compliance with regulatory requirements and ethical standards. Additionally, transparency and accountability are crucial to building trust with consumers.

In conclusion, data analytics has become an essential tool for businesses to succeed in today's digital economy. By leveraging data analytics, brands can gain valuable insights and make informed decisions. However, brands must also navigate the challenges of data analytics, including ensuring data quality, regulatory compliance, ethical considerations, and transparency. Overall, the benefits of data analytics outweigh the challenges, and brands that invest in data analytics will be better positioned to succeed in the long run.

7.10 Student activities

1. What are the different types of data analytics, and how do they differ from one another?
2. How can businesses ensure that the data they collect is accurate and of high quality?
3. What ethical considerations should businesses keep in mind when conducting data analytics?
4. How can predictive analytics be used to improve marketing strategies?
5. How can data visualisation tools be used to communicate insights to stakeholders effectively?
6. What is machine learning, and how can it be used in data analytics?
7. How can businesses leverage customer data to improve their products and services?
8. How can businesses use sentiment analysis to understand customer feedback?
9. How can businesses ensure that their data analytics strategies comply with regulatory requirements?
10. How can prescriptive analytics be used to optimise business operations?

References and further reading

Abdulquadri, A., Mogaji, E., Kieu, T. & Nguyen, P., 2021. Digital transformation in financial services provision: A Nigerian perspective to the adoption of chatbot. *Journal of Enterprising Communities: People and Places in the Global Economy*, 15(2), pp. 258–281.

Agbo, F. et al., 2020. Social media usage for computing education: The effect of tie strength and group communication on perceived learning outcome. *Journal of Education and Development Using Information and Communication Technology*, 16(1), pp. 5–26.

Anagnostopoulos, C. & Kolomvatsos, K., 2018. Predictive intelligence to the edge through approximate collaborative context reasoning. *Applied Intelligence*, 48, pp. 966–991.

Anagnostopoulos, C., Mpougiouris, P. & Hadjiefthymiades, S., 2005. Prediction intelligence in context-aware applications. *Proceedings of the 6th International Conference on Mobile Data Management*. https://doi.org/10.1145/1071246.1071266

Balakrishnan, J., Nwoba, A. & Nguyen, N., 2021. Emerging-market consumers' interactions with banking chatbots. *Telematics and Informatics*, 65, 101711.

Balthazar, P., Harri, P., Prater, A. & Safdar, N. M., 2018. Protecting your patients' interests in the era of big data, artificial intelligence, and predictive analytics. *Journal of the American College of Radiology*, 15(3), pp. 580–586. https://doi.org/10.1016/j.jacr.2017.11.035

Cardoso, D. & Ferreira, L., 2021. Application of predictive maintenance concepts using artificial intelligence tools. *Applied Sciences*. https://dx.doi.org/10.3390/app11010018

Chattopadhyay, A., Kupe, T., Schatzer, N. & Mogaji, E., 2022. Fireside chat with three vice chancellors from three continents. In: E. Mogaji, V. Jain, F. Maringe & R. Hinson, eds. *Re-imagining Higher Education in Emerging Economies*. Cham: Palgrave Macmillan, pp. 85–96.

Chylinski, M. et al., 2020. Augmented reality marketing: A technology-enabled approach to situated customer experience. *Australasian Marketing Journal*, 28(4), pp. 374–384.

Collins, G. S. & Moons, K. G., 2019. Reporting of artificial intelligence prediction models. *The Lancet*, 393(10181), pp. 1577–1579. https://doi.org/10.1016/s0140-6736(19)30037-6

Dwivedi, Y. K., Hughes, L., Ismagilova, E., Aarts, G., Coombs, C., Crick, T., ... & Williams, M. D., 2021. Artificial Intelligence (AI): Multidisciplinary perspectives on emerging challenges, opportunities, and agenda for research, practice and policy. *International Journal of Information Management*, 57, 101994.

Dhami, M. K, Mandel, D. R, Mellers, B. A. & Tetlock, P. E., 2015. Improving intelligence analysis with decision science. *Perspectives on Psychological Science*, 10(6), 753–757. https://doi.org/10.1177/1745691615598511

Dhruv, G., Hulland, J., Kopalle, P. & Karahanna, E., 2020. The future of technology and marketing: A multidisciplinary perspective. *Journal of the Academy of Marketing Science*, 48, pp. 1–8.

Dwivedi, Y. et al., 2022. Metaverse beyond the hype: Multidisciplinary perspectives on emerging challenges, opportunities, and agenda for research, practice and policy. *International Journal of Information Management*, 66, 102542.

Friedman, J. A., & Zeckhauser, R. 2012. Assessing uncertainty in intelligence. *Intelligence and National Security*, 27(6), pp. 824–847.

Gartner, 2023. What is data and analytics? [Online] Available at: https://www.gartner.com/en/topics/data-and-analytics

Halb, F., & Seebacher, U., 2020. Customer experience und touchpoint management. *B2B Marketing—A guidebook for the classroom to the boardroom*. New York: Springer.

Harth, N., Anagnostopoulos, C., & Pezaros, D., 2018. Predictive intelligence to the edge: impact on edge analytics. *Evolving Systems*, 9, pp. 95–118.

Hein, A. et al., 2020. Digital platform ecosystems. *Electronic Markets*, 30, pp. 87–98.

Hiran, K. K., Jain, R. K., Lakhwani, K. & Doshi, R., 2021. *Machine Learning: Master Supervised and Unsupervised Learning Algorithms with Real Examples (English Edition)*. New Delhi: BPB Publications.

Hodapp, D. & Hanelt, A., 2022. Interoperability in the era of digital innovation: An information systems research agenda. *Journal of Information Technology*, 37(4), pp. 407–427.

Kandampully, J., Bilgihan, A. & Li, D., 2022. Unifying technology and people: Revisiting service in a digitally transformed world. *The Service Industries Journal*, 42(1–2), pp. 21–41.

Klongthong, W., Muangsin, V., Gowanit, C. & Muangsin, N., 2020. Research article chitosan biomedical applications for the treatment of viral disease: A data mining model using bibliometric predictive intelligence. *Journal of Chemistry*, 2020, 6612034. https://doi.org/10.1155/2020/6612034

Koelzer, V. H., Sirinukunwattana, K., Rittscher, J. & Mertz, K. D., 2018. Precision immunoprofiling by image analysis and artificial intelligence. *Virchows Archive*. https://doi.org/10.1007/s00428-018-2485-z.

Koohang, A., Nord, J. H., Ooi, K. B., Tan, G. W. H., Al-Emran, M., Aw, E. C. X., ... & Wong, L. W. 2023. Shaping the metaverse into reality: a holistic multidisciplinary understanding of opportunities, challenges, and avenues for future investigation. *Journal of Computer Information Systems*, 63(3), 735–765.

Kopalle, P., Kumar, V. & Subramaniam, M., 2020. How legacy firms can embrace the digital ecosystem via digital customer orientation. *Journal of the Academy of Marketing Science*, 48, pp. 114–131.

Lee, W. J., Wu, H., Yun, H., Kim, H., Jun, M. B. G. & Sutherland, J. W., 2019. Predictive maintenance of machine tool systems using artificial intelligence techniques applied to machine condition data. 26th CIRP Life Cycle Engineering (LCE) Conference. https://doi.org/10.1016/j.procir.2018.12.019.

Lowe, R. J., 2017. Anti-money laundering – The need for intelligence. *Journal of Financial Crime*, 24(3), pp. 472–479. https://doi.org/10.1108/jfc-04-2017-0030

Majumder, S., Mondal, T. & Deen, M. J., 2017. Wearable sensors for remote health monitoring. *Sensors*, 17(1), pp. 130.

McKinsey, 2022. Marketing in the metaverse: An opportunity for innovation and experimentation [Online] Available at: https://www.mckinsey.com/capabilities/growth-marketing-and-sales/our-insights/marketing-in-the-metaverse-an-opportunity-for-innovation-and-experimentation

Meagher, P., 2023. The wells Fargo fake accounts scandal: A comprehensive overview [Online] Available at: https://www.learnsignal.com/blog/wells-fargo-fake-accounts-scandal-overview-2/#:~:text=The%20Wells%20Fargo%20fake%20accounts%20scandal%20first%20came%20to%20light,to%20meet%20unrealistic%20sales%20targets.

Mellers, B., Stone, E., Atanasov, P., Rohrbaugh, N., Metz, S. E., Ungar, L., ... & Tetlock, P., 2015. The psychology of intelligence analysis: Drivers of prediction accuracy in world politics. *Journal of Experimental Psychology: Applied*, 21(1), pp. 1–14.

Miric, M., Boudreau, K. & Jeppesen, L., 2019. Protecting their digital assets: The use of formal & informal appropriability strategies by App developers. *Research Policy*, 48(8), 103738.

Mogaji, E., 2021. *Brand Management*. Cham: Springer.

Mogaji, E., Olaleye, S. & Ukpabi, D., 2020. Using AI to personalise emotionally appealing advertisement. In: Nripendra P. Rana, Emma L. Slade, Ganesh P. Sahu, Hatice Kizgin, Nitish Singh, Bidit Dey, Anabel Gutierrez, Yogesh K. Dwivedi, eds. *Digital and Social Media Marketing: Emerging Applications and Theoretical Development*. Cham: Springers, pp. 137–150.

Mogaji, E., Soetan, T. & Kieu, T., 2020. The implications of artificial intelligence on the digital marketing of financial services to vulnerable customers. *Australasian Marketing Journal*, 29(3), pp. 235–242.

Mohapatra, S. K., Mishra, S., Tripathy, H. K., Bhoi, A. K. & Barsocchi, P., 2021. A pragmatic investigation of energy consumption and utilization models in the urban sector using predictive intelligence approaches. *Energies*, 14(13), 3900. https://doi.org/10.3390/en14133900

Morgan-Thomas, A., Dessart, L. & Veloutsou, C., 2020. Digital ecosystem and consumer engagement: A socio-technical perspective. *Journal of Business Research*, 121, pp. 713–723.

Olson, E., Olson, K., Czaplewski, A. & Key, T., 2021. Business strategy and the management of digital marketing. *Business Horizons*, 64(2), pp. 285–293.

Oosthuizen, K., Botha, E., Robertson, J. & Montecchi, M., 2021. Artificial intelligence in retail: The AI-enabled value chain. *Australasian Marketing Journal*, 29(3), pp. 264–273.

Ponzoa, J. & Erdmann, A., 2021. E-commerce customer attraction: Digital marketing techniques, evolution and dynamics across firms. *Journal of Promotion Management*, 27(5), pp. 697–715.

Sağkaya Güngö, A. & Ozansoy Çadırcı, T., 2022. Understanding digital consumer: A review, synthesis, and future research agenda. *International Journal of Consumer Studies*, 46(5), pp. 1829–1858.

Sampat, B., Mogaji, E. & Nguyen, N. P., 2023. The dark side of FinTech in financial services: A qualitative enquiry into FinTech developers' perspective. *International Journal of Bank Marketing*, Vol. ahead-of-print No. ahead-of-print. https://doi.org/10.1108/IJBM-07-2022-0328.

Seebacher, U., 2021. *Predictive Intelligence for Data-Driven Managers. Process Model, Assessment-Tool, It-Blueprint, Competence Model and Case Studies.* Springer. https://doi.org/10.1007/978-3-030-69403-6.

Sheth, J., 2020. Impact of Covid-19 on consumer behavior: Will the old habits return or die? *Journal of Business Research*, 117, pp. 280–283.

Soetan, T., Mogaji, E. & Nguyen, N., 2021. Financial services experience and consumption in Nigeria. *Journal of Services Marketing*, 35(7), pp. 947–961.

Thyago, P. C., et al., 2019. A systematic literature review of machine learning methods applied to predictive maintenance. *Computers & Industrial Engineering*, 137, 106024.

Wazurkar, P., Bhadoria, R. S. & Bajpai, D., 2017. Predictive analytics in data science for business intelligence solutions. In *2017 7th International Conference on Communication Systems and Network Technologies (CSNT)*. IEEE, pp. 367–370.

Wilson, H. J. & Daugherty, P. R., 2018. Collaborative intelligence: Humans and AI are joining forces. *Harvard Business Review*, 96(4), pp. 114–123.

Xu, K., Qu, Y. & Yang, K., 2016. A tutorial on the internet of things: From a heterogeneous network integration perspective. *IEEE Network*, 30(2), pp. 102–108.

CHAPTER 8

Regulating digital consumption

8.1 Background

Digital technology has become an integral part of our everyday life; it has shaped how we live, work, travel, and entertain our lives. We cannot underestimate the impact of technology, which sometimes can be bad, and this has raised a call for proper evaluation of if and how we should be using these technologies. It is not surprising that some countries have banned the use of certain technologies in their countries, some organisations prefer to use certain types of technologies, and even parents denying their children from using some types of technologies. This dilemma has called for the need to regulate digital consumption. This chapter provides an overview of the need for regulation, perhaps if it's a justifiable idea and who is responsible for this regulation. The chapter sheds light on some regulations and guidelines, highlights significant challenges, and presents practical implications for managers seeking to understand and manage consumer engagement in the digital environment.

8.2 Learning outcomes

By the end of this chapter, you should be able to:

- Describe the concept of regulating digital consumption.
- Recognise different things that can be regulated on digital platforms.
- Identify different stakeholders involved in regulating digital consumption.
- Understand the benefits of regulating digital consumptions.
- Describe different challenges in regulating digital consumption.

8.3 Introduction

Since its emergence in the 1990s, the character of the commercial Internet has changed dramatically—driving far-reaching changes in society and the economy as a result. The fast-moving digital innovation has transformed the nature of e-commerce and

DOI: 10.4324/9781003389842-8

disrupted sector after sector. It has also altered how consumers interact and transact with each other and with the marketplace. Today, a handful of companies control unimaginable portions of the world's economic activity and investment capital, resulting in a concentration of power and wealth in the hands of a few tech giants.

The widespread adoption of mobile devices and social media platforms has further amplified the influence of these companies, enabling them to gather vast amounts of data on individuals and shape public discourse. This has led to concerns about privacy, data protection, and the potential for manipulation of public opinion. The commercial Internet has also created new opportunities for entrepreneurs and small businesses but has also led to job displacement and widening economic inequality. Overall, the commercial Internet has brought about significant changes to the world we live in, both positive and negative, and its impact will continue to be felt for years to come.

Irrespective of these positive or negative impacts, there is a growing number of digital consumers that would be interested in digital technologies. Digital consumers come to different platforms to engage with themselves, brands, and other stakeholders. The need for continuous engagement has been discussed, aligning with the idea of Immersive time (ImT) on the metaverse (Mogaji et al., 2023), where it is beneficial for brands and developers to see that consumers are spending a long time on these platforms. One concern is regarding the monitoring of activities on these platforms, to ensure that no one is being exploited—balancing people's right to freedom of expression with online safety is a growing concern.

The digital platform can be a wild west web—where a lot of atrocities can happen. While we have recognised the benefits of digital transformation across our lives and business operation, we cannot ignore the dark side and challenges that come with it. This has therefore presented the need for regulating different activities on the platforms. It is known that digital businesses are operating in many cases without appropriate guardrails and as a manager, and it is imperative to reflect on these responsibilities, to see if your platform is safe enough to enhance a productive digital consumption. No doubt, digital technologies bring new and accelerated risks, and as digital technologies play an increasingly systemic role, our regulatory systems need to adapt to the ways they can be exploited to threaten our critical infrastructure, fundamental human rights, and consumer choice.

This chapter is set to discuss the regulations of digital consumption—to explore if the consumers' desires to keep consuming can be regulated, if brands can be regulated on the type of platforms they can use, and if the platform developers are regulated with regard to the platforms they are introducing. No doubt these thought-provoking questions will have an impact on the experiences of digital consumers but it's apparently for their good, welfare, and well-being. The chapter introduces some relevant and existing regulations that can guide brands working on digital platforms, highlights significant challenges, and provides practical recommendations for brands. It is anticipated that at the end of this chapter, you would have a better understanding of the regulations and put measures in place to enhance the digital consumer experiences on your digital platforms.

8.4 The problems

There are problems with our digital consumption, and we can't deny it—these problems come with the benefits of digital technologies. We need to have a better understanding of these problems and see how policies can be put in place to guarantee the well-being of digital consumers. Before we proceed into the problems, let's have a look at some quotes from prominent politicians working on addressing these problems.

> For too long, big tech has gotten away with being the land of the lawless. A lack of regulation online has left too many people vulnerable to abuse, fraud, violence and in some cases even loss of life—**Damian Collins MP, Chair of the Joint Committee on the draft Online Safety Bill**
>
> Digital technologies are key to our future prosperity, but we must also make sure that they are developed responsibly so we protect society and uphold the rights of our citizens—**The Rt Hon Oliver Dowden, Secretary of State for Digital, Culture, Media and Sport**
>
> Today's big tech companies have too much power — too much power over our economy, our society, and our democracy. They've bulldozed competition, used our private information for profit, and tilted the playing field against everyone else. And in the process, they have hurt small businesses and stifled innovation—**Elizabeth Warren, Senior United States Senator from Massachusetts—Here's how we can break up Big Tech | by Team Warren | Medium**

The quotes suggest a growing concern about the unchecked power and influence of big tech companies and the potential negative consequences that come with this power. Damian Collins MP and Elizabeth Warren both highlight the lack of regulation and control over big tech, with Warren specifically calling for the breaking up of these companies to prevent monopolistic behaviour. Though the focus of these politician's concerns may be on the big tech companies (some of which were discussed in Chapter 5), you need to be open-minded and have a holistic view of the digital platform ecosystem—your agency or boutique developer is not excluded in this discussion.

No doubt that big tech companies have accumulated vast amounts of data on individuals, giving them significant power over people's lives and livelihoods—Do you think that's a problem? Would you critically reflect if there is a problem in how much data they have collected, or we should be interested in HOW they use these data? Additionally, they have been criticised for their role in the spread of disinformation, the manipulation of public opinion, and the stifling of competition—again, reflect on this as a problem. Do you think they (tech companies) are the ones writing the hate speech online or we expect them to take responsibility and remove those people? Remember that 2000 abusive tweets were directed at four Black players following the England national football team's loss at the Euro 2020 final (Glynn & Brown, 2020).

Facebook was accused of playing a role in the mass murder of Rohingya Muslims in Myanmar in 2017. The platform was used to spread hate speech and incite violence against the Rohingya, which ultimately led to the displacement of over 700,000 people and the deaths of thousands. The United Nations found that Facebook had been 'a useful instrument for those seeking to spread hate' in Myanmar, and the company was criticised for not doing enough to address the issue. Facebook has since taken steps to combat hate speech and misinformation on its platform, but the situation in Myanmar serves as a stark reminder of the potential consequences of unchecked social media use and the need for responsible regulation and accountability (Stecklow, 2018).

While the importance of digital technologies cannot be denied, it is crucial to ensure that they are developed responsibly and with accountability. Oliver Dowden recognises this need for responsible development, but it remains to be seen whether governments and regulatory bodies will take meaningful action to hold big tech companies accountable.

These risks and challenges can impact consumer trust in digital transactions (Albayati et al., 2020). Cybersecurity threats, data breaches, identity theft, and fraudulent activities are some of the major risks that consumers face in digital transactions, which can lead to financial losses, reputational damage, and loss of personal information (Riquelme et al., 2019; Shree et al., 2021). Significant numbers of web users still refrain from online purchases because of fears relating to the misuse of personal data and the security of online payments (Adeola et al., 2021). Many people still feel they are being tracked and monitored and they are getting paranoid. These quotes reflect a growing concern about the unchecked power of platform developers and the need for increased regulation and accountability to prevent abuse, fraud, and the erosion of privacy and democracy. It is essential for governments and regulatory bodies to take meaningful action to ensure that digital technologies are developed responsibly and in the best interests of society as a whole.

Significantly, these problems can be summarised as it affects three key stakeholders.

8.4.1 Harm affecting children

There are serious risks and challenges that children face when using the Internet, including exposure to indecent images and potential exploitation by adults (Dong et al., 2020; Zhu et al., 2021). The Internet Watch Foundation (IWF) Annual Report 2020 reported record increases in self-generated child sexual abuse material. Rights' 'Pathways' research showed how the design and operation of major social media services led to children being exposed to extreme pro-suicide, eating disorder, and pornographic content. Remember digital consumers are all on this platform to engage. And in engagement, children are vulnerable. This exposure highlights the risks and challenges associated with children's access to the Internet. These images can have a profound and long-lasting impact on children's emotional, mental, and social development, and can lead to a range of negative consequences, such as depression, anxiety, and behavioural problems. Additionally, children who are exposed to indecent images may be more vulnerable to exploitation and abuse by online predators.

In addition, the issue of children self-harming through social media is another disturbing trend that highlights the negative impact that social media can have on vulnerable individuals. Social media can create a highly pressurised environment, where children feel the need to present a perfect image of themselves to others, often at the expense of their own mental health. This can lead to feelings of inadequacy, low self-esteem, and depression, which can contribute to self-harming behaviour. Furthermore, social media platforms may not have adequate measures in place to prevent self-harm content from being shared, and some may even sensationalise it. This can make it difficult for children to find support or help and can exacerbate their feelings of isolation and despair. There have been several reported cases of children and teenagers engaging in self-harm and even suicide due to social media pressures and cyberbullying. In 2017, a 14-year-old girl in the UK committed suicide after being exposed to graphic self-harm images on Instagram. In the same year, a 12-year-old girl in the United States took her own life after being bullied on social media. These are just a few examples of the serious consequences that can result from the negative impact of social media on children's mental health and well-being.

8.4.2 Harms affecting adults

Adults are not exempted from the problems on digital platforms which has called for more regulations (Flew et al., 2019). People are exposed to different forms of abuse and online harassment, involving persistent, unwanted behaviour directed at an adult which could be racism, sexual harassment, hate speech, threats, abuse against LGBTQ+ people, misogynistic abuse, and violence against women and girls. There is the harm of cyberbullying, where other platform users use these digital platforms to harass, intimidate, or embarrass someone, and we must also recognise how cyberbullying can be detrimental to an adult's mental and emotional well-being. One example is the case of Caroline Criado-Perez, a disabled British journalist and feminist activist who received a torrent of abusive tweets in 2013 after successfully campaigning to have Jane Austen featured on the £10 banknote. The abusive tweets included rape and death threats and were aimed at her disability as well as her gender. This incident led to the launch of the #ReclaimTheInternet campaign, which seeks to combat online abuse and harassment. Two of those abusers (platform users and digital consumers) were jailed for the Twitter abuse of feminist campaigner. There are also religious hate and anti-Semitism. A record number of anti-Semitic incidents were reported in the UK in May–June 2021, such that the Community Security Trust termed this period 'the month of hate'. Many of these incidents took place online. Addiction is also another harm that is associated with digital platforms. This addiction is not just about social media but the use of other digital platforms which could include gambling, gaming, or even pornography. Addiction to digital platforms is becoming increasingly common among adults. Spending excessive amounts of time online can have negative impacts on physical health, mental health, and relationships. The possibility of disinformation is also another problem that warrants the need for regulations. Digital consumers can be susceptible to disinformation, which can impact their decision-making and cause harm to themselves or others.

8.4.3 Harms affecting organisations

Organisations including companies and governed institutions are also experiencing some problems on digital platforms. This could range from limited inclusive designs for people with disabilities, disinformation on social media, or data breaches (Crowley, 2022). Company's data can be stolen or leaked, and this can result in identity theft, financial loss, and other serious consequences for digital consumers. TalkTalk suffered a significant data breach in October 2015, which exposed the personal and financial details of thousands of its customers. The cyberattack was believed to be one of the largest and most damaging breaches in UK history. The attackers gained access to TalkTalk's customer data through a vulnerability in the company's website. The compromised data included customers' names, addresses, dates of birth, email addresses, phone numbers, and financial information such as bank account and credit card details. In 2017, the credit reporting agency Equifax suffered a data breach that exposed the personal and financial information of millions of people, including names, Social Security numbers, birth dates, and addresses. The breach occurred because Equifax failed to apply a patch to a software vulnerability that had been identified earlier in the year. The question you may be asking here is what's the role of the regulators? What could the regulator do to ensure issues like cyberattacks do not happen?

From a political perspective, there were reports of Russian agents attempting to influence UK elections through social media. In 2018, the UK Parliament's Digital, Culture, Media and Sport (DCMS) Committee published a report that found evidence of Russian interference in the 2016 EU referendum and the 2017 UK general election. The report highlighted the use of social media platforms, such as Twitter and Facebook, to spread disinformation and propaganda. Russian agents were accused of creating fake accounts and groups, as well as buying ads and posts to target specific audiences with political messages designed to sway public opinion. The report also stated that social media companies had failed to adequately address the issue of foreign interference in UK elections, calling for greater regulation and transparency in their operations. The findings of the report have been widely debated and have led to calls for greater scrutiny of online advertising and political campaigning in the UK. Organisations need to be aware of the prospective harm that their stakeholders are exposed to, and see how regulations, policies, and procedures can help enhance the consumers' experiences on digital platforms.

8.5 The regulations

Different countries around the world are working on regulations to ensure the well-being of their citizens on digital platforms. While many governments have banned some platforms to outrightly protect their citizens (though we could still debate about the freedom of expression on different platforms), there are many countries who have endeavoured to come up with different regulations to protect their citizens. More like saying, if we can't stop you from using these digital platforms, we will provide you with regulations to guide you. Managers keen on understanding and managing consumer engagement in the digital environment need to be aware of these regulations and reflect on how it shapes their business practices and their engagement with digital consumers.

Though this is a growing list, this section aims to identify some relevant and popular regulations, and there is need to move beyond Europe and see what other countries are doing. It can be said that data protection regulations in Africa are generally less widespread and comprehensive than those in Europe and other regions, and enforcement can be limited in some cases. However, there is growing recognition of the importance of data protection in Africa, and more countries are expected to introduce or update data protection laws in the coming years. These regulations are bound to be reviewed and updated as the digital ecosystem evolves and likewise, the list is bound to grow as many other countries are working on theirs and as data protection and online safety are becoming increasingly important issues worldwide.

1. General Data Protection Regulation (GDPR), one of the most recognised regulations around the world, covers the European Union (and other platform developers engaging with digital consumers in Europe). It requires organisations to obtain explicit consent from individuals to collect and use their personal data. It gives

individuals the right to access, correct, and erase their personal data. The regulation requires organisations to report data breaches within 72 hours.

2. European Electronic Communications Code (EECC) was adopted and entered into force in December 2018. It sets an EU-level legal framework to coordinate national legislation on electronic communications networks and services. It ensures the provision of good quality, affordable, publicly available electronic communication services to end-users.

3. Digital Services Act (DSA) regulates the obligations of digital services that act as intermediaries in their role of connecting consumers with goods, services, and content. It will give better protection to consumers and to fundamental rights online, establish a powerful transparency and accountability framework for online platforms, and lead to fairer and more open digital markets. Harmonised across the EU and directly applicable, the new rules will make it easier to provide digital innovations across borders, while ensuring the same level of protection for all citizens in the EU.

4. The EU Platform to Business Regulation 2019/1150 ('P2B Regulation') was adopted in 2020. The primary purpose of the P2B Regulation is to ensure the fair and transparent treatment of business users by online platforms, giving them more effective options for redress when facing problems; and a predictable and innovation-friendly regulatory environment in which they can thrive.

5. Online Safety Bill is a draft bill from the UK which places a legal duty of care on social media companies to protect users from harm. The bill gives regulators powers to fine companies and block access to sites. It also requires companies to report illegal content to law enforcement.

6. California Consumer Privacy Act (CCPA) is a privacy law in the state of California, United States, that gives Californians the right to know what personal information businesses collect about them, the right to request that it be deleted, and the right to opt out of its sale.

7. Personal Information Protection and Electronic Documents Act (PIPEDA) is a federal law in Canada that regulates how private sector organisations handle personal information in the course of commercial activities.

8. Personal Data Protection Act (PDPA) is a data protection law in Singapore that governs the collection, use, and disclosure of personal data by organisations.

9. Cybersecurity Law is a law in China that regulates cybersecurity, including the protection of personal information. The regulation requires critical information infrastructure operators to store personal information and important data within China. It also gives the Chinese government broad powers to regulate online content.

10. General Data Protection Law (LGPD) is a data protection law in Brazil that regulates the collection, use, and storage of personal data by organisations.

11. Personal Data Protection Act (PDPA) is a data protection law in Malaysia that regulates the processing of personal data by both private and public sector organisations.

12. Privacy Act is a federal law in Australia that regulates how Australian government agencies handle personal information.

13. Protection of Personal Information Act (POPI Act)—POPIA from South Africa gives individuals the right to access and correct their personal data. It requires

organisations to obtain consent to collect and use personal data and expects organisations to report data breaches to the regulator and affected individuals.

14. Data Protection Act from Nigeria regulates the collection, use, and storage of personal data by organisations. The regulation requires organisations to obtain consent to collect, use, and disclose personal data. It gives individuals the right to access and correct their personal data.
15. Data Protection Act from Ghana.
16. Data Protection Act from Kenya, managed by the Data Protection Commissioner.
17. Data Protection Act from Tunisia managed by National Authority for the Protection of Personal Data.
18. Information Technology (IT) Act in India regulates electronic commerce and digital signatures in India and provides legal recognition for electronic documents.

Table 8.1 presents a summary of selected data protection regulations around the world, highlighting the regulatory body/agency or government department responsible for enforcing the regulation, the applicability to which organisations or individuals are subject to the regulation, and penalties for non-compliance: The fines, penalties, or legal consequences for organisations or individuals who violate the regulation. Note that this table includes only a few examples of digital regulations around the world and is not an exhaustive list.

8.6 Why regulate?

So, with these problems, it is evident for us to see why regulation is needed, and with all these regulations, you might be worrying why it's needed. It is imperative for managers to recognise that these regulations present justifiable reasons to effectively manage digital consumption on the digital platforms and to educate consumers, brands, and organisations on the value of having regulations in place. Well-designed regulation can have a powerful effect on driving growth and shaping a thriving digital economy and society, whereas poorly designed or restrictive regulation can dampen innovation. The right rules can help people trust the products and services they're using, which in turn can drive take-up and further consumption, investment, and innovation.

8.6.1 Ensure digital well-being

Digital well-being refers to the state of an individual's mental, physical, and emotional health in relation to their use of digital technologies such as social media, gaming, and other online platforms (Abeele, 2021). To maintain the desired level of well-being, regulators are putting these measures in place to ensure that everyone engaging on digital platforms is doing so safely. Referring back to the night club example, the Government here is the regulator who is challenging the Club owners to make sure they have CCTV, security guards, and metal detectors to protect the consumers. Regulators may not be fully involved in the development of digital platforms; they are simply responsible for the overall well-being of digital consumers. Regulators make sure children are not exposed to offensive images, people are not abused online, and companies manage their risks for cyberattack. Regulations can aim to promote the responsible use of digital technologies and prevent the negative consequences that can arise from excessive

Table 8.1 Summary of selected data protection regulations around the world

Regulation	Country	Launch Date	Regulatory Body	Applicability	Penalties for Non-Compliance
GDPR	European Union	May 2018	European Data Protection Board	Applies to all organisations that process personal data of EU residents	Up to 4% of global revenue or €20 million, whichever is greater
Online Safety Bill	United Kingdom	Draft Bill (still at committee stage as at March 2023)	UK Office of Communications (Ofcom)	Applies to social media companies and other online service providers	Fines of up to £18 million or 10% of annual global turnover
CCPA	United States (California)	January 2020	California Attorney General	Applies to businesses that meet certain revenue and data processing thresholds and collect personal data of California residents	Up to $7,500 per violation
PIPEDA	Canada	January 2001	Office of the Privacy Commissioner of Canada	Applies to private sector organisations that collect, use, and disclose personal information in the course of commercial activities	Up to $100,000 per violation
PDPA	Singapore	July 2014	Personal Data Protection Commission	Applies to organisations that collect, use, or disclose personal data in Singapore	Fines of up to 10% of an organisation's annual revenue or S$1 million, whichever is greater
Cybersecurity Law	China	June 2017	Cyberspace Administration of China	Applies to network operators and critical information infrastructure operators in China	Fines of up to RMB 1 million (approximately $154,000)
LGPD	Brazil	September 2020	National Data Protection Authority	Applies to all organisations that process personal data of Brazilian residents	Fines of up to 2% of a company's gross revenue in Brazil or R$50 million, whichever is lower

(Continued)

Table 8.1 (Continued)

Regulation	Country	Launch Date	Regulatory Body	Applicability	Penalties for Non-Compliance
POPIA	South Africa	July 2020	Information Regulator	Applies to all organisations that process personal data of South African residents	Fines of up to ZAR 10 million (approximately $675,000) or 10 years in prison
Data Protection Act	Nigeria	January 2019	National Information Technology Development Agency (NITDA)	Applies to all organisations that process personal data of Nigerian residents	Fines of up to 2% of an organisation's annual gross revenue or NGN 10 million (approximately $26,000), whichever is greater
Data Protection Act	Ghana	November 2012	Data Protection Commission	Applies to all organisations that process personal data of Ghanaian residents	Fines of up to GHS 2,000 (approximately $340) or up to two years in prison
Data Protection Act	Kenya	November 2019	Data Protection Commissioner	Applies to all organisations that process personal data of Kenyan residents	Fines of up to KES 5 million (approximately $45,000) or 1% of an organisation's annual gross revenue, whichever is higher
Data Protection Act	Tunisia	April 2004	National Authority for the Protection of Personal Data	Applies to all organisations that process personal data of Tunisian residents	Fines of up to TND 50,000 (approximately $18,000) or up to one year in prison

use or misuse of these platforms. For example, regulations can require platforms to provide users with tools to manage their time spent on the platform, limit the amount of data that is collected and shared with third parties, and ensure that content shared on the platform is not harmful or offensive. By providing users with tools to manage their time spent on the app, TikTok is acknowledging the potential risks of excessive use and promoting responsible use of digital technologies. It is also showing a commitment to the well-being of its users, which is important in today's digital landscape where people are spending increasing amounts of time on their devices. However, it is important to note that time limit features alone may not be sufficient in promoting digital well-being. Other measures such as content moderation, privacy protections, and educating users on the responsible use of digital technologies should also be considered. Nevertheless, the introduction of time limit features by TikTok is a positive step in the right direction towards promoting digital well-being. Ultimately, by regulating digital platforms to promote digital well-being, individuals can enjoy the benefits of digital technologies without compromising their mental and physical health.

8.6.2 Ensuring financial well-being

This can be considered a subset of digital well-being, but it is important and prominent, and it could be discussed separately. Money plays an integral part in our everyday life—we buy things online, send payments online, and save our money online through various fintechs and bank apps. With fintech bridging the gap between the highly regulated financial services sector and digital platforms being always of interest to digital consumers, regulations are important to reassure the consumers of their tractions, someone like an ombudsman to mediate between the brands, platforms developers and the digital consumer. The mediations could be to reduce financial crimes, money laundering, or simply to protect consumers making transactions online. In the UK, Payment Services Regulations 2017 regulate electronic payments and have led to a more secure and efficient payment system (Gov.uk, 2017). The regulations require digital payment service providers to take measures to prevent fraud and ensure the security of customers' funds. The European Union's 5th money laundering directive, or 5MLD for short, requires digital platforms to implement measures to prevent money laundering and terrorist financing. This helps to reduce financial crime and improve the overall integrity of the financial system (LexisNexis, 2023). The Dodd-Frank Act was enacted in the United States in response to the 2008 financial crisis. It includes a number of regulations aimed at increasing transparency and reducing risk in the financial system, including regulations for digital platforms such as crowdfunding portals (Hayes, 2023). Overall, regulating digital platforms has helped to reduce financial fraud and improve financial well-being by setting standards for security, transparency, and consumer protection. These regulations help to promote confidence in digital financial services, leading to increased adoption and greater financial inclusion.

8.6.3 Ethical considerations

Platform developers have a duty of care to the brands they work with and the customers they anticipate will engage on their platforms (Mogaji et al., 2023); however in some cases, the vested interest of the developers does not allow them to demonstrate their duty of care—they just want to get the platforms out there for people to use, get data from consumers, and monetise the information. This is where the regulators come in, to challenge bad practices, and remind the platform developers of their ethical responsibilities. Digital platforms collect vast amounts of personal data from users, including sensitive information like health and financial data. Regulations can help to protect user privacy by setting standards for data collection, use, and sharing, and by requiring companies to obtain user consent before collecting or sharing their data. The European Union's General Data Protection Regulation (GDPR) has set a higher standard for data protection and privacy, leading to ethical data practices on digital platforms. Under GDPR, companies must obtain user consent before collecting or using their data and must implement strict data protection measures. In the United States, the Children's Online Privacy Protection Act (COPPA) requires websites and online services to obtain parental consent before collecting personal information from children under 13. This regulation ensures that digital platforms are considering ethical considerations when it comes to collecting and using children's data. The regulation of digital platforms is important to ensure that these platforms are serving the interests of users and society as a whole, rather than just the interests of their own companies.

8.6.4 Avoiding misinformation

Regulation can also ensure that digital consumers are not misinformed, especially on social media. Digital platforms can be used to spread false information and harmful content, such as hate speech or disinformation campaigns. Regulation can help prevent the spread of such content and protect users from its negative effects. It is imperative to know that misinformation is not just on social media but could be on other digital platforms like the self-service kiosk, streaming services (Netflix, Apple TV), mobile apps, and websites. Imagine if you want to buy something on a website and there is wrong information, how would you feel? It is expected that platform developers and brands should ensure that their platform has the right information. Regulators would expect platform developers to implement content moderation policies and procedures to remove harmful or misleading content and ensure information on their platforms are correct and implement fact-checking measures to verify the accuracy of information shared on the platform. In addition, regulators would expect developers to use human moderators or automated systems to avoid this misinformation. Regulating digital platforms to prevent the spread of misinformation and harmful content is a complex issue that requires a multi-pronged approach. FactCheck.org, a prominent fact-checking organisation in the United States, has stated that their fact-checking process can take anywhere from a few hours to several days depending on the complexity of the issue. By implementing content moderation, fact-checking, transparency, and user education measures, digital platforms can help promote a healthier and more informed public discourse.

8.6.5 Promoting competition

Regulators have a holistic view of the ecosystem and they are responsible for maintaining healthy competition between the platform developers. Some digital platforms have become dominant players in their markets, making it difficult for competitors to enter and for users to switch to alternative platforms. Regulation can promote competition by ensuring a level playing field for all players in the market. Proposed legislation in Europe, Asia, and the United States may impose strict restrictions on how large technology companies can interact with smaller competitors and limit their utilisation of artificial intelligence technologies such as facial recognition (Schechner, 2022). It has been reported that the United States' Federal Trade Commission (FTC) is seeking to block Meta from acquiring Within Unlimited and its popular virtual reality dedicated fitness app, Supernatural. The European Union (EU) had to approve Apple's planned acquisition of British music discovery app Shazam when EU antitrust investigation showed it would not harm competition. Likewise, the UK Competition and Markets Authority (CMA) had to intervene and clear online food delivery company Takeaway.com's takeover of UK rival Just Eat, citing concerns that the acquisition would result in a significant reduction in competition and choice for consumers. It is anticipated that tech companies and developers will inspire the new wave of M&A deals, and regulators are expected to get more involved (Harvey, 2020). Overall, the trend of regulators scrutinising tech company mergers and acquisitions is likely to continue as concerns about anti-competitive behaviour and harm to consumers persist.

8.6.6 National security

This may have a political undertone, especially in those countries where one or two digital platforms have been banned; it is however important to recognise that regulating digital consumption can actually be for national security. This could be for reducing the spread of misinformation and propaganda, which can be used by malicious actors to sow discord and undermine national security. By requiring digital platforms to verify the accuracy of information and take down false or misleading content, regulators can help protect citizens from being misled or manipulated by foreign adversaries. From an international policy perspective, international cooperation is necessary to ensure that regulations are consistent across countries and that digital platforms cannot simply move to a different jurisdiction to avoid regulation. Following the 2016 US presidential election, concerns were raised about foreign interference in the democratic process. In response, countries like the United States and France have passed legislation requiring digital platforms to disclose information about political advertising and make efforts to prevent the spread of disinformation. This has helped to improve the integrity of elections and prevent foreign interference. The UK has passed legislation requiring digital platforms to remove terrorist content within a specified timeframe. According to a report by the UK Home Office, this legislation has resulted in the removal of over 300,000 pieces of terrorist content from online platforms. In the wake of the Christchurch mosque shootings in New Zealand, countries like Australia have passed legislation requiring digital platforms to remove violent and extremist content. This has helped to prevent the spread of hate speech and extremist content, which can contribute to radicalisation and pose a threat to national security.

From a device perspective (see Section 3.7 on difference between platform and devices), regulators also have a role to play, to ensure that the platforms are not hosted on devices that can jeopardise national security. For example, US Défense Department issued a new policy that prohibits the use of mobile devices made by Chinese tech companies like Huawei and ZTE, citing concerns about the potential for these devices to be used for espionage or cyberattacks. The UK government also warned that Huawei technology must be removed from the UK's 5G public networks by the end of 2027 under legal documents prepared by the world-leading National Cyber Security Centre (NCSC) and handed to broadband and mobile operators in the country. Similarly, the UK government had also banned the use of TikTok on government-issued mobile devices due to concerns over the security of the app. While the ban on TikTok may have a limited impact on the app's overall user base, it reflects a growing concern among governments around the world about the security risks associated with certain digital platforms and the need to take action to protect national security.

8.7 Who is regulating?

Regulating digital platforms can be a very daunting work—an ongoing, ever-demanding, and ever-evolving work, especially as the digital environment is changing and evolving, platform developers getting more innovative and consumers asking for more platforms, and regulators often have to catch up with these innovations. This section aims to identify key stakeholders responsible for regulating digital platforms.

8.7.1 The government

The government has a duty of care to its citizens, and it is not surprising to see different countries working on developing legislation, acts, and laws to control how consumers engage on digital platforms. From China to UAE and even Nigeria banning some digital platforms to EU, the UK, and the United States developing regulations, the governments are playing one role or the other to regulate digital consumption. The Chinese government has banned several major digital platforms, such as Facebook, Google, Twitter, and YouTube, due to concerns over their content and potential influence on Chinese society. Similarly, the Iranian government has blocked access to popular social media platforms like Twitter, Facebook, and Instagram, as well as messaging apps like Telegram and WhatsApp, perhaps in an effort to regulate how the citizen engage on digital platforms.

The government will often carry out extensive public policy and parliamentary process, engaging with different stakeholders including developers, brands, and users, to make sure everyone is involved in the development of the policy. The government can also give a regulatory power to implement these regulations. For example, the UK online safety bill aims to make the UK 'the safest place in the world to be online' and proposed a new regulatory regime with Ofcom as an independent regulator for providers of online user-to-user and search services. The governments can use antitrust laws to prevent digital platforms from becoming too dominant in their respective markets. This can involve breaking up companies, limiting their ability to acquire competitors, or imposing regulations to prevent anti-competitive behaviour. Governments can regulate how digital platforms moderate user-generated content to prevent harmful or illegal content from being shared. Governments can impose taxes on digital platforms to generate revenue and level the playing field with traditional businesses that are subject to more stringent tax regulations.

8.7.2 Regulatory bodies

In most cases, the government will delegate the regulations of digital platforms to regulatory bodies. These bodies are often empowered by the Act of parliament, to give authority to the regulator bodies to enact the law, review it when necessary, and even punish those who are flaunting the laws. Regulators for digital platforms can vary by country and region, but generally, government agencies such as the Federal Trade Commission (FTC) in the United States, the European Commission in the European Union, and the Ministry of Economy, Trade and Industry (METI) in Japan, among others, are responsible for ensuring the safety of digital consumers. Table 9.1 presents a list of regulatory bodies from different countries around the world. These regulatory bodies are tasked with enforcing laws and regulations that govern digital platforms, including data privacy, cybersecurity, consumer protection, and antitrust laws. They may investigate and take legal action against digital platforms that engage in illegal or unethical practices, such as misrepresenting their products or services, engaging in unfair competition, or violating users' privacy rights.

As seen with the UK Online Safety Bill, the Office of Communications, commonly known as Ofcom, the government-approved regulatory and competition authority for the broadcasting, telecommunications, and postal industries of the UK, has powers to demand information and data from tech companies, including on the role of their algorithms in selecting and displaying content, so it can assess how they are shielding users from harm. Ofcom as a regulator will be able to enter companies' premises to access data and equipment, request interviews with company employees, and require companies to undergo an external assessment of how they're keeping users safe. Ofcom can require that service providers use 'accredited technology' to identify harmful content and 'swiftly take down that content'. In the United States, the Department of Justice (DOJ) and Federal Trade Commission (FTC) have launched antitrust investigations into several large tech companies, including Google, Facebook, Amazon, and Apple. The regulators would have to check if these companies are engaging in anti-competitive behaviour that has harmed consumers and other businesses.

It is imperative to know that the regulators don't just regulate social media, they regulate digital consumptions on other digital platforms. E-commerce platforms like Amazon, Alibaba, and eBay are heavily regulated by governments to ensure that consumer rights are protected and that the products sold on these platforms meet certain safety standards. Online marketplaces like Uber, Airbnb, and TaskRabbit are subject to a variety of regulations, including licensing requirements, insurance regulations, and tax laws. Gaming platforms like Steam, Xbox Live, and PlayStation Network are regulated to ensure that the games they offer are appropriate for their intended audiences and that they meet certain technical and security standards. Streaming services like Netflix, Hulu, and Amazon Prime Video are subject to regulations around content and copyright, as well as regulations related to data privacy and security. Messaging apps like WhatsApp, WeChat, and Facebook Messenger are subject to regulations around data privacy and security, as well as regulations around content moderation to prevent the spread of harmful or illegal content.

8.7.3 Tech self-regulating

Here we see digital developers taking responsibility to regulate themselves, as often the digital platform developers would argue that they can regulate themselves better instead of the government and policymakers encroaching into their territory. Many tech companies including Meta and Twitter have long resisted calls for their platforms to be regulated but promised to regulate themselves (Bridge, 2022). From the social media platforms, Facebook established an independent oversight board to review and make decisions on controversial content moderation issues. The board is composed of experts from a range of backgrounds and is designed to provide an independent review process for user appeals and content decisions. Google introduced a set of privacy principles, aimed at providing clear and transparent guidance on how the company handles user data. The principles include a commitment to user control, transparency, and security, and are designed to ensure that users have greater control over their data and how it is used. Likewise, Twitter has the civic integrity policy, aimed at combating misinformation and election interference on the platform. The policy includes clear guidelines on what constitutes misinformation and how it will be addressed, as well as measures to promote transparency and accountability in political advertising.

From an AI perspective, the Microsoft Fairness Toolkit is intended to help developers identify and mitigate bias in AI systems and to ensure that these systems are fair and unbiased. IEEE Global Initiative on Ethics of Autonomous and Intelligent Systems is another effort towards self-regulations as it's based on a multi-disciplinary initiative focused on developing standards and guidelines for AI that are transparent, accountable, and human-centric. There is Partnership on AI, which is a multi-stakeholder organisation focused on promoting AI that is ethical, transparent, and socially responsible. In addition to government regulators and tech companies regulating themselves, there are also self-regulatory organisations (SROs) that oversee digital platforms. These organisations are industry-led and may establish guidelines and best practices for their members to follow. Examples of SROs include the Interactive Advertising Bureau (IAB) and the Digital Advertising Alliance (DAA), which set standards for online advertising and data collection.

While these examples demonstrate that tech developers are taking steps to regulate themselves, it is important to note that self-regulation alone may not be sufficient to address all the challenges and issues associated with digital platforms. Government and policymakers have an important role to play in setting standards and enforcing compliance, and in ensuring that the interests of users are protected and promoted. UK's digital secretary, Oliver Dowden, MP said in a speech in 2021 on the draft Online Safety Bill that 'The era of self-regulation for big tech has come to an end (UK Parliament, 2021). The companies are clearly responsible for services they have designed and profit from and need to be held to account for the decisions they make'. In his speech, Dowden called for a new regulatory framework to hold big tech companies accountable for the services they provide and the decisions they make, arguing that the era of self-regulation for these companies has come to an end. This submission raises the question of if and how tech companies can regulate themselves especially as they may prioritise commercial interests over user protection, leading to inadequate regulation and oversight and the regulations may not be consistent across the industry, leading to uneven and fragmented approaches to protecting user rights and ensuring ethical standards. For example, the same regulation for a main digital platform developer may not be applicable to a freelancer developer based in another country and working for a brand in the

UK. In addition, self-regulation may lack the legitimacy and accountability that comes with government oversight, leading to questions about the effectiveness and credibility of the self-regulatory system. Notwithstanding, it is imperative to develop codes of conduct and best practices and support collaborative approaches to promoting the responsible and ethical use of digital platforms.

8.7.4 The organisation

Organisations can also regulate how their staff engage on digital platforms. Organisations can provide policies and procedures that prohibit their staff from using a particular platform, and organisations can insist that their staff use a particular platform. Organisations can create a policy that outlines acceptable digital consumption practices, such as guidelines for social media use, email etiquette, and the use of personal devices during work hours. Organisations can monitor their staff's digital activities to ensure that they are complying with the organisation's policies and to identify any potential security risks or breaches. Organisations can block access to certain websites or apps that are not work-related or that pose security risks. Even for Universities for example, certain platforms are provided for teaching and learning even when there are alternatives. That's why you see some Universities prefer to use Microsoft Teams instead of using Zoom. Some organisations will not allow their staff to use social media on the work phone or laptop. Organisations can encourage their staff to take breaks from digital consumption, such as by taking regular breaks from screens, encouraging physical activity, and setting boundaries around work-related communication outside of working hours. It's important for organisations to strike a balance between regulating digital consumption and respecting their staff's privacy and autonomy. By developing policies and training programs that promote responsible digital consumption, organisations can help their staff use digital technologies more effectively and safely, while also protecting the organisation from potential risks or liabilities.

8.7.5 The digital consumer

The digital consumers themselves also have a responsibility to regulate their digital consumption. As iterated in Section 9.4, adults as digital consumers are exposed to harm on digital platforms but they are also able to control how they engage—they can choose to log out, choose to report the individual causing harm, or even choose to delete the app. Just like going to a night club and you see someone spiking your drink, you won't drink it and then call an ambulance, instead you will dispose the drink, possibly report the person and leave the club. Digital consumers are expected to use many of the tools provided by platform developers to improve their experiences on the platforms. With many digital platforms now including reporting tools that allow users to report inappropriate content or behaviour, digital consumers can use these features to enhance their experiences in the digital environment. Ultimately, there is the need for self-awareness and motivation, where consumers can choose to disengage, delete their social media account, or go on vacation with no phones. Digital consumers can also choose to regulate how much time they use on different platforms. Many digital platforms, including Apple's iOS and Google's Android operating systems, now include screen time controls that allow users to set limits on their app usage. These controls can help users to manage their time and reduce excessive use of digital platforms.

Likewise, as earlier discussed in Chapter 3 about digital consumer and analytics, there are digital platforms, such as Facebook and Instagram, that now include usage reports that allow users to see how much time they are spending on the app each day. This can help users to be more aware of their app usage and make informed decisions about how they use their time online. As a digital consumer, you can choose not to shop online and go to the high street to spend your cash. Choosing to detox and disengage from digital platforms does not mean you cease to be a digital consumer, it's all about taking responsibility for your well-being. In addition, digital consumers can engage with other platforms to help them regulate their activities. Some digital platforms, such as Calm and Headspace, have created well-being apps that can help users to manage stress, anxiety, and other mental health issues. These apps can help users to build healthy habits and manage their time more effectively. For those who may still choose to engage with the apps, they can benefit from focus mode, which allows users to temporarily pause notifications and limit distractions. This can help users to stay focused on important tasks and reduce the temptation to check their devices unnecessarily.

Reflective question

How can an organisation strike a balance between regulating their staff's digital consumption to promote productivity and security, while also respecting their staff's autonomy and privacy in their personal lives?

8.7.6 Parents and guardian

As iterated in Section 9.4, children are facing problems on digital platforms and parents have the responsibility to make sure their children are protected from harm. Parents and Guardians have a responsibility to regulate how their children consume digital technology, they can choose to provide digital devices and access to digital platforms at certain age, and they can choose to reduce screen time and stop them from downloading some apps (Holiday et al., 2022). Though the platform developers may have said children of a certain age cannot access the app, there are instances where children are bypassing this age barrier and using the platforms, though many digital platforms, including social media sites and video-sharing apps, have introduced age verification measures to prevent children from accessing age-inappropriate content. Parents should be using these measures to regulate their children's activities.

If children may want to insist on some platforms, there are child-friendly versions which can be more appropriate. For example, there are Facebook's Messenger Kids and YouTube Kids. These versions are designed to be age-appropriate and include additional safety features to protect children online. It is essential that parents, educators, and policymakers work together to protect children from the risks associated with online exposure to indecent images. This can be done through a combination of education, regulation, and technology solutions. Parents can play a crucial role in educating their children about safe Internet use and monitoring their online activity.

Parent has a responsibility to protect their children from exposure to indecent images; this could also be about restricting access to some website through the Wi-Fi in the house. With platform developers providing parental control features that allow parents to set limits on their child's online activity, including screen time and content access, parents can use these technologies to regulate how their children access technology. For example, YouTube Kids has a range of parental controls that allow parents to restrict certain types of content and monitor their child's activity. Additionally, parents, educators, and mental health professionals can play an important role in educating children about healthy social media use, promoting positive self-esteem and self-image, and providing access to resources and support for those who may be struggling. Overall, addressing the issue of children self-harming through social media requires a multifaceted approach that involves collaboration and support from various stakeholders. Overall, addressing this issue requires a collaborative effort to ensure that children are protected and have access to a safe and positive online experience.

8.8 Challenges in regulating digital consumption

Regulating digital platforms can be very challenging—for the regulators to enforce the rule, developers to understand the rule and shape their design, and brands to work with stakeholders and be sure they are not flaunting the rules. This section highlights some challenges for regulating digital platforms, creating awareness about it, and identifying how possible they can be addressed. Understanding these challenges is important for managers keen on managing consumer engagement in the digital environment.

8.8.1 Developers' hostility

Platform developers can be very protective of their territory and hostile to regulations, and there are possibilities that they can jeopardise the regulatory process. In 2016, the US Federal Bureau of Investigation (FBI) asked Apple to unlock an iPhone used by one of the San Bernardino terrorists. Apple initially refused, citing concerns about the security of its products and customer privacy. The FBI eventually found another way to unlock the phone, but the case highlighted the potential for tension between developers and government regulators (Nakashima & Albergotti, 2021). In the early 2000s, Microsoft faced a lengthy antitrust case brought by the US government and several states. The case alleged that Microsoft had engaged in anti-competitive practices by bundling its Internet Explorer browser with Windows, making it harder for competitors like Netscape to gain market share. The case dragged on for years, which some argue slowed down innovation in the browser market and gave Google an opportunity to gain dominance with its Chrome browser. In 2018, Amazon faced criticism for developing and marketing facial recognition technology that some argued was biased against people of colour (Paul, 2020). The technology was used by law enforcement agencies, raising concerns about potential racial profiling and civil rights violations. Amazon initially resisted calls for regulation or oversight of its facial recognition technology but eventually backed away from selling the technology to law enforcement agencies. WhatsApp has promised encryption of messages on their platform, a data confidentiality mechanism designed to help Internet users keep their online data and communications private and secure, but you need to reflect on what developers are proposing to safeguard the consumers and the demands of the government and regulators.

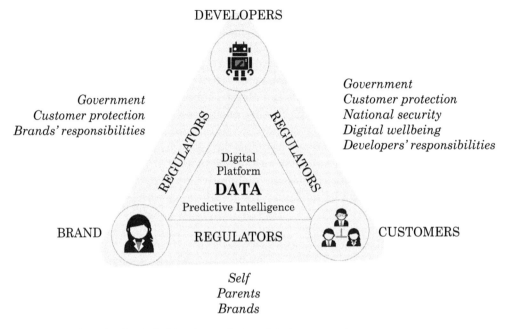

Figure 8.1 The role of stakeholders in regulating digital consumption

8.8.2 The evolving digital platforms

Digital platforms are constantly evolving, and regulators may struggle to keep up with new technologies and threats. It is crucial for regulators to stay informed and adapt regulations as necessary to address emerging threats and technological developments. The evolvement has now made technologies available to different people in different parts of the world, and digital platforms are often global in nature, meaning that they operate across multiple countries and jurisdictions. This can create challenges for regulators who need to navigate different legal frameworks and cultural norms. While regulating digital platforms can play an important role in ensuring national security, it is important to approach regulation critically and consider the potential benefits and drawbacks.

8.8.3 Expensive and complex task

Monitoring and enforcing these regulations can be very expensive, it requires human resources, time, and effort to make sure that the stakeholders, including brands, developers, and consumers are aware of the regulations and are able to change their business practices to align with the new regulations. Digital platforms can be difficult to regulate and enforce due to their complex and decentralised nature. It can be challenging for regulators to track and monitor the actions of individuals and organisations that operate in digital spaces. Moreover, government regulators often have limited resources and expertise when it comes to regulating digital platforms, which can make it difficult to keep up with the fast pace of technological change and effectively monitor and enforce regulations. In addition, digital platforms can be complex and multi-faceted, with different features and functions that may require different types of regulation.

For example, a social media platform may have features for messaging, video sharing, and live streaming, each of which may require different types of regulation. Overall, regulating digital platforms is a challenging and complex task that requires a nuanced and collaborative approach, as well as ongoing monitoring and adaptation to keep up with the fast pace of technological change.

8.8.4 Government responsibilities

Different countries have different levels of expectations when it comes to regulating digital consumption. Considering the world is becoming a global village where everyone is connected, there are inherent challenges with how governments are regulating technologies. For example, you might have WhatsApp in the UK but are unable to use it in the UAE. You might then be questioning if WhatsApp is bad, why would the UK accept it and the UAE is rejecting it? This reflective question can go for any of those restricted digital platforms. While some countries may be strict with their digital platform regulations, there are other countries that can be lenient or not putting much attention to data protection of their citizens. There are possible challenges with managing cross-border issues in digital platform development. Digital platforms operate globally, and government regulation may not be uniform across all jurisdictions. This can pose challenges in terms of enforcing regulation, preventing regulatory arbitrage, and ensuring that digital platforms operate in accordance with local laws and norms.

8.8.5 Ensuring digital liberty

Many people have complained and raised concerns about how digital platforms are being banned in some countries, and there is always the defence of national security. Balancing the digital consumers' freedom and liberty to use any digital platform and the governments' desire to control citizen activities is always a challenge and dilemma for regulators. You begin to ask, why do you cross the line between ensuring the well-being of consumers or becoming a dictator state, telling consumers what to use and what not to use? It is also important to reiterate denying digital consumers this digital liberty can have unintended consequences, such as driving innovation and investment away from certain countries or industries. Regulators must carefully consider the potential impact of regulations on innovation and competition to ensure that they do not stifle economic growth. Governments and organisations have a responsibility to protect digital liberties, which are an essential part of human rights in the digital age. This includes ensuring that people have access to the Internet, protecting their privacy and personal data, and preventing censorship or surveillance that might restrict their freedom of expression or access to information. Instead of denying people their digital liberty, we should work towards creating policies, regulations, and technologies that enable and protect digital liberties while ensuring safety, security, and accountability.

8.9 Conclusion

This chapter has provided an overview of regulating digital consumption. The fact that digital consumers are enjoying their time in the digital environment is not enough justification to regulate activities. There are inherent challenges affecting children, adults, brands, and various organisations and these have warranted the need for regulations. Digital platform regulations are an increasingly important topic in the modern era, as the power and influence of tech giants such as Facebook, Google, and Amazon have grown exponentially. While these companies have brought many benefits to consumers, they have also faced criticism for a range of issues, including privacy violations, data breaches, content moderation, and antitrust concerns. As a result, governments around the world are taking a closer look at how to regulate digital platforms in order to protect users and promote a fair and competitive marketplace.

Different regulatory bodies have been set up to develop, monitor, and enforce the regulations. Digital platform regulation is a complex and rapidly evolving area that requires careful consideration of the various trade-offs and impacts involved. While there is a clear need for regulation to address the harms and challenges posed by digital platforms, it is important to ensure that any regulations are well-designed, evidence-based, and able to achieve their intended goals without unintended consequences. Policymakers must recognise the need to carefully balance national security concerns with free speech rights, ensuring global cooperation, staying informed about emerging technologies, and considering the potential unintended consequences of regulation, and regulators can work to effectively address national security threats while promoting innovation and economic growth. It is also important to balance this with the need for innovation and growth in the digital sector. Over-regulation can stifle innovation and limit the potential benefits that digital technology can bring.

In conclusion, regulating digital platforms can be a daunting task, and both government regulators and developers have important roles to play in ensuring that digital platforms are safe, fair, and effective. While government regulation can help protect consumers and promote competition, it must be balanced with the need for innovation and the rights of developers. At the same time, developers must be willing to work collaboratively with regulators, be transparent about their operations and practices, and be willing to address potential harms and biases in their platforms. By working together, regulators and developers can help ensure that digital platforms continue to be valuable tools for innovation, communication, and social interaction, while also protecting the interests of users and society as a whole. It is important to recognise that there are many other types of digital platform regulations that are currently being discussed or implemented around the world. However, the effectiveness of these regulations can vary depending on a range of factors, including the specific regulatory approach, the ability of companies to comply, and the potential unintended consequences of regulation.

8.10 Student activities

1. Should social media platforms be held responsible for the content posted by their users? Why or why not?
2. Should the government regulate algorithms used by digital platforms to reduce bias and discrimination? Why or why not?
3. How can we best regulate digital platforms to protect consumer privacy?
4. What policies could be put in place to reduce the spread of fake news and misinformation online?

5. What are some different perspectives on digital platform regulation from industry associations, advocacy groups, and government agencies?

6. What are some potential solutions for addressing the challenges posed by digital platform regulation?

7. How does content moderation impact free speech on digital platforms?

8. What are the benefits of regulating digital consumption for children and vulnerable adults?

9. How can different stakeholders work together to develop and implement regulatory frameworks for digital platforms? What are some challenges that stakeholders might face in these processes, and how can they be addressed?

10. How can we develop innovative solutions to address specific challenges related to digital platform regulation, such as data privacy or algorithmic transparency? What are some potential obstacles to implementing these solutions, and how can they be overcome?

11. How can we effectively advocate for policy reforms related to digital platform regulation?

12. What are some key considerations to keep in mind when communicating these recommendations to policymakers and the wider public?

References and further reading

Abdulquadri, A., Mogaji, E., Kieu, T. & Nguyen, P., 2021. Digital transformation in financial services provision: A Nigerian perspective to the adoption of chatbot. *Journal of Enterprising Communities: People and Places in the Global Economy*, 15(2), pp. 258–281.

Abeele, M., 2021. Digital wellbeing as a dynamic construct. *Communication Theory*, 31(4), pp. 932–955.

Adeola, O. et al., 2021. Marketing bank services to financially vulnerable customers: Evidence from an emerging economy. *International Journal of Bank Marketing*, 39(3), pp. 402–428.

Agbo, F. et al., 2020. Social media usage for computing education: The effect of tie strength and group communication on perceived learning outcome. *International Journal of Education and Development using Information and Communication Technology*, 16(1), pp. 5–26.

Albayati , H., Kim, S. & Rho, J., 2020. Accepting financial transactions using blockchain technology and cryptocurrency: A customer perspective approach. *Technology in Society*, 62(1), 101320.

Balakrishnan, J., Nwoba, A. & Nguyen, N., 2021. Emerging-market consumers' interactions with banking chatbots. *Telematics and Informatics*, 65, 101711.

Bridge, G., 2022. Survey: The dark side of news consumption on social media [Online] Avail—able at: https://variety.com/vip/survey-the-dark-side-of-news-consumption-on-social-media -1235349747/

Chattopadhyay, A., Kupe, T., Schatzer, N. & Mogaji, E., 2022. Fireside chat with three vice chancellors from three continents. In: E. Mogaji, V. Jain, F. Maringe & R. Hinson, eds. *Re-imagining Higher Education in Emerging Economies*. Cham: Palgrave Macmillan, pp. 85–96.

Chemma, N., Abdelli, M. & Awasthi, A., 2022a. Management and information technology in the digital era: Conclusion and research agenda. In: N. Chemma, M. El Amine Abdelli, A. Awasthi, & E. Mogaji, eds. *Management and Information Technology in the Digital Era*. Bingley: Emerald, pp. 233–237.

Chemma, N., Abdelli, M. & Awasthi, A., 2022b. Management and information technology in the digital era: Introduction to edited collection on challenges and perspectives. In: *Management and information technology in the digital era.* Bingley: Emerald, pp. 1–6.

Chylinski, M. et al., 2020. Augmented reality marketing: A technology-enabled approach to situated customer experience. *Australasian Marketing Journal*, 28(4), pp. 374–384.

Crowley, K., 2022. Why deep learning holds the key to preventing cyberattacks before they can strike. *Cyber Security: A Peer-Reviewed Journal*, 6(2), pp. 148–153.

Dhruv, G., Hulland, J., Kopalle, P. & Karahanna, E., 2020. The future of technology and marketing: A multidisciplinary perspective. *Journal of the Academy of Marketing Science*, 48, pp. 1–8.

Dong, H., Yang, F., Lu, X. & Hao, W., 2020. Internet addiction and related psychological factors among children and adolescents in China during the coronavirus disease 2019 (COVID-19) epidemic. *Frontiers in Psychiatry*, 11, p. 751.

Dwivedi, Y. et al., 2022. Metaverse beyond the hype: Multidisciplinary perspectives on emerging challenges, opportunities, and agenda for research, practice and policy. *International Journal of Information Management*, 66, 102542.

Flew , T., Martin, F. & Suzor, N., 2019. Internet regulation as media policy: Rethinking the question of digital communication platform governance. *Journal of Digital Media & Policy*, 10(1), pp. 33–50.

Glynn, E. & Brown, D., 2020. Discrimination on football Twitter: The role of humour in the othering of minorities. *Sport in Society.* https://doi.org/10.1080/17430437.2022.2144726, pp. 1–12.

Gov.uk, 2017. The payment services regulations 2017 [Online]. Available at: https://www.legislation.gov.uk/uksi/2017/752/contents/made

Harvey, D., 2020. How technology has inspired the new wave of M&A deals [Online]. Available at: https://www.markssattin.co.uk/general/2020-11/how-technology-has-inspired-the-new-wave-of-m-a-deals

Hayes, A., 2023. Dodd-Frank Act: What it does, major components, criticisms [Online]. Available at: https://www.investopedia.com/terms/d/dodd-frank-financial-regulatory-reform-bill.asp

Hein, A. et al., 2020. Digital platform ecosystems. *Electronic Markets*, 30, pp. 87–98.

Hodapp, D. & Hanelt, A., 2022. Interoperability in the era of digital innovation: An information systems research agenda. *Journal of Information Technology*, 37(4), pp. 407–427.

Holiday, S., Norman, M. & Densley, R., 2022. Sharenting and the extended self: Self-representation in parents' Instagram presentations of their children. *Popular Communication*, 20(1), pp. 1–15.

Jelovac, D., Ljubojević, C. & Ljubojević, L., 2022. HPC in business: The impact of corporate digital responsibility on building digital trust and responsible corporate digital governance. *Digital Policy, Regulation and Governance*, 24(6), pp. 485–497.

Kandampully, J., Bilgihan, A. & Li, D., 2022. Unifying technology and people: Revisiting service in a digitally transformed world. *The Service Industries Journal*, 42(1–2), pp. 21–41.

Khalil, A., Abdelli, M. & Mogaji, E., 2022. Do digital technologies influence the relationship between the COVID-19 crisis and SMEs' resilience in developing countries? *Journal of Open Innovation: Technology, Market, and Complexity*, 8(2), pp. 100–109.

Khan, I., Ahmad, M. & Majava, J., 2021. Industry 4.0 and sustainable development: A systematic mapping of triple bottom line, circular economy and sustainable business models perspectives. *Journal of Cleaner Production*, 297, 126655.

Kopalle, P., Kumar, V. & Subramaniam, M., 2020. How legacy firms can embrace the digital ecosystem via digital customer orientation. *Journal of the Academy of Marketing Science*, 48, pp. 114–131.

LexisNexis, 2023. 5th EU anti-money laundering directive [Online]. Available at: https://risk
.lexisnexis.com/global/en/insights-resources/white-paper/what-you-need-to-know-about-the
-fifth-eu-aml-directive

McKinsey, 2022. Marketing in the metaverse: An opportunity for innovation and experimentation [Online]. Available at: https://www.mckinsey.com/capabilities/growth-marketing-and-
sales/our-insights/marketing-in-the-metaverse-an-opportunity-for-innovation-and
-experimentation

Miric, M., Boudreau, K. & Jeppesen, L., 2019. Protecting their digital assets: The use of formal
& informal appropriability strategies by App developers. *Research Policy*, 48(8), 103738.

Mogaji, E., 2021. *Brand Management*. Cham: Springer.

Mogaji, E., Restuccia, M., Lee, Z. & Nguyen, N., 2023. B2B brand positioning in emerging
markets: Exploring positioning signals via websites and managerial tensions in top-performing
African B2B service brands. *Industrial Marketing Management*, 108, pp. 237–250.

Mogaji, E., Soetan, T. & Kieu, T., 2020. The implications of artificial intelligence on the digital
marketing of financial services to vulnerable customers. *Australasian Marketing Journal*,
29(3), pp. 235–242.

Mogaji, E., Wirtz, J., Belk, R. & Dwivedi, Y., 2023. Immersive Time (ImT). *International
Journal of Information Management*, 72, 102659.

Morgan-Thomas, A., Dessart, L. & Veloutsou, C., 2020. Digital ecosystem and consumer
engagement: A socio-technical perspective. *Journal of Business Research*, 121, pp.
713–723.

Nakashima, E. & Albergotti, R., 2021. The FBI wanted to unlock the San Bernardino shooter's
iPhone. It turned to a little-known Australian firm [Online]. Available at: https://www
.washingtonpost.com/technology/2021/04/14/azimuth-san-bernardino-apple-iphone-fbi/

Olson, E., Olson, K., Czaplewski, A. & Key, T., 2021. Business strategy and the management of
digital marketing. *Business Horizons*, 64(2), pp. 285–293.

Oosthuizen, K., Botha, E., Robertson, J. & Montecchi, M., 2021. Artificial intelligence in retail:
The AI-enabled value chain. *Australasian Marketing Journal*, 29(3), pp. 264–273.

Paul, K., 2020. Amazon to ban police use of facial recognition software for a year [Online]. Available at:
https://www.theguardian.com/technology/2020/jun/10/amazon-rekognition-software-police-
black-lives-matter#:~:text=When%20it%20was%20first%20released,effect%20on%20non
%2Dwhite%20people.

Ponzoa, J. & Erdmann, A., 2021. E-commerce customer attraction: Digital marketing techniques,
evolution and dynamics across firms. *Journal of Promotion Management*, 27(5), pp. 697–715.

Riquelme, I., Román, S., Cuestas, P. & Iacobucci, D., 2019. The dark side of good reputation
and loyalty in online retailing: When trust leads to retaliation through price unfairness.
Journal of Interactive Marketing, 47(1), pp. 35–52.

Sağkaya Güngö, A. & Ozansoy Çadırcı, T., 2022. Understanding digital consumer: A review,
synthesis, and future research agenda. *International Journal of Consumer Studies*, 46(5),
pp. 1829–1858.

Schechner, S., 2022. Big tech braces for a wave of regulation [Online]. Available at: https://www
.wsj.com/articles/big-tech-braces-for-wave-of-regulation-11642131732

Sheth, J., 2020. Impact of Covid-19 on consumer behavior: Will the old habits return or die?
Journal of Business Research, 117, pp. 280–283.

Shree, S., Pratap, B., Saroy, R. & Dhal, S., 2021. Digital payments and consumer experience in
India: A survey based empirical study. *Journal of Banking and Financial Technology*, 5(1),
pp. 1–20.

Soetan, T., Mogaji, E. & Nguyen, N., 2021. Financial services experience and consumption in
Nigeria. *Journal of Services Marketing*, 35(7), pp. 947–961.

Stecklow, S., 2018. Facebook removes Burmese translation feature after Reuters report [Online].
Available at: https://www.reuters.com/article/cbusiness-us-facebook-myanmar-hate-speec-idCA
KCN1LM200-OCABS

UK Parliament, 2021. No longer the land of the lawless: Joint Committee reports [Online]. Available at: https://committees.parliament.uk/committee/534/draft-online-safety-bill-joint -committee/news/159784/no-longer-the-land-of-the-lawless-joint-committee-reports/

Wirtz, J., Kunz, W., Hartley, N. & Tarbit, J., 2023. Corporate digital responsibility in service firms and their ecosystems. *Journal of Service Research*, 26(2), pp. 173–190.

Zhu, C., Huang, S., Evans, R. & Zhang, W., 2021. Cyberbullying among adolescents and children: A comprehensive review of the global situation, risk factors, and preventive measures. *Frontiers in Public Health*, 9, 634909.

CHAPTER 9

Dark side of digital consumption

9.1 Background

Despite the bright sides of digital consumption, we cannot ignore the dark sides. The developers working on the good sides can also work on the dark sides. The consumers enjoying the good sides of digital consumption can also experience the dark sides, which can be traumatising. It is imperative for managers interested in understanding and managing consumer experiences in a digital environment to be mindful of these dark sides. This chapter builds on the idea of regulations discussed in the previous chapter and recognises that when regulations are out of the way, these dark sides are experiences. The regulations are like a gatekeeper and barriers to mitigate these dark sides. This chapter provides an overview of dark sides, contextualised relevant examples of dark sides from the triple bottom line framework, recognising the impact on people, profit, and the planet. The chapter offers an understanding of the role of developers and brands in promoting responsible digital consumption and developing practical strategies and steps they can take to protect consumers. It concludes by offering hope for the future, suggesting that even though there are negative aspects of digital consumption, there are also steps that can be taken to mitigate these negative effects.

9.2 Learning outcomes

By the end of this chapter, you should be able to:

- Describe the concept of dark sides in digital consumption.
- Identify different examples of dark sides in digital consumption.
- Recognise the implication of dark sides on key stakeholders.
- Understand the impact of dark sides on digital consumption.
- Describe practical action plans for stakeholders to manage the dark sides of digital consumption.

DOI: 10.4324/9781003389842-9

9.3 Introduction

Digital consumption allows brands, customers, and developers to engage on platforms. Everyone has benefited from the bright sides of digital platforms and consumption—innovative business solutions which enhanced business operations, job opportunities for many tech developers, entertainment, and enhanced life satisfaction for consumers. Digital platforms have bridged the gap between brands and consumers, with manifold opportunities for sales, engagement, and data from user-generated content (Paniagua et al., 2017). Digital platforms create efficient ways of working and organising, to develop new products and services, and to address and influence users, customers, clients, and the broader public. Engagement between firms and consumers is being democratised (Kietzmann et al., 2011). Everyone is on the same level playing ground to engage. You can send a tweet to a president, virtually explore San Francisco through a headset, buy things online for friends in another city, and join online classes from your room.

Though research and practice have mostly focused on the 'bright side' of digital consumption, there are increasingly observable concerns around the dark sides of digital consumption. These dark sides of digital consumption have significantly influenced cognitive, emotional, social, and mental health outcomes (Immordino-Yang et al., 2012). These dark sides are experienced on different types of platforms, suggesting the need for managers and developers to be aware of things that can affect consumer experiences on digital platforms (Talwar et al., 2019). The dark sides (which can also be described as negative effects of digital consumption) refer to things that will discourage a consumer not to use a platform, things that could stop a brand from adopting the digital platform for their consumer engagement, and also things that can stop a developer working on a platform. Recognise these three stakeholders as we explore the impact of dark sides in digital consumption.

This chapter explores dark sides in the context of the triple bottom line framework, recognising the impact on people, profit, and the planet (Khan et al., 2021), suggesting that everyone—either the brand, consumer, or developers, is affected. The chapter recognises different dark sides from different platforms, provided some relevant theoretical underpinning into dark sides of digital platforms, especially across some common platforms, and offers relevant implications on action plans going forward. Managers have to take more responsibilities in recognising these dark sides and putting measures to address them.

It is expected that at the conclusion of the chapter, you should have an increased awareness of the negative effects of digital consumption on people (digital consumers), profit (brands and developers), and the planet (digital sustainability). This chapter will enhance a deeper comprehension of the ways in which the dark sides of digital consumption can affect individuals and strategies to manage these dark sides. Ultimately this chapter is about increased critical thinking skills and the ability to analyse the positive and negative aspects of digital consumption, and to make informed decisions about how to engage with digital media in a responsible and healthy way.

9.4 Defining the dark side of digital consumption

Dark sides of digital consumption can be described as the negative consequences that consumers and communities face from engaging on digital platforms. This definition is adapted from Baccarella et al.'s (2018, p. 433) definition of the 'dark side' of social media. It is imperative that the dark side of digital consumption is not limited to social media (a form of shared media, see Chapter 5) but all forms of digital platform that supports digital consumption. Social media (and other digital platforms) has a dark side to it which is looming larger by the day, and it is damaging the freedom and well-being of communities and individuals (Baccarella et al., 2018). The dark side of digital consumption refers to the negative consequences and harmful effects that result from our increasing reliance on and consumption of digital technologies and platforms. This can include a wide range of issues, such as decreased privacy, cyberbullying, addiction, social isolation, increased energy consumption and carbon footprint, the spread of misinformation and fake news, and the displacement of workers due to automation, among others. These negative effects can impact individuals, society as a whole, and the environment, and require thoughtful consideration and action to address.

With digital consumption, the degree of brightness or darkness is often a subjective matter, as it depends on various factors such as individual perspectives, cultural norms, and social values. What one person might view as a positive aspect of digital consumption, such as access to information and the ability to connect with others online, another person might view as a negative aspect, such as privacy concerns or the risk of addiction. Moreover, the impact of digital consumption can also vary depending on the context and the particular technology or platform being used. For example, social media platforms can have both positive and negative effects on mental health, depending on factors such as how they are used, the content being shared, and the individual's personal circumstances. Digital consumption can be a double-edged sword, both for users and brands (Mogaji & Nguyen, 2022). Like any other consumption and phenomena—including fast food, capital markets, crowdsourcing, sharing economy, and even dating, there can be negative or detrimental consequences on society, but individuals may want to explore it differently. For example, how many hours on gaming defines addiction? Even though there may not be a fixed number, the negative impact cannot be overemphasised.

The digital revolution is changing the way we live and interact, but it is neither sustainable nor equitable. Despite the numerous wonders that have accompanied the digital revolution, upon reflection, Tapscott (2016) arrived at a somewhat disheartening realisation: The anticipated 'promise' of a more equitable, just, and sustainable world through digital advancement has gone unfulfilled. Tapscott (2016) further noted that a number of tech giants, including Google, Amazon, and others, have become dominant players in various industries, in part due to their ability to operate more efficiently with fewer employees. Meanwhile, service aggregators like Uber, Lyft, and Airbnb hold significant power to disrupt traditional industries such as taxis and hotels, potentially leading to job losses. Additionally, data harvesting companies like Facebook are accumulating vast amounts of data that position them to exert control over multiple industries. The consequences of many technological innovations, intentional and unintentional, are usually not dichotomous, but simultaneously have both bright and dark sides. The upward spiral in demand for hardware is rapidly increasing the extraction of ramping-up extraction of rare earth minerals and other precious metals including cobalt (Kuntsman & Rattle, 2019; Town et al., 2022). There are inherent challenges that our digital consumption has presented us, it is imperative that we acknowledge them and make effort to address them.

9.5 Dark sides of digital consumption and the triple bottom line (TBL)

This chapter section critically evaluates these dark sides by connecting it to the triple bottom line. Triple bottom line (TBL) is a framework that considers the social, environmental, and economic impacts of an organisation's activities (Elkington, 2008). The three 'bottom lines' in this framework refer to the three areas of impact: People, planet, and profit. The TBL approach recognises that businesses and organisations have a responsibility to not only generate economic profit but also to consider their impact on society and the environment. As the TBL approach encourages organisations to balance these three bottom lines, the dark side of digital consumption is explored in this context, to evaluate the actions of brands and developers, how they are negatively impacting broader society and environment, and hopefully change their business practices.

9.5.1 Dark side on people

Digital consumption can have negative impacts on people's well-being and social interactions, including addiction to social media and digital devices, cyberbullying, and decreased face-to-face communication. These issues can affect people's mental health, relationships, and sense of community. These are reasons why people may not want to use digital platforms to engage with brands and other digital consumers. Think about this, if you have had a bad experience at a night club, you may not want to go back, you don't trust the people, and even the club owner to protect you. Likewise, people are facing significant problems and experiencing the dark sides of digital consumption. Many researches have established these dark sides—from social media, mobile money, gaming, and shopping (Conti et al., 2018; Mogaji & Nguyen, 2022; Okazaki et al., 2021; Bhutani & Behl, 2023; Baccarella et al., 2018). There are concerns over cyberbullying, harassment, hate speech, misinformation, and possible over-information and information overload. Where there is an app for everything, content abounds everywhere and there is the inability to make choice due to overload of information. This is known as decision paralysis or analysis paralysis. It occurs when there are too many options to choose from, or when there is too much information to process. This can lead to feelings of anxiety and stress and can even result in procrastination or avoidance of the decision altogether.

The digital divide between Global North and Global South is also another dark side of digital platforms (Lythreatis et al., 2022). The Global North generally refers to developed countries with advanced economies, while the Global South includes developing and underdeveloped countries with lower economic growth rates. Richer countries in North America, Western Europe, and East Asia house well over 90% of the world's data centres, while Latin American and African states are home to less than 2%. A significant dark side is the unequal access to technology and the Internet, which is prevalent in the Global South. According to the International Telecommunication Union's (ITU) latest data (2021), about 46% of the global population do not have access to the Internet. In the Global North, around 82% of the population has access to the Internet, while in the Global South, only around 35% of the population has access. This significant gap in Internet access highlights the unequal access to technology and the Internet, which is prevalent in the Global South. This divide is due to various factors, including the lack of infrastructure, high cost of devices and Internet connectivity, limited education, and language barriers. As a result, people in the Global South may not have the same opportunities to access information, education, and job opportunities as those in the Global North (Chattopadhyay et al., 2022). Moreover, the digital divide perpetuates existing inequalities, as those without access to digital platforms are further marginalised and left behind. This can lead to a significant economic and social disadvantage, affecting the ability of individuals and communities to participate in the global economy and society.

Beyond access to digital technology posing as a dark side, the design and development of these digital platforms can also perpetuate inequality which affects people, this could be someone who is a dwarf and struggles to use the self-service machine at the station because it's very high, visually impaired digital consumer not able to access a website, or an individual who may have difficulty accessing a touchscreen device if they have limited finger mobility or strength. In June 2022, Robert Jahoda, a visually impaired user, sued DraftKing for inaccessibility. Jahoda claims the company's website was not compatible with popular screen-reading software. Digital platforms can be designed with accessibility in mind, such as by incorporating keyboard shortcuts or providing alternative methods of input (e.g., voice commands or touchpads). Additionally, platforms can provide alternative text or audio descriptions of visual content to make them accessible to users with visual impairments.

The future of society, work, and interaction with other people is changing (Hampton, 2016; Khalil et al., 2022; Chemma et al., 2022). Where we work, how we engage, how we meet our friends and family are changing. Not surprisingly this is a concern about how digital platforms alleviate and exacerbate feelings of loneliness. Study shows that 71% of people spend more time with their smartphone than their romantic partner and most people (54%) prefer the company of their smartphone compared to the company of their partner (SellCell, 2021). Even with the growing adoption of self-checkouts at supermarkets, there are talking lanes—a designated lane or checkout line where customers can engage in conversation with the cashier or other customers, this allows people to move out from the bubble of digital platforms and engage with others. Research has suggested that excessive social media use can lead to feelings of loneliness and depression, especially among young people (Boursier et al., 2020; Cauberghe et al., 2021). This may be because social media can create unrealistic expectations about what social interactions should look like, or because it can lead to social comparison and feelings of inadequacy. Many people are also losing their jobs because of AI, automation, and cheaper labour from other parts of the world. Moreover, many people are getting unfair decisions because many AI and automated decision-making systems are often deployed as a background process, unknown and unseen by those they impact, and many vulnerable people are being affected by these dark sides of digital platforms.

9.5.2 Dark side on planet

Digital consumption can contribute to environmental problems such as increased energy consumption, e-waste, and pollution, which can harm the planet and its ecosystems. It can also lead to increased consumption and waste, as digital devices and services often encourage a culture of disposability. With the growing demand for modern digital technologies (from tablets and smartphones to televisions and electric cars), there is pressure on natural resources, including minerals, metals, fossil fuels, and water. These resources are required for the manufacturing and operation of various digital devices and infrastructure, such as smartphones, computers, servers, data centres, and communication networks (Bilal et al., 2014; Yuan et al., 2022).

The electricity for powering data centres around the world is also increasing, and with Internet traffic increasing by 23% in 2021 and the vast and distributed digital infrastructure, there is a scaling up in energy consumption and carbon emissions (Telegeography, 2022). In 2021, the energy consumption of data transmission networks worldwide was estimated to be between 260 and 340 TWh, accounting for approximately 1.1–1.4% of the world's total electricity usage (IEA, 2022). Likewise, the production of smartphones and other electronic devices requires the extraction of rare earth elements, which are found in limited quantities and often in environmentally sensitive areas. The production of electric cars requires the mining of lithium, cobalt, and nickel, which can have significant environmental and social impacts.

A study showed that training a large AI model, that is, feeding data into the system and making predictions, can emit more than 284 tonnes of CO_2. Data centres, which are the backbone of the Internet and cloud services, consume vast amounts of electricity to power and cool the servers. Similarly, in the case of Bitcoin and other cryptocurrencies which rely on blockchain technology, the validation process requires vast amounts of electricity, which translates into a significant level of carbon emissions. It is essential to promote sustainable practices and responsible resource management in the design, production, and disposal of digital technologies. This can include the use of recycled materials, the development of more energy-efficient devices, and the adoption of renewable energy sources.

Another perspective on dark side of technology is the number of devices that consumers have. Don't be surprised if many people have two or three mobile phones lying around the house which they are not using. This is an emerging trend of digital consumers where they will always want to have new gadgets. According to a 2022 report by the Global E-waste Statistics Partnership (GESP), the world generated 53.6 million metric tons of e-waste in 2019, and this is projected to increase to 74.7 million metric tons by 2030 (Baldé et al., 2022). Mobile phones account for a significant portion of e-waste. According to a Mazuma post, 150+ million smartphones reach landfills every year, creating a devastating effect on the environment (Mazuma, 2023). It is also important to encourage consumers to use digital technologies in a more sustainable manner, such as reducing e-waste through proper disposal and recycling, and reducing energy consumption through more efficient use of devices.

9.5.3 Dark side on profit

The negative effect of digital consumption has a significant impact on profit—the profit of the developers working on the platforms and the profits of brands using these platforms to engage their consumers. The dark side of digital consumption can have economic impacts such as increased corporate power and market dominance, decreased competition, and economic inequality. This can lead to fewer choices for consumers and less innovation, as well as negative impacts on workers and communities. The impact of cyberbullying, harassment, and misinformation on consumer cannot be overemphasised. These negative experiences can have a profound and lasting effect on the mental health, emotional well-being, and even physical safety of individuals. Consumers will not be willing to engage on these platforms if things are not done properly and if they are not safe and their well-being is not guaranteed. This dark side can lead to a loss of trust and credibility among consumers. Platform developers and start-up founders need to know that this dark side can result in reduced usage of their products and services, which can ultimately lead to a decline in revenue. These negative experiences can lead to a decline in user engagement, which can impact the effectiveness of targeted advertising and other revenue-generating activities on digital platforms. in 2017, YouTube faced a major advertising boycott after it was revealed that ads were being displayed alongside extremist and inappropriate content. Several major advertisers pulled their ads from the platform, leading to a loss of revenue for YouTube and parent company Google. More recently, Twitter faced criticism for its handling of misinformation and hate speech on the platform, leading to a decline in user engagement and a loss of advertising revenue. Moreover, tech companies may face legal and regulatory consequences if they are found to be facilitating or condoning such behaviour on their platforms. This can result in fines, legal fees, and reputational damage, which can have a significant impact on the profitability of the company.

The tech industry has been known for its rapid growth and constant innovation. However, as the industry evolves and changes, there are certain dark sides that emerge, such as outsourcing and laying off staff. Outsourcing is a common practice in the tech industry, where companies contract work to third-party vendors or move jobs to countries with lower labour costs. With COVID-19 changing how we work, highlighting the possibilities of working from home, there are possibilities of recruiting staff from different parts of the world to do the work. While outsourcing may benefit companies by reducing costs, it can have negative consequences for employees, who may lose their jobs or be forced to accept lower wages. In addition to outsourcing, tech companies may also lay off staff as part of cost-cutting measures. These layoffs can have a significant impact on the affected employees, as they may struggle to find new jobs in a highly competitive industry. Alfonseca and Zahn (2023) reported on tech companies that have made cuts in 2023 and how it affects the dynamics in the industry. Amazon will lay off an additional 9,000 workers, Yahoo will lay off 20% of its workforce. Twilio, a cloud computing company, announced that it will be reducing its staff by approximately 17%, which equates to around 1,500 employees. Zoom laid off roughly 1,300 employees, which amounts to 15% of the company's workforce. Payments company PayPal is cutting 7% of its staff, which amounts to about 2,000 employees. SAP, the biggest software company in Europe, will lay off 2.5% of its global workforce, which amounts to about 2,800 employees. Spotify, the Sweden-based music streaming platform, will lay off 6% of its workforce, which amounts to about 600 employees. Alphabet Inc., the parent company of Google, will lay off 12,000 jobs from its global workforce, impacting approximately 6% of the company's employees while Microsoft plan to lay off 10,000 employees, affecting nearly 5% of Microsoft's global workforce. As a dark side of digital consumption, layoffs in the tech industry can lead to feelings of job insecurity and anxiety among employees. Layoffs can also have a negative impact on the profitability of the organisation. When companies lay off workers, they may also be losing valuable talent and experience that cannot be easily replaced. This can impact the quality of the company's products or services, leading to a decline in customer satisfaction and revenue. Additionally, layoffs can also damage the company's reputation, as they may be seen as a sign of instability or a lack of concern for employees. This can lead to decreased morale among remaining employees, making it difficult to attract and retain top talent in the future.

You can have staff sabotaging digital platforms which can cause significant damage to a company's reputation and profits in several ways. The actions of a staff member had serious consequences for the company's reputation and profits. Customers and stakeholders may lose trust in the company's ability to protect their data and maintain secure systems, leading to loss of business and revenue. Additionally, legal and regulatory consequences may arise from such incidents, further impacting the company's reputation and financial stability. In Kenya, a former employee of Kenya's Independent Electoral and Boundaries Commission (IEBC) was accused of hacking into the commission's systems during the 2017 presidential elections. The individual allegedly accessed and manipulated election results, which led to the nullification of the election by the Kenyan Supreme Court (Reuters, 2017). This incident not only resulted in financial loss but also undermined the credibility of the IEBC and the democratic process in Kenya. In the UK, a former employee of the tech company Sage was jailed for sabotaging the company's systems in 2016. The individual accessed and destroyed payroll data of nearly 300 companies, causing significant financial loss and reputational damage to Sage (Whitfield, 2016). While these examples may have jeopardised the brand, there are possible positive outcomes from staff sabotaging bad practices.

Timnit Gebru was a research scientist and co-lead of the ethical artificial intelligence team at Google, where she worked on issues such as bias and fairness in machine learning systems. In December 2020, Gebru was fired by Google after she published a paper discussing the risks of large language models, which are a type of artificial intelligence system that has been shown to produce biased and harmful outputs. Gebru claimed that her dismissal was the result of her raising concerns about Google's treatment of underrepresented minorities in the company. Developers need to be aware of the impact of their business operations and how they manage the working relationships of their staff and possibly provide policies that support whistle-blowers in exposing ethical issues and ensuring greater transparency and accountability in the tech industry. Table 9.1 presents a summary of the dark sides of digital consumption conceptualised with the triple bottom line and possible solutions.

9.6 Dark sides of digital consumption and digital platforms

While the dark side of digital consumption has been explored in the context of the triple bottom line, this section aims to critically evaluate the dark side in the context of digital platforms, specifically to recognise the platform as an avenue for brands, consumers, and developers to engage and interact. By exploring these dark sides, managers will be able to challenge their developers to address it, and they will be able to plan to mitigate the dark sides and ultimately manage digital consumer expectations.

9.6.1 Paid platform

This is a platform that has been provided by a developer, and a brand has paid for it to make sure for a certain time or make use of certain features; you can see this as a subscription platform, like the Shopify for e-commerce, Google Drive for cloud storage, or Monday.com for project management. It is imperative to reflect on what are the dark

Table 9.1 Summary of the dark sides of digital consumption conceptualised with the triple bottom line and possible solutions

Triple Bottom Line	Dark Sides of Digital Consumption	Possible Solutions
People	▪ Digital consumption can have negative impacts on well-being and social interactions. ▪ Dark sides of digital consumption include addiction, cyberbullying, and decreased face-to-face communication. ▪ Concerns exist over cyberbullying, harassment, hate speech, and misinformation. ▪ The digital divide between the Global North and Global South is significant. ▪ Design and development of digital platforms can perpetuate inequality. ▪ Excessive social media use can lead to feelings of loneliness and depression. ▪ Automation and AI are leading to job loss and unfair decision-making.	▪ Promote digital literacy and responsible digital consumption. ▪ Encourage face-to-face communication and social interaction. ▪ Develop policies to prevent cyberbullying and trolling. ▪ Promote media literacy and critical thinking skills to combat misinformation. ▪ Increase transparency and regulation around data collection and usage. ▪ Close the digital divide through increased access to technology and digital literacy programs. ▪ Encourage digital detox and mindfulness practices to promote mental health.
Planet	▪ Digital consumption can harm the environment through energy consumption, e-waste, and pollution. ▪ Digital devices and services promote a culture of disposability and increased consumption and waste. ▪ The demand for modern digital technologies leads to pressure on natural resources. ▪ Data centres' electricity consumption is increasing, resulting in higher carbon emissions. ▪ The production of digital devices requires rare earth elements found in limited quantities and sensitive areas. ▪ Cryptocurrencies like Bitcoin require significant amounts of electricity, leading to carbon emissions.	▪ Promote energy efficiency and renewable energy sources. ▪ Implement circular economy practices to reduce e-waste and encourage recycling. ▪ Develop sustainable supply chains for rare earth minerals. ▪ Encourage responsible consumption through education and awareness campaigns. ▪ Promoting sustainable practices and responsible resource management can reduce the negative environmental impact of digital technologies.

(Continued)

Table 9.1 (Continued)

Triple Bottom Line	Dark Sides of Digital Consumption	Possible Solutions
Profit	■ Digital consumption has negative economic impacts including increased corporate power, decreased competition, and economic inequality, which can impact the profit of platform developers and brands that use them. ■ Cyberbullying, harassment, and misinformation can harm mental health, emotional well-being, and physical safety of individuals, leading to a loss of trust and credibility among consumers and resulting in reduced usage of products and services, leading to a decline in revenue. ■ Legal and regulatory consequences may result from facilitating or condoning such behaviour on platforms, leading to fines, legal fees, and reputational damage. ■ Negative experiences can lead to a loss of income, such as YouTube's advertising boycott and Twitter's decline in user engagement and advertising revenue. ■ The negative impact of digital consumption can lead to fewer choices for consumers, less innovation, and negative impacts on workers and communities.	■ Enforce antitrust laws to prevent market concentration. ■ Encourage competition through regulatory frameworks and incentives. ■ Promote consumer education and awareness. ■ Implement policies to promote economic equality. ■ It is essential to promote responsible behaviour and accountability among digital platform developers, brands, and users to mitigate the negative impact of digital consumption. ■ By promoting transparency, user privacy, and ethical practices, it is possible to build trust and credibility among consumers and build a more sustainable digital economy and society.

sides of these types of platforms, and who is responsible? Would that be the developer? and what you expect the brands (paying for the platform) to do? One of the dark sides is the high cost of having these platforms which may be discouraging for many businesses, with consumers reflecting on the choices and seeking alternatives. Brands may explore if they need to keep paying for Zoom or migrate to Google Meets. The lack of value can also be considered a dark side, especially when it comes to how much restrictions are on the platforms for the brands. In addition, control over ownership, content, and operations for brands on paid platforms can present a dark side.

In January 2021, the social media platform Parler was removed from the app stores of Apple and Google and suspended by Amazon Web Services due to concerns over the platform's content moderation policies and the potential for the platform to incite violence. This highlights the potential risks of limited control on a paid platform. Even Donald Trump was removed from Twitter and it's not surprising to see that he had to go create his own platform—Truth Social. Technical challenges can also pose a problem for brands, in setting up in the long run, especially where there is a service failure, and brands that have bought that platform will have to deal with the aftermath of that problem. Political clamps on these paid platforms can also pose a dark side for brands and consumers. In October 2020, Nigerian social media users criticised the Nigerian government's handling of protests against police brutality on the social media platform Twitter, which led to a government crackdown on social media users and the temporary suspension of Twitter in Nigeria.

9.6.2 Earned platform

Earned platforms refer to platforms that are being used by the brand but being controlled by other brands or developers, and often they don't pay for these platforms like the paid platform, more like a brand choosing to work with an influencer or coming unto a podcast to share information about their platform. Imagine a vegetarian who has just launched an app which allows vegetarians to date themselves (call it Tinder for Vegetarians) and decides to appear on a Vegetarian talk show on YouTube or podcast. This adoption of the talk shows' platform could also be a form of media planning and product placement. While earned digital platforms can provide many benefits, such as increased brand awareness and customer engagement, there are also several potential dark sides or drawbacks, including negative reviews and comments from consumers on the hosting platforms, especially if they don't like the brands. So, in the case of the Tinder for Vegetarians dating app, consumers who would be listening to the podcast may not like the idea of creating an app for vegetarians and they may leave negative feedback or reviews, which could damage the company's reputation. There could also be cyberbullying or harassment, which can damage the mental health of the brand owner, staff, and those who may have appeared on the podcast and negatively impact the company's reputation. In addition, the lack of control over the narrative of those earned media can pose a dark side to digital consumers. The brand (Tinder for Vegetarians) may not have control over how their brand is presented or perceived on earned digital platforms (the YouTube channel and podcast), as users generate and share content outside their control.

The prospects of false or misleading information can also be a dark side, especially in cases where the metrics are over-inflated, where the platform provides unsubstantiated metrics of engagement. Earned digital platforms may be vulnerable to the spread of false or misleading information and unethical activities, which could harm the reputation and credibility of companies associated with them. In 2019, the NBA faced backlash for its relationship with Chinese tech giant Tencent, which has been accused of censoring content critical of the Chinese government. Some commentators criticised the NBA for being complicit in China's efforts to suppress free speech and human rights, while others defended the league's business interests in China. Managers would be expected to make their due diligence to ensure they are working with the right platform, with shared interests and common values.

9.6.3 Shared platform

These are the social media platforms which offer a free and open platform for brands and consumers to engage. This is like renting a room in a shared apartment, and things that are affecting the apartment will surely have an impact on the tenants—the brands having a social media profile page. In March 2019, the Internet company Mozilla announced that it would be suspending its advertising on Facebook in response to the Cambridge Analytica scandal. Mozilla also stated that it would be taking a more cautious approach to social media advertising in the future and would be exploring other ways to promote its products and services. Shared digital platforms may collect and store large amounts of personal data from users, which can raise privacy concerns and lead to the misuse or mishandling of sensitive information, and brand managers are expected to be aware and reflect on the ethical collection of the data, for example, how is the company using the data of all their social media followers, how are they aggregating these data—from Instagram to Facebook and Twitter? While this may be right, as part of the accepted terms and conditions, brands need to reflect on their ethical stance. Companies and consumers may become dependent on a shared digital platform, which can limit their ability to switch to alternative platforms or services—it was not surprising to see Lush the UK-based beauty brand announced that it would be closing its social media accounts in the UK, stating that it wanted to focus on other, more personal ways of connecting with its customers. The company stated that it would be putting more effort into building relationships with its customers through its website, email newsletters, and in-store experiences. Likewise, MTN Group, a South African-based mobile telecommunications company, recognised the need to avoid huge reliance on social media as a platform and has been known to invest heavily in experiential marketing campaigns, such as music festivals and sports events, as a way to connect with customers in a more personal and memorable way.

9.6.4 Co-created platform

Co-created platforms are those platforms created for a certain project and a certain time period by two or more brands with their own existing platforms. For example, you could be having an event and need an app for the event or the collaboration of Beyoncé (as a brand) to work with Adidas (another brand) to create Ivy Park—another brand with its own platforms. While co-created digital platforms can offer many benefits, such as greater user engagement and innovation, there are also several potential dark sides or drawbacks fragmentation and complexity as there are many stakeholders working on it and duties can actually overlap—knowing who is responsible for what. Co-created digital platforms may face challenges in maintaining quality control, as multiple stakeholders may have different priorities or standards. Co-created digital platforms may lack standardisation or consistency, which can lead to confusion or inconsistency in user experience, it is not surprising therefore to see co-created brands choosing to stay with one company instead of creating a completely new digital platform. Likewise, co-created digital platforms may face intellectual property issues, such as disputes over ownership or use of content or technology. It is therefore imperative for brands to be mindful of possible infringement, for each brand co-creating to know what they are responsible for. The mobile payment system, M-Pesa was co-created by the British telecommunications company, Vodafone, and the Kenyan mobile network operator, Safaricom. While the platform has been hugely successful in Kenya and other African countries, there have been disputes over revenue sharing and intellectual property ownership between Vodafone and Safaricom. In 2020, Vodafone sued Safaricom over the use of the M-Pesa brand name and the ownership of the platform's intellectual property. Safaricom and South Africa's Vodacom later acquired the co-created brand—M-Pesa from Britain's Vodafone. Another example of a possible dark side for legal implications is in the music streaming service, Tidal. Tidal was co-created by the rapper Jay-Z and a consortium of other musicians, and the platform has faced legal issues over the ownership of its streaming rights and the payment of royalties to artists. In 2018, Tidal was sued by several artists who claimed that the platform had not paid them the royalties they were owed. The lawsuit was settled out of court, but it highlights the potential legal issues that can arise in co-created digital platforms.

9.6.5 Owned platform

These are platforms that are owned by the brands and have been created by the platform developers. Though the brands have control over their own platform, there are several potential dark sides or drawbacks that managers need to be aware of and put measures to address them. Considering brands are responsible for their own platform—they are not covered by the security infrastructure of paid media, and their platforms are vulnerable to cyberattacks or hacking, which could lead to the theft of sensitive data, such as customer information or financial data. In 2018, Hong Kong-based airline Cathay Pacific Airways announced that it had suffered a major data breach affecting over 9 million customers worldwide. The breach exposed personal data including names, passport numbers, email addresses, and dates of birth. In May 2017, the Indian food delivery and restaurant discovery platform Zomato suffered a data breach that exposed the personal data of 17 million users, including email addresses, passwords, and usernames. Data breaches can have severe consequences for individuals and organisations alike, and it is crucial for companies to take steps to protect their customers' data and respond quickly and effectively to any breaches that occur. Considering brands choose who to design their platforms, they need to be mindful of who is working on the platforms as one of the dark sides could be working with developers who are not very competent and this could lead to creating poorly designed platforms, which are difficult to navigate, or slow to load, and can frustrate users and discourage them from returning.

Maintenance and upkeep of the platforms are also important, to ensure that the platform remains secure, functional, and up-to-date, which can be time-consuming and costly. Information on these platforms should be correct as many digital platforms may find it misleading. For example, if your company is no longer opening on Saturdays, you need to update the website and let consumers know, so that you don't have people coming in on Saturdays and leaving frustrated and then posting on social media that your website is misleading because the website says you are open on Saturdays, but you are not open. Ensuring accessible design can also be a dark side; as brands may not be very conversant about the requirement for developing accessible platforms, these platforms not being accessible to users with disabilities can lead to legal or ethical concerns and exclude potential customers or users. Rafael Cordero, a blind user, filed a lawsuit against Electronic Arts (EA) in 2019, alleging that the design of its website is not fully usable and accessible to blind and visually impaired users and is in violation of the Americans with Disabilities Act (ADA). These are some of the dark sides that can open the brands to lawsuits. Brands (working with developers) need to ensure that their platforms are accessible to people with disabilities, particularly those that provide essential services like online shopping. For individuals with visual impairments, the ability to shop online can be essential for accessing a wide range of products and services, and inaccessible websites can create barriers to independent living.

Government policies can also pose a dark side for platform owners, recognising the need for platform owners to be aware of policies that can affect their business operations. In March 2021, the Nigerian ride-hailing company Gokada announced that it was shutting down its ride-hailing and delivery services due to a lack of funds, following a ban on motorcycles in Lagos and the economic impact of the COVID-19 pandemic. This kind of unpredictable government policy highlights the potential risks of financial sustainability and regulatory challenges for platform owners. Table 9.2 presents a summary of the dark sides of digital consumption conceptualised with the different types of platforms and possible solutions

9.7 What will be your role going forward?

9.7.1 Customers

Digital consumers need to be aware of the dark side. It is important they are educated about it and know what to look out for. Digital consumers should be able to recognise the red flags and be able to act. Digital consumers need to be careful of their engagement on the platform; they need to be careful of how they share their personal data. Digital consumers need to take responsibility for their well-being, if things are not right, they should act appropriately—either by using the tools provided by the developer or leaving the platform. Be in charge—digital consumers have a right to their privacy; they have control over their level and intensity of engagement on the digital platform. Digital consumers should also report to the regulators if things are not going well on the platform. Digital consumers should be able to verify information on social media, be mindful of apps they download, and be mindful of websites where they are shopping and putting their card details. As iterated in the previous chapter, digital consumers should also look out for their friends, older relatives, children, and vulnerable adults. Importantly, digital consumers need to be good digital citizens—not to join others in perpetuating the negative things on figural platforms—you don't want to experience the dark sides, don't present the dark side to other people. Be courteous as you engage.

Table 9.2 Summary of the dark sides of digital consumption conceptualised with the different types of platforms and possible solutions

Platforms	Dark Sides of Digital Consumption	Possible Solutions
Paid platform	■ High cost can discourage businesses from using paid platforms. ■ Lack of value in relation to restrictions on platforms can be a dark side. ■ Limited control over ownership, content, and operations on paid platforms can pose risks. ■ Technical challenges in setting up and dealing with service failures can be a problem for brands. ■ Political clamps on paid platforms can negatively impact brands and consumers. ■ Platforms may face content moderation issues and risk being removed from app stores, as seen with Parler and Donald Trump's removal from Twitter. ■ Brands need to be mindful of the risks and make informed. decisions when choosing paid platforms.	■ Businesses can consider alternative options or negotiate with developers for more affordable plans. ■ Brands to assess the value of paid platforms to ensure that they are worth the cost and meet their needs. ■ Developers can provide more transparent policies on content moderation and ownership to improve brand control and avoid potential risks. ■ Brands can diversify their platform usage to minimise the impact of service failures and technical challenges. ■ Governments can ensure that political clamps on paid platforms do not infringe on freedom of expression or limit access to information. ■ Developers can work to address technical challenges and improve the reliability of their platforms to minimise risks for brands. ■ Brands can collaborate with developers and other stakeholders to establish standards and guidelines for platform usage that prioritise safety, reliability, and transparency.
Earned platform	■ Negative reviews and comments from consumers on hosting platforms. ■ Cyberbullying or harassment of brand owner, staff, or podcast guests. ■ Lack of control over the narrative and perception of the brand on earned platforms. ■ Prospects of false or misleading information, especially in cases of inflated metrics. ■ Vulnerability to the spread of false or unethical activities. ■ Risk of harm to the reputation and credibility of companies associated with earned platforms. ■ Need for managers to do their due diligence in ensuring shared interests and values within the platform.	■ Conduct thorough research on the hosting platform and its users before appearing on it. ■ Build a strong brand identity and community outside of the hosting platform to reduce dependence on it. ■ Set up monitoring tools to track online mentions of the brand and respond promptly to negative comments or reviews. ■ Build a positive relationship with the hosting platform and its users by engaging with them and providing valuable content. ■ Create clear guidelines for user-generated content to ensure that it aligns with the brand's values and messaging. ■ Partner with reputable influencers or content creators who share the same values and vision as the brand. ■ Utilise data analytics to track the impact of earned media and adjust the strategy accordingly.

(Continued)

Table 9.2 (Continued)

Platforms	Dark Sides of Digital Consumption	Possible Solutions
Shared platform	▪ Personal data collected and stored by shared digital platforms can raise privacy concerns and lead to misuse or mishandling of sensitive information. ▪ Over-reliance on social media platforms can limit a company's ability to connect with customers through other channels, such as their website or in-store experiences. ▪ Brands and consumers may become overly dependent on social media platforms, which can limit their ability to switch to alternative platforms or services. ▪ The misuse of social media can lead to the spread of false information, hate speech, cyberbullying, and other harmful content. ▪ Social media can have a negative impact on mental health and well-being. ▪ The constant stream of information and notifications on social media can be addictive and lead to decreased productivity and attention span.	▪ Ensure ethical data collection and handling practices, including clear and transparent terms and conditions for users to provide informed consent. ▪ Diversify marketing strategies beyond social media platforms, such as investing in experiential marketing campaigns to build more personal connections with customers. ▪ Monitor and address privacy concerns related to data collection and storage on shared digital platforms. ▪ Implement crisis management plans to respond promptly to negative comments, reviews, or cyberbullying on earned digital platforms. ▪ Build strong relationships with customers through personalised experiences, such as email newsletters, in-store experiences, and direct communication channels, to reduce dependence on shared digital platforms. ▪ Conduct due diligence before partnering with or appearing on earned digital platforms to ensure alignment with brand values and avoid association with unethical practices or false information. ▪ Continuously review and adapt digital marketing strategies to mitigate risks and capitalise on new opportunities, including exploring alternative social media platforms or emerging technologies.

(Continued)

Table 9.2 (Continued)

Platforms	Dark Sides of Digital Consumption	Possible Solutions
Co-created platform	■ Co-created digital platforms can suffer from fragmentation and complexity, with many stakeholders and overlapping duties. ■ Maintaining quality control can be challenging, as different stakeholders may have different priorities or standards. ■ Lack of standardisation or consistency can lead to confusion or inconsistency in user experience. ■ Intellectual property issues, such as disputes over ownership or use of content or technology, can arise. ■ Legal implications can also arise, as seen in examples like M-Pesa and Tidal, where co-created platforms faced legal issues over revenue sharing, intellectual property ownership, and payment of royalties.	■ Establish clear guidelines and roles for each stakeholder involved in the co-created platform to avoid fragmentation and overlap of duties. ■ Ensure quality control by setting a standard for the platform's content and user experience and have a process in place for reviewing and approving contributions from stakeholders. ■ Strive for standardisation and consistency across the platform to prevent confusion among users. ■ Create a clear agreement and framework for intellectual property ownership and usage to avoid legal disputes. ■ Consider the option of merging existing platforms instead of creating a completely new one to maintain consistency and reduce complexity.
Owned platform	■ Vulnerability to cyberattacks and data breaches, which can lead to the theft of sensitive data. ■ Poorly designed platforms that are difficult to navigate or slow to load can frustrate users and discourage them from returning. ■ Maintenance and upkeep of the platform can be time-consuming and costly. ■ Inaccurate information on the platform can mislead consumers and lead to frustration. ■ Inaccessibility of the platform to users with disabilities can lead to legal or ethical concerns and exclude potential customers or users. ■ Unpredictable government policies can pose financial sustainability and regulatory challenges for platform owners.	■ Secure the platform from cyber-attacks and data breaches by implementing appropriate security measures. ■ Hire competent developers to create and maintain the platform and ensure its accessibility to people with disabilities. ■ Keep the platform up-to-date and accurate to avoid legal and ethical concerns, such as misleading information. ■ Have contingency plans and alternative revenue sources to mitigate the risks of unpredictable government policies. ■ Engage with customers and respond quickly and effectively to any breaches or issues to maintain their trust and loyalty.

9.7.2 Brands

Brands have a huge role in managing the dark sides, especially as they serve as the conduit for developers who want to share their platforms with digital consumers. Managers need to know these dark sides and how it affects their consumers and business operations. It is imperative that brands beef up security on their digital platform—you see companies also using two-factor authentication and password management when staff are assessing the platforms. Managers need to be careful of who has access to what and the level of control or access. Education is also important for the staff, to know these dark sides and the threat to business. Staff could be tested on a fictitious phishing email, to see if staff will click a link or if they are aware of what to do. Brands need to have policies and procedures in place to manage any form of threat or attack. Staff must know what to do when they are been attacked. There is need to create awareness about what to do in time of attack. Brands also need to be good, and ethics is important; another reminder that these companies need to do the right thing with data management, and respect the rules, regulations, and guidelines. Brands also need to be very selective about the platform developers they work with. They need to be mindful of the past precedence—carry out due diligence, ask questions and references, be sure that their values align, and are aware of the security measures to have in place. Brands should not hesitate to re-evaluate the business arrangement, especially if things are not working well with consumers and well-being is being jeopardised. Brands should also address consumer misbehaviour on digital platforms—block, remove, and report to authority.

9.7.3 Developers

As with the consumers and brands, you would expect the platform developers to be aware of the dark side of digital platforms, especially on their own platform, and they need to be aware of threats to their platforms, the consumers, and stakeholders. Developers need to be alert, to stay ahead of the game, especially freelancer and agency developers, and they need to be aware of the latest trends in digital safety and integrate that for their customers. Dark side agents are often one step ahead; abusive words emerge every day and measures should be in place to address these issues, including updating algorithms to pick them up. Brands have a responsibility to engage with the regulators, to ensure that they follow the provided guidelines and beef up security on the platform. Remember stakeholders have huge expectations. Brands will be expected to provide a safe haven for brands and consumers engaging on the platform. Developers need to reassure brands and consumers of safe platforms, putting measures in place to remove trolls, attacks, or cyberbullying.

Ethics is important for digital platform providers. We can't stop talking about it. Brands are expected to do the right thing with data management—reflecting on how they collect, store, and process data. Developers reflect on their algorithm and how it can affect vulnerable people. Developers would be expected to be inclusive in their design and access to the platform, ensuring that the design (of the digital platform) works for everyone. Ensuring anyone of any ability can access the platform regardless of ability. Algorithm should be inclusive, platform access should be inclusive, and use of language and user interface design as iterated in the previous section; this dark side is not just about the impact on their profits but how it affects people and the environment.

While developers are aware of issues on their platform that can discourage people and affect their profit, they need to have that holistic understanding, especially around digital sustainability, making effort to protect the environment. Brands need to consider the impact of e-waste, energy for data centre, and impact of business activities on the environment. Reduce carbon emissions, allow customers to return digital devices, and support recycling.

9.7.4 Regulators

Though the previous chapter has specifically focused on the role of the regulators in regulating digital platforms and managing the dark sides, it is imperative to recognise their roles as gatekeepers in addressing the dark sides. Regulators need to be aware of what they are regulating. As Mogaji and Nguyen (2022) noted on the dark sides of mobile money in Nigeria, there was confusion if the platform should be regulated by the Central Bank or the Telecommunication regulators. Regulators need to have clear jurisdiction and be able to address it well. Likewise, the regulators need to be aware and be at alert, considering how fast digital platforms are evolving, regulators need to stay ahead of the game. Know what to look for, know when and how to act. Importantly, regulators can help by providing guidelines to advise and educate stakeholders. Policies and procedures should be provided for the stakeholders; however, it's not just having it in place but enforcing it and knowing that the brands and developers know what to do.

9.8 Conclusion

The bright side of digital consumption has benefited brands, customers, and developers by enhancing business operations, job opportunities, and entertainment. Digital platforms bridge the gap between brands and consumers and democratise engagement. However, there are increasing concerns about the dark sides of digital consumption. These dark sides have negative effects on cognitive, emotional, social, and mental health outcomes, and they discourage consumers, brands, and developers from using digital platforms.

The dark side of digital consumption refers to the negative consequences that individuals, society, and the environment face due to increasing reliance on digital technologies and platforms. These negative effects can include decreased privacy, cyberbullying, addiction, social isolation, increased energy consumption, the spread of misinformation, and displacement of workers. The degree of brightness or darkness is often subjective, and the impact of digital consumption can vary depending on the context and particular technology or platform being used.

Despite the numerous wonders of digital consumption, there is a realisation that the anticipated 'promise' of a more equitable, just, and sustainable world through digital advancement has gone unfulfilled. The digital revolution is neither sustainable nor equitable, and there is a need for managers to take responsibility for recognising and addressing the dark sides of digital consumption. Ultimately, this chapter is about increased critical thinking skills and the ability to analyse both the positive and negative aspects of digital consumption and to make informed decisions about how to engage with digital media responsibly and healthily.

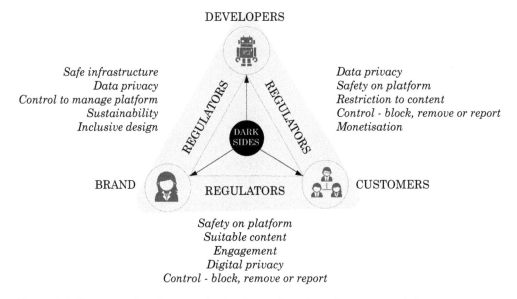

Figure 9.1 The connections between the developers, brands, and consumers, their engagement on digital platforms, and the role of regulators in managing the dark side

Figure 9.1 illustrates the connections between the developers, brands, and consumers and their engagement on digital platforms. The role of regulators in managing these dark sides is also presented. The chapter focuses on the roles of customers, brands, developers, and regulators in managing the dark sides of digital platforms. Digital consumers should be educated about the risks and take responsibility for their privacy, personal data, and engagement on the platform. Brands should improve security on their platforms, have policies and procedures in place to manage threats or attacks, and be selective about the platform developers they work with. Developers should be aware of the threats to their platforms, alert, and proactive in addressing them, as well as ensure inclusivity, ethical algorithms, and digital sustainability. Regulators should have clear jurisdiction, stay ahead of the game, and address the dark sides appropriately.

9.9 Student activities

1. What are some of the negative consequences of social media addiction, and how can we mitigate them?
2. What is cyberbullying, and how does it impact victims and society as a whole?
3. How can excessive use of digital devices affect our physical health, and what steps can we take to prevent or reduce these negative effects?
4. What is the impact of excessive screen time on our mental health, and how can we develop healthy digital habits?
5. How do algorithms and social media platforms reinforce bias and discrimination, and what can be done to address these issues?
6. How does digital piracy harm creators and the wider economy, and what can be done to combat it?

7. What are some of the potential dangers of online dating and socialising, and how can we stay safe while using these platforms?
8. How does digital content consumption affect our ability to focus and retain information, and what strategies can we use to improve our digital literacy?
9. What are some of the ethical considerations surrounding data privacy and digital surveillance, and how can we protect our personal information online?
10. How can we balance the benefits of technology and digital media with the potential negative effects on our physical and mental health, relationships, and society as a whole?

References and further reading

Abdulquadri, A., Mogaji, E., Kieu, T. & Nguyen, P., 2021. Digital transformation in financial services provision: A Nigerian perspective to the adoption of chatbot. *Journal of Enterprising Communities: People and Places in the Global Economy*, 15(2), pp. 258–281.

Agbo, F. et al., 2020. Social media usage for computing education: The effect of tie strength and group communication on perceived learning outcome. *Journal of Education and Development using Information and Communication Technology*, 16(1), pp. 5–26.

Alfonseca, K. & Zahn, M., 2023. Tech layoffs 2023: Companies that have made cuts [Online] Available at: https://abcnews.go.com/Business/tech-layoffs-2023-companies-made-cuts/story?id=96564792

Baccarella, C., Wagner & Kietzmann, J., 2020. Averting the rise of the dark side of social media: The role of sensitization and regulation. *European Management Journal*, 38(1), pp. 3–6.

Baccarella, C., Wagner, T., Kietzmann, J. & McCarthy, I., 2018. Social media? It's serious! Understanding the dark side of social media. *European Management Journal*, 36(4), pp. 431–438.

Balakrishnan, J., Nwoba, A. & Nguyen, N., 2021. Emerging-market consumers' interactions with banking chatbots. *Telematics and Informatics*, 65, 101711.

Baldé, C. et al., 2022. Global transboundary E-waste flows monitor 2022 [Online] Available at: https://api.globalewaste.org/publications/file/286/Global-Transboundary-E-waste-Flows-Monitor-2022.pdf

Bhutani, C. & Behl, A., 2023. The dark side of gamification in interactive marketing. In: *The Palgrave Handbook of Interactive Marketing*. Cham: Springer International Publishing, pp. 939–962.

Bilal, K., Malik, S., Khalid, O. & Hameed, A., 2014. A taxonomy and survey on green data center networks. *Future Generation Computer Systems*, 36(2014), pp. 189–208.

Chattopadhyay, A., Kupe, T., Schatzer, N. & Mogaji, E., 2022. Fireside chat with three vice chancellors from three continents. In: E. Mogaji, V. Jain, F. Maringe & R. Hinson, eds. *Re-imagining Higher Education in Emerging Economies*. Cham: Palgrave Macmillan, pp. 85–96.

Chemma, N., Abdelli, M. & Awasthi, A., 2022a. Management and information technology in the digital era: Introduction to edited collection on challenges and perspectives. In: N. Chemma, M. El Amine Abdelli, A. Awasthi & E. Mogaji, eds. *Management and Information Technology in the Digital Era*. Bingley: Emerald, pp. 1–6.

Chemma, N., Abdelli, M. & Awasthi, A., 2022b. Management and information technology in the digital era: Conclusion and research agenda. In: N. Chemma, M. El Amine Abdelli, A. Awasthi, and E. Mogaji, eds. *Management and Information Technology in the Digital Era*. Bingley: Emerald, pp. 233–237.

Chylinski, M. et al., 2020. Augmented reality marketing: A technology-enabled approach to situated customer experience. *Australasian Marketing Journal*, 28(4), pp. 374–384.

Conti, M., Dehghantanha, A., Franke, K. & Watson, S., 2018. Internet of Things security and forensics: Challenges and opportunities. *Future Generation Computer Systems*, 78, pp. 544–546.

Dhruv, G., Hulland, J., Kopalle, P. & Karahanna, E., 2020. The future of technology and marketing: A multidisciplinary perspective. *Journal of the Academy of Marketing Science*, 48, pp. 1–8.

Dwivedi, Y. et al., 2022. Metaverse beyond the hype: Multidisciplinary perspectives on emerging challenges, opportunities, and agenda for research, practice and policy. *International Journal of Information Management*, 66, 102542.

Elkington, J., 2008. The triple bottom line: Sustainability's accountants: In M.V. Russo, eds. *Environmental Management. Readings and Cases*. Thousand Oaks: SAGE Publications, pp. 49–67.

Flew, T., Martin, F. & Suzor, N., 2019. Internet regulation as media policy: Rethinking the question of digital communication platform governance. *Journal of Digital Media & Policy*, 10(1), pp. 33–50.

Hampton, K., 2016. Persistent and pervasive community: New communication technologies and the future of community. *American Behavioral Scientist*, 60(1), pp. 101–124.

Hein, A. et al., 2020. Digital platform ecosystems. *Electronic Markets*, 30, pp. 87–98.

Hodapp, D. & Hanelt, A., 2022. Interoperability in the era of digital innovation: An information systems research agenda. *Journal of Information Technology*, 37(4), pp. 407–427.

IEA, 2022. Data centres and data transmission networks [Online] Available at: https://www.iea.org/reports/data-centres-and-data-transmission-networks

Immordino-Yang, M., Christodoulou, J. & Singh, V., 2012. Rest is not idleness: Implications of the brain's default mode for human development and education. *Perspectives on Psychological Science*, 7(4), pp. 352–364.

Jelovac, D., Ljubojević, C. & Ljubojević, L., 2022. HPC in business: The impact of corporate digital responsibility on building digital trust and responsible corporate digital governance. *Digital Policy, Regulation and Governance*, 24(6), pp. 485–497.

Kandampully, J., Bilgihan, A. & Li, D., 2022. Unifying technology and people: Revisiting service in a digitally transformed world. *The Service Industries Journal*, 42(1–2), pp. 21–41.

Kanungo, R., Gupta, S., Patel, P. & Prikshat, V., 2022. Digital consumption and socio-normative vulnerability. *Technological Forecasting and Social Change*, 182, 121808.

Khalil, A., Abdelli, M. & Mogaji, E., 2022. Do digital technologies influence the relationship between the COVID-19 crisis and SMEs' resilience in developing countries? *Journal of Open Innovation: Technology, Market, and Complexity*, 8(2), pp. 100–109.

Khan, I., Ahmad, M. & Majava, J., 2021. Industry 4.0 and sustainable development: A systematic mapping of triple bottom line, Circular Economy and Sustainable Business Models perspectives. *Journal of Cleaner Production*, 297, 126655.

Kietzmann, J., Hermkens, K. & McCarthy, I., 2011. Social media? Get serious! Understanding the functional building blocks of social media. *Business Horizons*, 54(3), pp. 241–251.

Koklic, M., Kukar-Kinney, M. & Vida, I., 2022. Consumers' de-ownership as a predictor of dark-side digital acquisition behavior: Moderating role of moral intensity and collectivism. *Journal of Business Research*, 138, pp. 108–116.

Kopalle, P., Kumar, V. & Subramaniam, M., 2020. How legacy firms can embrace the digital ecosystem via digital customer orientation. *Journal of the Academy of Marketing Science*, 48, pp. 114–131.

Kuntsman, A. & Rattle, I., 2019. Towards a paradigmatic shift in sustainability studies: A systematic review of peer reviewed literature and future agenda setting to consider environmental (Un) sustainability of digital communication. *Environmental Communication*, 13(5), pp. 567–581.

Lythreatis, S., Singh, S. & El-Kassar, A., 2022. The digital divide: A review and future research agenda. *Technological Forecasting and Social Change*, 175, 121359.

Mazuma, 2023. Mobile phone recycling facts and figures [Online] Available at: https://www.mazumamobile.com/blog/general/mobile-phone-recycling-facts-and-figures/#:~

:text=150%2B%20million%20smartphones%20reach%20landfills,to%20fix%20the %20world's%20ecosystem

McKinsey, 2022. Marketing in the metaverse: An opportunity for innovation and experimentation [Online] Available at: https://www.mckinsey.com/capabilities/growth-marketing-and-sales/our -insights/marketing-in-the-metaverse-an-opportunity-for-innovation-and-experimentation

Miric, M., Boudreau, K. & Jeppesen, L., 2019. Protecting their digital assets: The use of formal & informal appropriability strategies by app developers. *Research Policy*, 48(8), 103738.

Mogaji, E., 2021. *Brand Management*. Cham: Springer.

Mogaji, E. & Nguyen, N., 2022. The dark side of mobile money: Perspectives from an emerging economy. *Technological Forecasting and Social Change*, 185, 122045.

Mogaji, E., Soetan, T. & Kieu, T., 2020. The implications of artificial intelligence on the digital marketing of financial services to vulnerable customers. *Australasian Marketing Journal*, 29(3), pp. 235–242.

Mogaji, E., Wirtz, J., Belk, R. & Dwivedi, Y., 2023. Immersive Time (ImT). *International Journal of Information Management*, 72, October 2023, 102659.

Morgan-Thomas, A., Dessart, L. & Veloutsou, C., 2020. Digital ecosystem and consumer engagement: A socio-technical perspective. *Journal of Business Research*, 121, pp. 713–723.

Okazaki, S., Plangger, K., Roulet, T. & Menéndez, H. D., 2021. Assessing stakeholder network engagement. *European Journal of Marketing*, 55(5), pp. 1359–1384.

Olson, E., Olson, K., Czaplewski, A. & Key, T., 2021. Business strategy and the management of digital marketing. *Business Horizons*, 64(2), pp. 285–293.

Oosthuizen, K., Botha, E., Robertson, J. & Montecchi, M., 2021. Artificial intelligence in retail: The AI-enabled value chain. *Australasian Marketing Journal*, 29(3), pp. 264–273.

Paniagua, J., Korzynski, P. & Mas-Tur, A., 2017. Crossing borders with social media: Online social networks and FDI. *European Management Journal*, 35(3), pp. 314–326.

Pellegrino, A., Abe, M. & Shannon, R., 2022. The dark side of social media: Content effects on the relationship between materialism and consumption behaviors. *Frontiers in Psychology*, 13(1), pp. 17–45.

Ponzoa, J. & Erdmann, A., 2021. E-commerce customer attraction: Digital marketing techniques, evolution and dynamics across firms. *Journal of Promotion Management*, 27(5), pp. 697–715.

Reuters, 2017. Kenya election commission investigating hacking claims [Online] Available at: https://www.reuters.com/article/uk-kenya-election-commission-idUKKBN1AP0VE

Sağkaya Güngö, A. & Ozansoy Çadırcı, T., 2022. Understanding digital consumer: A review, synthesis, and future research agenda. *International Journal of Consumer Studies*, 46(5), pp. 1829–1858.

SellCell, 2021. Smartphone relationship survey: 71% of people spend more time with their phone than their romantic partner [Online] Available at: https://www.sellcell.com/blog/smartphone -relationship-survey/

Sheth, J., 2020. Impact of Covid-19 on consumer behavior: Will the old habits return or die? *Journal of Business Research*, 117, pp. 280–283.

Soetan, T., Mogaji, E. & Nguyen, N., 2021. Financial services experience and consumption in Nigeria. *Journal of Services Marketing*, 35(7), pp. 947–961.

Talwar, S. et al., 2019. Why do people share fake news? Associations between the dark side of social media use and fake news sharing behavior. *Journal of Retailing and Consumer Services*, 51, pp. 72–82.

Tapscott, D., 2016. After 20 years, it's harder to ignore the digital economy's dark side [Online] Available at: https://hbr.org/2016/03/after-20-years-its-harder-to-ignore-the-digital -economys-dark-side

Telegeography, 2022. The state of the network [Online] Available at: https://www2.telegeography .com/hubfs/LP-Assets/Ebooks/state-of-the-network-2022.pdf

Town, G., Taghizadeh, S. & Deilami, S., 2022. Review of fast charging for electrified transport: Demand, technology, systems, and planning. *Energies*, 15(4), pp. 1276–1287.

Verbeke, A. & Hutzschenreuter, T., 2021. The dark side of digital globalization. *Academy of Management Perspectives*, 35(4), pp. 606–621.

Whitfield, G., 2016. Sage employee arrested at Heathrow airport in connection with data breach [Online] Available at: https://www.chroniclelive.co.uk/business/business-news/sage-employee-arrested-heathrow-airport-11765342

Wirtz, J., Kunz, W., Hartley, N. & Tarbit, J., 2023. Corporate digital responsibility in service firms and their ecosystems. *Journal of Service Research*, 26(2), pp. 173–190.

Yuan, H., Feng, K., Li, W. & Sun, X., 2022. Multi-objective optimization of virtual energy hub plant integrated with data center and plug-in electric vehicles under a mixed robust-stochastic model. *Journal of Cleaner Production*, 363, 132365.

CHAPTER 10

Contemporary issues of digital consumption

10.1 Background

Digital consumption, which refers to the use of digital technologies to consume various types of content and services, has become an integral part of our daily lives. As technology evolves, there are both opportunities and challenges that arise related to digital consumption. The digital divide is one critical issue that technology can exacerbate, limiting individuals' ability to access critical resources such as education and healthcare. Data privacy and security are also significant concerns as technology has the potential to collect, analyse, and share personal information. As technology advances rapidly, it can be challenging for individuals and organisations to keep up with the latest developments, requiring ongoing training and upskilling to remain competitive. It is essential for individuals and organisations to reflect on the potential issues related to digital consumption and take steps to mitigate negative impacts, such as bridging the digital divide, promoting data privacy and security, and investing in ongoing training and upskilling to adapt to a rapidly changing digital landscape. In this chapter, we will explore some of the contemporary issues of digital consumption. These are issues that managers, developers, and consumers need to be aware of as we engage with digital technologies going forward. This issue can be both positive and negative; it goes beyond just the good sides or the dark sides to but critically reflect on how digital technology will shape our work, life, and business going forward. What would life look like by 2030? What are those things that would have changed? What are those things that would have to change? How about our jobs? As a student, how can you position yourself for a career in the future?

DOI: 10.4324/9781003389842-10

10.2 Learning outcomes

By the end of this chapter, you should be able to:

- Describe the concept of contemporary issues of digital consumption.
- Identify the contemporary issues of digital consumption.
- Understand why stakeholders should be aware and mindful of these contemporary issues.
- Recognise how these contemporary issues affect key stakeholders.
- Identify what stakeholders can do to address these contemporary issues.

10.3 Introduction

The exploration of digital consumer engagement in the digital environment has been an important journey through this book, highlighting the opportunities and challenges that come with this new era of consumption. This is the last chapter, and as we look to the future, it is clear that digital engagement will continue to play an important role in our lives, and we must be prepared to adapt and innovate in response to emerging trends and challenges. This chapter brings us to the end of the theoretical and practical exploration of digital consumer engagement in the digital environment. The book has been a journey from the understanding of digital consumers to the platform they engage, the brand providing the platform for engagement, and also the developers working on the platform. This journey has also explored the regulatory requirements to manage the inherent dark sides of digital consumption. The book has recognised diverse platforms for different forms of engagement, but the question remains what lies ahead for digital consumption. What does the future hold and how can we be prepared for this future?

This chapter focuses on the contemporary issues in digital consumption, highlighting some emerging trends and issues that can shape digital consumption going forward—these are issues that can either bring positive changes or come with negative implications (Mogaji, 2021). On the positive side, digital technologies have the potential to improve efficiency, communication, and access to information. However, there are also negative issues. For example, excessive use of social media and digital devices can lead to addiction and negative impacts on mental health. Additionally, privacy concerns and the potential for data breaches are a growing concern as more personal information is stored online.

In today's increasingly digitised world, the way we consume and interact with technology is rapidly evolving (Bailey et al., 2022). From the rise of artificial intelligence and automation to the emergence of new decentralised technologies like blockchain and cryptocurrency, there are numerous contemporary issues and trends shaping the future of digital consumption. Alongside these technological developments, we are also seeing changes in the way that consumers engage with brands and companies, as well as new regulatory challenges around data privacy and security. In this context, it is important to understand the key themes and implications of these emerging trends, and how they are likely to shape the future of digital consumption for different stakeholders (Balakrishnan et al., 2021; Dwivedi et al., 2022; Koohang et al., 2023).

The success of digital consumption in the future will depend on how effectively stakeholders manage these issues and work together to address emerging challenges and opportunities. This includes students and professionals in the tech industry continuing to develop and refine their skills, brands and platforms becoming more engaging and personalised in their offerings, and developers leveraging new technologies and cross-functional collaboration to innovate and improve digital experiences. At the same time, regulators must remain vigilant and responsive to emerging threats and challenges and work to develop and enforce standards that protect consumers and ensure ethical and responsible digital engagement (Almeida Teixeira et al., 2019). Ultimately, the future of digital consumption will depend on how effectively stakeholders navigate these complex and evolving issues and work together to create a safe, secure, and engaging digital environment that delivers value and benefits to all.

With the growing prospects for digital transformation, we should be bothered about these issues. We should be aware and ready to act. These issues have a significant impact on our lives, work, and society as a whole. As digital technologies become more prevalent and integrated into our daily lives, it is important to understand both the positive and negative effects they can have. Aligning with the three target audience for this book discussed in Chapter 1—the student, staff, and start-up founders, this chapter reflects on their expectations with regard to these contemporary issues.

Reflective questions

How would you describe the future of digital consumption? What can you predict will happen?

What should we be concerned about, going forward with digital consumption?

10.4 Contemporary issues

The rapid pace of technological change and the widespread adoption of digital technologies have created a range of complex issues related to digital consumption, requiring ongoing attention and thoughtful solutions (Rasool et al., 2020). The issues emerging from digital consumption and engagement are indeed enormous, and they require ongoing attention and discussion. From privacy concerns to the potential for addiction and mental health impacts, there are many important factors to consider when it comes to digital consumption. As we continue to rely more and more on digital technologies for communication, work, and entertainment, these issues will only become more pressing. Addressing these issues will require collaboration between stakeholders across sectors, including businesses, governments, and individuals, to ensure that the benefits of emerging technologies are maximised, and the risks are mitigated. Considering the enormous nature of these issues, this section has summarised them into three key themes, and by focusing on these key themes, we can better understand the challenges and opportunities presented by the digital era and work together to address the most pressing issues facing consumers, businesses, and society as a whole.

10.4.1 Ethical and social implications of emerging technologies

With the rapid advancement of technologies like AI, blockchain, and computer-generated content, there are significant social and ethical questions that must be addressed.

For example, with the growing size of big data, AI will keep shaping digital consumption going forward, but it has been recognised that AI has the potential to be biased or misused, which can have negative impacts on individuals or communities. Similarly, blockchain can be used to promote transparency and security, but there are also concerns about its potential impact on privacy and anonymity (Hancock et al., 2020). The development and use of computer-generated content raises questions about authenticity and ownership, while the control of data has significant implications for privacy and ownership. There are also huge concerns and possibilities around online tracking and targeted advertising—considering consumers have accepted the terms and conditions, shouldn't they be targeted (Mogaji et al., 2020). How do you strike the balance between providing a random advertisement to everyone or personalising the advertisement based on people's interests? Consumers will be more appreciative of targeted advertisements that meet their immediate needs, but another concern is when does personalisation of an advertisement become a burden. Data breaches and security threats and the ethical concerns around the collection and use of personal data by companies are also ongoing issues with digital consumption. The rise of deepfakes can also be considered an emerging issue; these are digital manipulations of audio, video, or images, using advanced machine learning techniques to create highly realistic and often convincing fake media (Whittaker et al., 2021). Deepfakes can be used for a range of purposes, including political propaganda, disinformation, and revenge porn. The emergence of deepfakes raises a number of important questions related to privacy, security, and authenticity. For example, how can we ensure that digital media is authentic and trustworthy when it is increasingly easy to manipulate and falsify? How can we protect individuals from the potential harms of deepfakes, such as reputational damage or emotional distress? And what role should governments, tech companies, and other stakeholders play in regulating the use of deepfakes? Addressing these questions will require ongoing collaboration and innovation among stakeholders from a range of fields, including technology, law, media, and ethics (Davis & Arrigo, 2021). It will be important to develop new technologies and standards for detecting and mitigating the impact of deepfakes, as well as to educate consumers and the public about the risks and challenges posed by this emerging technology.

10.4.2 Transformation of digital consumption and creation

The emergence of technologies like the metaverse and 5G is transforming how we experience and consume digital content, while the rise of user-generated content is changing how content is created and distributed. The metaverse refers to a virtual world where users can interact with each other and digital content in a more immersive way than traditional 2D interfaces, such as websites or mobile apps (Dwivedi et al., 2022; Koohang et al., 2023; Jain et al., 2023). This concept has gained traction in recent years with the rise of virtual and augmented reality technology, as well as the increasing popularity of online gaming and social media platforms. With 5G, users can access digital content more quickly and with less lag, making it easier to stream high-quality video, engage with virtual reality or augmented reality experiences, and participate in real-time communication with others (Mogaji et al., 2023). This has significant implications for how we consume and interact with digital content, as well as the potential for new types of content and experiences to emerge. These changes are creating new opportunities for businesses and individuals to reach audiences and consumers, but they also raise important questions about the authenticity and ownership of content. The rise of AI-generated content also has the potential to transform how content is created and consumed, with implications for the role of human labour in content creation.

Virtual and augmented reality, edge computing and the Internet of Things, voice assistants and natural language processing, quantum computing, and its potential impact on encryption and security are issues that will transform digital consumption going into the future. With augmented reality, consumers are able to try on some clothes without stepping into the store, consumers are able to see how furniture will fit into their empty room, and the Internet of Things allows people to control things in their house even when they are on holiday. Wearable technology and quantified self-movement are future opportunities for digital consumption. Consumers may have difficulty adapting to new technologies and experiences, brands need to provide user-friendly and accessible technology, tech developers need to consider accessibility and inclusivity, and regulators need to ensure emerging technologies adhere to ethical and legal standards.

The rise of social media platforms has created a new landscape for content creation and consumption (Chemma et al., 2022). With the ability to create and share content easily, anyone can become a content creator and potentially reach a large audience. Children aspiring to be YouTubers and TikTokers. As consumers engage more on this digital platform, they will begin to take ownership of their content (and data) and more chances for monetising their content. However, the question remains if content creation will be a sustainable career for the future. This shift towards user-generated content has disrupted traditional media industries and has created new opportunities for brands to reach consumers in more authentic and engaging ways. However, this also means that brands and content creators must work harder to stand out in a crowded digital space and build a loyal following. Brands are also not stopping in creating content to engage consumers—from social media to websites, emails, newsletters, and blogpost, looking into the future, there are possibilities that these contents will be created using ChatGPT and other AI generative content.

Social media influencers play a crucial role in digital consumption and engagement on platforms, and they often serve as trendsetters and evangelists for brands (Vrontis et al., 2021). The working relationship with influencers will likely evolve as computer-generated influencers (CGI) begin to grow. These fictional computer-generated 'people' have the realistic characteristics, features, and personalities of humans (Conti et al., 2022). They are created using advanced computer algorithms and graphics software to create realistic, lifelike representations of people that can be used in advertising and marketing campaigns. One of the main advantages of computer-generated models and influencers is that they can be customised and tailored to fit specific brand messaging and values. They can also be more cost-effective than traditional models and influencers, as they do not require as much time and effort to manage or coordinate. However, there are also some potential drawbacks to using computer-generated models and influencers. For example, some consumers may view these models as inauthentic or misleading, which could damage brand reputation and trust. Additionally, there is a risk that these models could be used to perpetuate unrealistic beauty standards or other harmful stereotypes.

Overall, the use of computer-generated models and influencers is a complex issue that involves considerations around ethics, brand reputation, and consumer perception. It is important for brands to carefully weigh the potential benefits and risks before deciding to use these models in their marketing and advertising campaigns. Some examples are KFC's virtual influencer campaign launched in 2019, featuring a computer-generated influencer named 'Colonel Sanders'. The campaign was aimed at promoting the brand's new Kentucky Fried Chicken and Waffles dish. Lil Miquela is a virtual influencer created by Brud, a Los Angeles-based artificial intelligence (AI) company. She is presented as a 19-year-old music artist and social media influencer, with a growing social media following and partnerships with several brands. Shudu Gram is a virtual fashion model created by British photographer Cameron-James Wilson, and she has been featured in several fashion campaigns. Reflecting on these emerging issues, you want to ask if the machine (CGIs) will take over the jobs of influencers. What is the impact of CGIs on content creation? These are some of the questions to consider as we explore these contemporary issues in digital consumption.

10.4.3 Ownership and control of data and digital assets

With the increasing digitisation of our lives, there is a growing need to ensure that individuals have control over their own data and that it is stored and used responsibly. Blockchain technology has the potential to enable decentralised data storage and ownership, while the control of data has significant implications for privacy and security. Cryptocurrency is a decentralised digital currency that operates independently of a central bank or government and is based on a technology called blockchain. Blockchain technology allows for secure and transparent transactions, making it an attractive option for individuals and businesses looking for an alternative to traditional financial systems. Cryptocurrency's potential to decentralise financial systems and provide greater control over one's financial assets aligns with the theme of ownership and control of data and digital assets (Howson & de Vries, 2022). Additionally, the use of blockchain technology raises ethical and social questions related to issues such as transparency, privacy, and security. Therefore, while cryptocurrency can be associated with both the third theme and the second theme (transformation of digital consumption and creation), its potential to provide greater control over digital assets places it primarily under the third theme. Consumers have a stake in the ownership and control of their own data and digital assets. This may involve concerns about privacy, or the desire to have greater control over their digital identity. Addressing these issues will require a balance between protecting individual privacy and data ownership, while also enabling the responsible use of data for social and economic benefit.

Consumers may face a steep learning curve and risk of fraud or financial loss with cryptocurrencies, brands need to consider the environmental impact of blockchain and cryptocurrency, tech developers need to prioritise security and efficiency in blockchain systems, and regulators need to balance innovation with regulation to prevent misuse and illegal activities (Goodell et al., 2023). Regulators will however have a role to play in ensuring that individuals have the necessary legal protections to control their own data and digital assets. This may involve setting standards or guidelines for data privacy or intellectual property rights (Flew et al., 2019; Mogaji & Nguyen, 2022).

Other emerging trends to consider under the ownership and control of data and digital assets are Central bank digital currencies (CBDCs) and their potential impact on the financial system, the regulation of cryptocurrencies and blockchain technology, decentralised finance (DeFi), and peer-to-peer lending and intellectual property issues in the blockchain space, such as patent wars and copyright infringement. As discussed in Chapter 9 about the dark side of digital consumption on the planet. It is imperative to recognise the environmental impact and sustainability concerns in cryptocurrency mining.

Reflective question

What are other contemporary issues in digital consumption you would like to share?

10.5 Why bother about these issues?

It is not just enough to have awareness of these contemporary issues but to reflect on what can be done to position the brand effectively and strategically. From a business perspective, understanding contemporary issues in digital consumption is crucial for staying competitive and meeting the needs of consumers. Companies that are able to effectively leverage digital technologies can gain a competitive advantage and reach new audiences (Mogaji et al., 2023). However, failing to address issues such as privacy and security can lead to loss of customer trust and reputational damage. Understanding contemporary issues in digital consumption is important for individuals, businesses, and society as a whole. By staying informed about the positive and negative impacts of digital technologies, we can make more informed decisions about how we use them and ensure that they are developed and used in a responsible and ethical way. Aligning with the three target audience for this book discussed in Chapter 1, this section highlights some reflections for stakeholders with regard to managing these contemporary issues.

10.5.1 Student

10.5.1.1 Enhance your education

As students engage with contemporary issues in digital consumption, they must develop their cognitive skills and critical thinking abilities in order to collect and evaluate factual evidence and discern what points they believe are correct and why. In a world where information is readily available at our fingertips, it is essential that students learn how to distinguish between reliable and unreliable sources of information (Chattopadhyay et al., 2022). Additionally, students must develop the ability to think critically about the implications of digital consumption on their own lives, work, and society as a whole. They should ask questions such as: What are the potential benefits and drawbacks of digital technologies? How can we ensure that digital technologies are developed and used in a responsible and ethical way? How can we protect our privacy and security online? By engaging with these questions and developing their critical thinking skills, students can become informed and responsible digital citizens who are prepared to navigate the complex digital landscape of the future.

Table 10.1 A summary of these contemporary issues with implications on stakeholders

Theme	Implications for Consumers	Implications for Brands	Implications for Tech Developers	Implications for Regulators
Ethical and Social Implications of Emerging Technologies *Emerging technologies raise a range of ethical and social questions related to issues such as privacy, security, and impact on society.*	Consumers are directly impacted by these ethical and social questions and may have concerns about their digital rights and well-being.	Brands must ensure that they are using emerging technologies in a responsible and ethical manner, taking into account the potential impact on their customers and society as a whole.	Tech developers must take into account the ethical and social implications of their work, and ensure that they are designing and building technology that is aligned with the values and needs of society.	Regulators must set standards and guidelines for the development and use of emerging technologies, ensuring that they are used in a responsible and ethical manner, and protecting the rights and well-being of individuals and society as a whole.
Transformation of Digital Consumption and Creation *Emerging technologies are transforming the ways in which we consume and create digital content, opening up new possibilities for communication, creativity, and expression.*	Consumers are experiencing a range of new forms of digital consumption and creation, which may require new skills, knowledge, and tools.	Brands must adapt to the changing landscape of digital consumption and creation and may need to develop new platforms, devices, or content to meet the evolving needs and desires of their customers.	Tech developers are creating the underlying technologies that enable new forms of digital consumption and creation and must stay at the forefront of innovation to remain competitive.	Regulators may need to adapt existing regulations to account for the changing landscape of digital consumption and creation and ensure that individuals have access to the necessary tools and resources to participate in these new forms of digital engagement.
Ownership and Control of Data and Digital Assets *Emerging technologies are creating new possibilities for ownership and control of digital assets, such as data, intellectual property, and financial assets.*	Consumers are seeking greater control over their own data and digital assets and may be concerned about issues such as privacy, security, and intellectual property rights.	Brands must respect the digital rights of their customers and ensure that they are not overstepping boundaries or violating laws related to data privacy or intellectual property.	Tech developers are creating technologies that enable individuals to own and control their own data and digital assets and must ensure that these technologies are secure, transparent, and accessible to everyone.	Regulators must set standards and guidelines related to data privacy and intellectual property rights, ensuring that individuals have the necessary legal protections to control their own data and digital assets.

10.5.1.2 *Take a stance*

Students should be encouraged to debate and take a stance on contemporary issues in digital consumption. By engaging in debates and discussions, students can develop their critical thinking skills and learn to articulate their views on complex topics. As you may be aware, contemporary issues in digital consumption often present an abundance of information and support for all sides, making it important for students to understand the different perspectives and develop their own informed opinions (Jain et al., 2022). For example, in the context of using AI to generate content versus hiring a human author, students might consider questions such as: What are the potential benefits and drawbacks of using AI to generate content? How does the quality of content generated by AI compare to that produced by humans? What are the ethical implications of using AI to generate content, such as concerns around job displacement or the authenticity of content? What are the financial considerations of using AI versus hiring human authors? If your boss asked you to write a report, would you use ChatGPT or would you write it without any assistance from AI? These are some critical reflections for students to be aware of (Jain et al., 2023). By exploring these and other questions, students can develop a deeper understanding of contemporary issues in digital consumption and become more informed and engaged citizens (Sharma et al., 2022).

10.5.1.3 *Acquire skills*

In order to survive the challenges posed by contemporary issues in digital consumption, it is important for individuals to develop the right skill set to remain competitive in the job market and advance in their careers. One important step is to stay informed about the latest developments in technology and understand how they may impact your industry or profession. This will allow you to identify areas where you can add value and leverage technology to improve your work. In addition, it is important to develop skills that are less likely to be automated by AI or machine learning. For example, skills such as creativity, problem-solving, communication, and leadership are highly valued in the workplace and are less likely to be replaced by machines. Continuous learning and upskilling are also essential to stay competitive and remain relevant in the job market. This can involve taking courses or attending training programs to develop new skills or deepen your expertise in a particular area. Ultimately, the key to surviving and thriving in the face of the impending force of AI on work is to be proactive and adaptable. By staying informed, developing in-demand skills, and continuously learning, individuals can position themselves for success in the digital age.

10.5.2 Start-ups

10.5.2.1 *Artificial intelligence*

AI tools are becoming increasingly important in digital consumption and are being used by businesses to improve their operations, provide better customer service, and make data-driven decisions. Chatbots as AI-powered virtual assistants can communicate with customers and answer their queries. They can help businesses provide 24/7 customer support, handle large volumes of inquiries, and provide personalised recommendations to customers. For example, a chatbot can help a customer book a hotel room or order food from a restaurant. Natural Language Processing (NLP) is an AI technique that allows machines to understand and analyse human language. It is used to analyse social media sentiment and customer feedback to improve products and services (Chemma et al., 2022b). For example, NLP can be used to analyse customer reviews and feedback to identify common complaints and issues that need to be addressed. Machine learning algorithms can be used to analyse customer data and provide insights into consumer behaviours, preferences, and patterns. This can help businesses identify trends and make data-driven decisions. For example, machine learning algorithms can be used to analyse customer data to identify products that are likely to be popular and adjust inventory accordingly (Khalil et al., 2022). AI-powered image and video recognition tools can be used to analyse visual content and identify objects, people, and activities. This can be used in various applications such as product recognition and recommendation, security, and content moderation. Predictive analytics (as discussed in Chapter 7) uses data, statistical algorithms, and machine learning to identify the likelihood of future outcomes based on historical data. This can be used in various applications such as predicting customer behaviour and demand, fraud detection, and risk assessment.

10.5.2.2 Informed consumer

Start-up founders and platform developers need to be mindful of contemporary issues in digital consumption and understand the concerns of their consumers. While innovation is important, it should not come at the expense of consumer well-being. Start-ups and platform developers should strive to balance the drive for innovation with ethical considerations, including the impact on consumers (Bailey et al., 2022). This can involve engaging with consumers and soliciting feedback to understand their needs and concerns, as well as conducting thorough risk assessments to identify potential harms or negative consequences of their innovations. In addition, showing empathy and a genuine concern for consumer well-being can be a key differentiator for start-ups and platform developers. By prioritising the needs of their consumers and working to address their concerns, these companies can build trust and loyalty, which can ultimately drive long-term success. While profitability is important for start-ups and platform developers, it should not be the sole driving force behind innovation. Companies that prioritise ethical considerations and consumer well-being can still be profitable and may even be more successful in the long run by building a loyal and engaged customer base.

10.5.2.3 Improving the society

Start-ups need to consider the impact of their platform on the environment and society as a whole. For example, they can explore the use of sustainable materials in their products, implement eco-friendly practices in their operations, and support social initiatives that align with their values. By doing so, they can improve their brand reputation, attract socially conscious consumers, and contribute positively to the world (Kandampully et al., 2022). Additionally, start-ups can leverage AI tools to optimise their operations, reduce waste, and conserve resources. For instance, they can use AI-powered sensors to monitor energy usage in their facilities, use machine learning algorithms to optimise logistics and reduce emissions, and implement predictive maintenance strategies to minimise equipment downtime and extend the lifespan of their assets. Ultimately, start-ups that prioritise sustainability and social responsibility can not only make a positive impact on the world but also differentiate themselves from their competitors and gain a competitive advantage in the market. Improving the society is more than just sustainability but the well-being of consumers as well (Abdulquadri et al., 2021; Adeola et al., 2021). As the use of digital platforms continues to increase, so does the potential for negative behaviours such as cyberbullying and trolling. Start-ups and platform developers need to take responsibility for ensuring that their platforms are safe and free from inappropriate content. This can be done by implementing strong moderation policies and tools, providing easy ways for users to report inappropriate behaviour, and taking swift action against offenders. Additionally, platforms can use AI tools to help detect and flag potentially harmful content, as well as to identify and intervene in cases of cyberbullying (Flew et al., 2019). Parents and educators can also be supported to play a role in promoting responsible digital behaviour and helping young people to recognise and avoid harmful content and behaviour online (Holiday et al., 2022). It's important for everyone involved to work together to create a safe and supportive digital environment for all users.

10.5.2.4 Immersive time on digital platform

Digital addiction and excessive use of technology has become a growing concern in today's society, and it is the responsibility of platform developers to address this issue (Mogaji et al., 2023; Wirtz et al., 2023). One way to do this is by incorporating features that encourage users to take breaks or limit their usage, such as setting time limits, sending reminders, or providing resources on digital wellness. For example, Instagram has introduced a 'You're all caught up' feature which informs users when they have seen all the new posts since their last visit, encouraging them to log off and take a break. Another example is the Forest app, which helps users stay focused and away from their phone by planting virtual trees that grow when they stay off their phone. By incorporating such features and promoting digital wellness, platform developers can help ensure a healthier and more sustainable digital consumption. As Mogaji et al (2023) discussed in their paper on immersive time on the metaverse, there is a growing need for corporate digital responsibility (Wirtz et al., 2023) where platform developers can warm their consumers about taking a break. How much time do you expect digital consumers to spend on digital platforms. How much time do you expect children to use on social media. Should children time on social media be regulated? (By who? An app to automatically lock the phone or the parents?) Would the time spent reduce? These are some of the questions platform developers will have to deal with as they reflect on the contemporary issues of digital consumption.

10.5.2.5 Authenticating information

The issue of misinformation or fake news is a growing concern in today's digital age. Start-ups need to take responsibility for the content that is being shared on their platforms and take steps to combat misinformation. One way to do this is by using AI-powered tools that can detect and flag potentially false or misleading content. Additionally, start-ups can collaborate with fact-checking organisations to ensure that the content being shared on their platforms is accurate and reliable. It is also important for start-ups to promote media literacy and critical thinking among their users, encouraging them to fact-check information and question sources before accepting information as true. From a consumer protection perspective, should digital consumers be asked to submit their government-issued identification cards before opening and using a social media profile? No doubt, this can be a controversial issue. While it can help with identifying and potentially mitigating issues related to fake profiles, identity theft, and online harassment, it can also raise privacy and security concerns. Many consumers may be hesitant to submit their personal identification information to social media platforms, especially considering the numerous data breaches and security incidents that have occurred in recent years. It can also be challenging to implement and enforce such requirements globally, given the varying laws and regulations in different countries. Therefore, any decision to implement this requirement would need to weigh the benefits of increased security and authenticity against the potential privacy concerns and the possible impact on user adoption and engagement. Ultimately, it would be up to the social media platform to communicate the benefits of such requirements and ensure transparency around how the information is collected, used, and protected.

> **Reflective question**
>
> **Would you be willing to provide your ID card/passport before opening a social media account?**

10.5.2.6 Innovations beyond social media

Start-up companies need to start evaluating innovations beyond social media as the demands of consumers are changing. Start-up companies and platform developers need to continuously evaluate and adapt to changing consumer demands (Kandampully et al., 2022). While social media remains an important platform for consumer engagement, there are other emerging technologies that start-ups can explore to innovate and reach consumers. Facebook has recognised the declining user numbers and engagement on social media platforms and not surprising to see Facebook (Meta) investing heavily in virtual and augmented reality technology, with the goal of creating a fully immersive metaverse where people can interact with each other and digital content in new and engaging ways. Google had a social media platform called Google+ that was launched in 2011. However, due to low user engagement, Google announced that it would be shutting down the platform. The shutdown was completed in April 2019. Twitter has launched features like Twitter Blue, a subscription service that offers additional features to users for a fee. TikTok is to be banned from UK parliamentary devices. Tech companies and platform developers need to start thinking beyond social media as a platform to engage their consumers. Virtual and augmented reality (VR/AR) technologies are becoming more accessible and can offer new and immersive ways to engage consumers. Additionally, voice-enabled technologies like smart speakers and virtual assistants are becoming more common in households and offer opportunities for start-ups to provide personalised and convenient services to consumers. It is important for start-ups to stay up-to-date with emerging technologies and to be open to exploring new ways to engage consumers beyond traditional social media platforms.

> **Reflective question**
>
> What other social media platform do you predict will emerge in the next few years?

Staff

10.5.2.7 Well-being of consumers

Employed staff at companies and organisations, including managers and owners, need to reflect on their business decisions as they navigate contemporary issues in digital consumption. One of the key considerations for companies is how emerging technologies may impact their staffing levels and workforce. While technologies such as AI and automation can improve efficiency and reduce costs, they can also lead to job displacement for some workers. Companies need to carefully consider the impact of their technology investments on their employees and explore ways to upskill or retrain workers whose jobs may be impacted by automation (Mogaji & Nguyen, 2022). In addition, companies need to balance their financial decisions with the needs of their staff. This may involve making difficult decisions about investments in technology versus investments in human resources, as well as exploring alternative work arrangements such as remote work or flexible schedules to support employee well-being.

10.5.2.8 Ensuring equitable access and safety

Moving on from just ensuring well-being of consumers, specifically ensuring equitable access and safety for everyone on the platform is another critical consideration for staff and organisations as they navigate contemporary issues in digital consumption, especially as consumers are getting more demanding (see previous examples of visually impaired consumers suing a company because of the inaccessible website). Equitable access refers to ensuring that all users, regardless of their background, location, or socioeconomic status, have equal opportunity to access and engage with the platform. This may involve addressing issues such as language barriers, access to technology, and connectivity, as well as ensuring that the platform is designed in a way that is user-friendly and accessible to all. Ensuring safety on the platform is also essential to protect users from harm and create a positive user experience. This may involve implementing measures such as content moderation, reporting systems for abuse or harassment, and privacy controls that enable users to control their own data and protect their personal information. Organisations also need to be proactive in addressing emerging concerns around equitable access and safety, particularly in the context of marginalised communities or groups that may be disproportionately impacted by digital consumption. This may involve partnering with community organisations, conducting user research and feedback sessions, and actively soliciting feedback from diverse user groups to ensure that the platform is meeting their needs and addressing their concerns (Soetan et al., 2021; Agbo et al., 2020). Ultimately, ensuring equitable access and safety on the platform is not only the right thing to do from a social and ethical perspective but also critical to the long-term success and sustainability of the platform. By fostering a positive user experience that prioritises safety and inclusivity, organisations can build strong relationships with users and create a platform that is trusted, valued, and resilient.

10.5.2.9 *Ethical implications of technology*

Another important consideration for companies is the ethical implications of their technology investments. For example, Fashion brand Levi Strauss & Co has announced a partnership with digital fashion studio Lalaland.ai to make custom artificial intelligence (AI) generated models in what it says will increase diversity among its models (Schneider, 2023). While Levi Strauss & Co can generate cheaper, more deviser and affordable models using AI, should they be paying human models. But remember AI models will not be buying jeans? While these technologies may seem cheaper, companies need to be mindful of these issues and work to mitigate potential harm, such as by ensuring diverse and inclusive development teams and conducting regular ethical assessments of their technology investments (Balakrishnan et al., 2021). Ultimately, the key for companies is to approach these decisions with a holistic view that considers both the financial implications and the impact on their employees and broader society. By prioritising ethical considerations and investing in the skills and well-being of their workforce, companies can build a more sustainable and successful future.

10.5.2.10 *Data access*

Access to data is a critical consideration for staff and organisations as they navigate contemporary issues in digital consumption. With increasing concerns around privacy and data security, consumers are becoming more selective about the types of data they share with companies and brands. In order to build trust with consumers and access the data they need, organisations need to be transparent about their data practices and demonstrate a clear value proposition for why consumers should share their data (Mogaji et al., 2020). This may involve offering personalised experiences or incentives in exchange for data, such as access to exclusive content or discounts. At the same time, organisations need to be mindful of ethical considerations around data collection and use. This includes ensuring that data is collected and used in a transparent and secure manner, as well as respecting consumers' right to control their own data and opt out of data collection and use. Staff, managers, and organisations also need to be proactive in addressing emerging concerns around data privacy and security. This may involve implementing robust data protection and security measures, such as data encryption and two-factor authentication, as well as conducting regular audits and assessments to identify and address potential vulnerabilities. Ultimately, the key for staff and organisations is to approach data access and privacy with a consumer-centric perspective that prioritises transparency, trust, and ethical considerations.

10.5.2.11 *Cookies-less world*

A 'cookies-less world' refers to the shift away from the use of HTTP cookies, which are small data files that websites store on a user's device to track their activity and remember their preferences (Thomas, 2021). This shift is happening due to increased privacy concerns among consumers and regulatory pressures to protect user data. Major web browsers like Google Chrome and Apple Safari have made changes to block third-party cookies, and new privacy regulations like the EU's General Data Protection Regulation (GDPR) and California's Consumer Privacy Act (CCPA) are imposing stricter rules on data collection and sharing. In this new world, companies will need to find new ways to collect and analyse data from their customers while respecting their privacy rights. Some of the alternative methods include first-party data collection, contextual targeting, and identity-based targeting (Mogaji et al., 2020). First-party data collection involves gathering data directly from customers through their interactions with a company's website, social media pages, or apps. Contextual targeting involves displaying ads based on the content of the webpage or app that the customer is viewing. Identity-based targeting involves using authenticated customer data, such as email addresses or login information, to target ads. Companies can also use data partnerships with other companies or leverage machine learning algorithms to gain insights from customer behaviour without relying on cookies. By building strong relationships with consumers and demonstrating a commitment to responsible data practices, organisations can access the data they need to drive innovation and growth while also safeguarding consumer privacy and security.

10.5.2.11 Online brand activism

In the age of social media, consumers have more power than ever before to influence the reputation of a brand online (Batista et al., 2022). Hashtags and boycotts can go viral quickly, and brands must be prepared to respond to them appropriately. Some brands choose to take a stand on political and social issues, while others prefer to remain neutral. One example of a brand taking a stand on a political and social issue that was well accepted by the public is Nike's 'Dream Crazy' campaign featuring former NFL quarterback Colin Kaepernick. The campaign launched in 2018 and featured a photo of Kaepernick with the tagline 'Believe in something. Even if it means sacrificing everything'. Kaepernick had gained national attention for kneeling during the national anthem before NFL games as a protest against police brutality and racial injustice. Nike's campaign sparked controversy, with some consumers burning their Nike products in protest. However, the campaign was also well-received by many, particularly among younger consumers who support Kaepernick's message. The campaign resulted in a significant increase in sales for Nike, and the company was praised for taking a stand on an important social issue. Either way, it's important for brands to be aware of the potential risks and rewards of engaging in these conversations and to have a well-thought-out strategy in place (Béal et al., 2023). Brands need to invest in supporting consumer engagement on digital platforms to maintain a positive brand reputation and build customer loyalty. This can include responding to customer inquiries and requests on social media, monitoring and responding to customer reviews on app stores and review websites like Trustpilot, and engaging with customers through email marketing campaigns and loyalty programmes. By providing prompt and helpful customer support, brands can create a positive experience for their customers and encourage them to continue using and recommending the brand to others (Khalil et al., 2022). This can also help to mitigate any negative feedback or reviews and prevent potential PR crises.

10.6 What future holds

Predicting the future of technology and digital consumption can be challenging, as these fields are constantly evolving and advancing. However, there are some potential trends and developments that may shape the future of these contemporary issues. For example, artificial intelligence is expected to continue to advance and be integrated into more aspects of our lives, potentially leading to increased automation and efficiency, but also potentially impacting employment and privacy. Metaverse may also continue to grow and evolve, potentially leading to new forms of digital interaction and socialisation, but also raising concerns about privacy and addiction.

Blockchain and cryptocurrency may continue to gain in popularity and usage, potentially leading to more decentralised and secure systems of data management and transactions, but also raising questions about regulation and environmental sustainability. Content creation, computer-generated images, and generative content may continue to advance, potentially leading to new forms of art and entertainment, but also raising concerns about authenticity and ownership. The development and adoption of 5G technology may continue to increase, potentially leading to faster and more reliable connectivity, but also raising concerns about the environmental impact and potential health risks.

Overall, while the future of these contemporary issues is uncertain, it is likely that they will continue to shape and impact our daily lives in a significant way. It is important for stakeholders—students, staff employed in a company, and start-up founders—to stay informed and engaged with these issues as they continue to evolve and develop.

10.6.1 Students

Keep yourself informed about these issues—don't be afraid but be prepared to address these issues. Join the debate, join the conversation—how would AI change how we consume digital technologies? Should students be allowed to use Chat GPT? Have an opinion. Though this can change based on your level of exposure, education, and enlightenment. Approach these issues with an open mind and a willingness to learn, as the field of AI is constantly evolving, and there is always something new to discover (Chattopadhyay et al., 2022; Sharma et al., 2022). Keeping yourself informed and joining the conversation is a great start. Additionally, acquiring skills in areas such as data analysis, programming, and ethical considerations in AI can help you stand out in the job market and contribute to the development of responsible AI technologies. Volunteering with tech developers, platforms, and brands is also a great way to gain practical experience and experiment with your skills.

10.6.2 Brands

As consumers become more aware of their data privacy and security, brands must prioritise transparency and accountability in their data practices. This includes being transparent about what data is being collected and how it is being used, as well as providing options for consumers to control their data (Almeida Teixeira et al., 2019; Balakrishnan et al., 2021). In terms of offering value on digital platforms, brands need to focus on creating engaging and personalised experiences for consumers. This can involve leveraging emerging technologies like virtual reality and the metaverse to create immersive experiences that offer unique value to consumers. However, it's important for brands to remember that these technologies should not be used simply for the sake of being trendy, but rather should be used strategically to enhance the overall brand experience. Finally, brands must be mindful of the changing needs and expectations of their consumers (Gambetti & Biraghi, 2023). This means constantly listening to feedback and adapting to new trends and technologies as they emerge. By prioritising transparency, value, and consumer needs, brands can build stronger and more meaningful relationships with their customers in the digital age.

10.6.3 Developers

Developers need to keep innovating, innovating, and innovating. Developers need to stand out with more innovation. They don't need to rest on their oars and achievement. Developers should also focus on developing skills in emerging technologies, such as artificial intelligence, blockchain, and virtual reality. This can involve taking courses or tutorials, participating in hackathons, and working on personal projects to build practical experience. Collaboration is key to building better products and services in the digital age, and developers who work in cross-functional teams are often able to produce more robust and innovative solutions. By bringing together designers, developers, and other stakeholders, teams can ensure that products and services are designed with the user in mind and are able to address a broader range of needs and use cases (Mogaji et al., 2023). Third-party developers can also benefit from expanding their digital offerings and investing in human resources to drive up innovation. By staying up-to-date with the latest trends and technologies, and by collaborating with other developers and stakeholders, third-party developers can build a stronger reputation for innovation and deliver more value to their clients and customers. Building trust with consumers and brands is also essential, particularly in the age of data privacy and security concerns. Developers who prioritise security and privacy in their products and services, and who are transparent about their data practices, are more likely to build trust with consumers and brands. This can help to drive adoption of their products and services and can also contribute to a positive reputation in the industry.

In summary, stakeholders need to stay informed and aware of these issues as they continue to evolve and impact our daily lives. This includes staying up-to-date with new developments and advancements in technology, understanding the potential risks and benefits of using these technologies, and being aware of your rights as a consumer. It is also important to stay informed about the ethical considerations and responsible use of technology, as well as the environmental impact of digital consumption. Engaging in conversations and dialogue with experts in these fields can also be helpful in developing a deeper understanding of these complex issues and their potential impact on society.

10.7 Conclusion

The contemporary issues in digital consumption are complex and multifaceted, with implications for various stakeholders. Consumers have a right to privacy and control over their data but also face challenges navigating new technologies and digital experiences. Brands must balance providing innovative and user-friendly technology with ethical considerations and responsibility for the environmental impact of their products. Tech developers play a crucial role in creating and improving digital technologies, but must also prioritise security, accessibility, and inclusivity. Regulators must balance innovation with regulation, ensuring the protection of consumers while fostering innovation and growth. As illustrated in Figure 10.1, there are future aspirations and

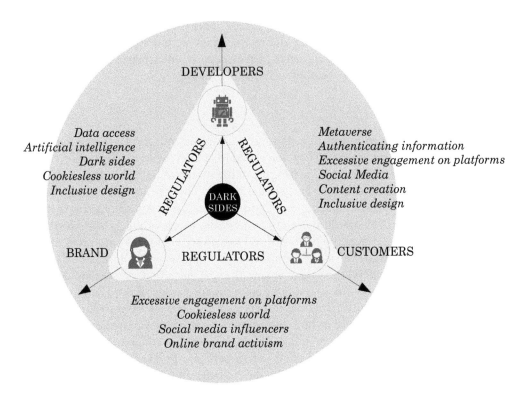

Figure 10.1 The future aspirations and contemporary issues for developers, brands, and consumers as they engage on digital platform.

contemporary issues for developers, brands, and consumers as they engage on digital platforms.

Artificial intelligence, metaverse, blockchain, content creation, computer-generated images, 5G, control of data, and chatbots are just a few of the emerging issues in digital consumption. These issues highlight the potential for technology to transform our lives in both positive and negative ways. As we continue to navigate these complex and rapidly evolving issues, it is essential that we approach them with a collaborative and interdisciplinary mindset, working together to find solutions that prioritise the well-being of consumers, the responsible use of technology, and the sustainable development of our digital world.

Based on current trends and emerging technologies, it is postulated that the future of digital consumption is likely to be shaped by three main themes: Ethical and Social Implications of Emerging Technologies, Transformation of Digital Consumption and Creation, Ownership and Control of Data and Digital Assets. For consumers, this could mean more personalised and seamless experiences that integrate with different aspects of their lives. However, it could also raise concerns about privacy and the use of personal data. Brands will need to adapt to changing consumer preferences and invest in new technologies to remain competitive but will also face pressure to be transparent and ethical in their use of data and emerging technologies. For tech developers, there will be ample opportunities to innovate and develop new products and services that can drive the next phase of digital transformation. However, they will also need to navigate complex regulatory environments and ensure that their innovations are safe, secure, and accessible to all. Finally, regulators will need to balance the need for innovation with protecting the public interest, ensuring that emerging technologies do not exacerbate existing inequalities and are deployed in ways that are safe, transparent, and equitable.

As we look towards the future of digital consumption, it is clear that the intersection of technology and society will continue to evolve and shape the way we interact with the world around us. It will be up to all stakeholders to work together to ensure that the benefits of these technologies are realised, while mitigating any potential risks or negative impacts.

10.8 Student activities

1. What is your understanding about contemporary issues of digital consumption?
2. How can technology be used to create more sustainable practices in digital consumption?
3. What are some potential ethical concerns surrounding the use of AI in digital consumption, such as personalised advertising and recommendation algorithms?
4. How can companies effectively protect users' personal data and privacy in a world where data breaches and hacks are becoming more common?
5. What impact has the rise of influencer culture had on digital consumption? Is it a positive or negative influence overall?
6. What role can virtual and augmented reality play in the future of digital consumption, and what are some potential benefits and risks of these technologies?
7. How can digital consumption contribute to social justice movements and advocacy efforts?
8. What can be done to bridge the digital divide and ensure equal access to digital resources and opportunities for all communities, regardless of socioeconomic status or geographic location?
9. How can a brand have prepared for the future of digital consumption?
10. With cashless societies and online transaction, how do you envisage donation to homeless people on the street?

References and further reading

Abdulquadri, A., Mogaji, E., Kieu, T. & Nguyen, P., 2021. Digital transformation in financial services provision: A Nigerian perspective to the adoption of chatbot. *Journal of Enterprising Communities: People and Places in the Global Economy*, 15(2), pp. 258–281.

Adeola, O. et al., 2021. Marketing bank services to financially vulnerable customers: Evidence from an emerging economy. *International Journal of Bank Marketing*, 39(3), pp. 402–428.

Agbo, F. et al., 2020. Social media usage for computing education: The effect of tie strength and group communication on perceived learning outcome. *Journal of Education and Development Using Information and Communication Technology*, 16(1), pp. 5–26.

Almeida Teixeira, G., Mira da Silva, M. & Pereira, E., 2019. The critical success factors of GDPR implementation: A systematic literature review. *Digital Policy, Regulation and Governance*, 21(4), pp. 402–418.

Bailey, D. et al., 2022. We are all theorists of technology now: A relational perspective on emerging technology and organizing. *Organization Science*, 33(1), pp. 1–18.

Balakrishnan, J., Nwoba, A. & Nguyen, N., 2021. Emerging-market consumers' interactions with banking chatbots. *Telematics and Informatics*, 65, 101711.

Batista, J., Barros, L., Peixoto, F. & Botelho, D., 2022. Sarcastic or assertive: How should brands reply to consumers' uncivil comments on social media in the context of brand activism? *Journal of Interactive Marketing*, 57(1), pp. 141–158.

Béal, M., Grégoire, Y. & Carrillat, F., 2023. Let's laugh about it! using humor to address complainers' online incivility. *Journal of Interactive Marketing*, 58(1), pp. 34–51.

Chattopadhyay, A., Kupe, T., Schatzer, N. & Mogaji, E., 2022. Fireside chat with three vice chancellors from three continents. In: E. Mogaji, V. Jain, F. Maringe & R. Hinson, eds. *Re-imagining Higher Education in Emerging Economies*. Cham: Palgrave Macmillan, pp. 85–96.

Chemma, N., Abdelli, M. & Awasthi, A., 2022a. Management and information technology in the digital era: Introduction to edited collection on challenges and perspectives. In: *Management and Information Technology in the Digital Era*. Bingley: Emerald, pp. 1–6.

Chemma, N., Abdelli, M. & Awasthi, A., 2022b. Management and information technology in the digital era: Conclusion and research agenda. In: *Management and Information Technology in the Digital Era*. Bingley: Emerald, pp. 233–237.

Chylinski, M. et al., 2020. Augmented reality marketing: A technology-enabled approach to situated customer experience. *Australasian Marketing Journal*, 28(4), pp. 374–384.

Conti, M., Gathani, J. & Tricomi, P., 2022. Virtual influencers in online social media. *IEEE Communications Magazine*, 60(8), pp. 86–91.

Davis, S. & Arrigo, B., 2021. The Dark Web and anonymizing technologies: Legal pitfalls, ethical prospects, and policy directions from radical criminology. *Crime, Law and Social Change*, 76(4), pp. 367–386.

Dhruv, G., Hulland, J., Kopalle, P. & Karahanna, E., 2020. The future of technology and marketing: A multidisciplinary perspective. *Journal of the Academy of Marketing Science*, 48, pp. 1–8.

Dwivedi, Y. et al., 2022. Metaverse beyond the hype: Multidisciplinary perspectives on emerging challenges, opportunities, and agenda for research, practice and policy. *International Journal of Information Management*, 66, 102542.

Flew, T., Martin, F. & Suzor, N., 2019. Internet regulation as media policy: Rethinking the question of digital communication platform governance. *Journal of Digital Media & Policy*, 10(1), pp. 33–50.

Gambetti, R. & Biraghi, S. 2023. Branded activism: Navigating the tension between culture and market in social media. *Futures*, 145, 103080.

Goodell, J., Alon, I., Chiaramonte, L. & Dreassi, A., 2023. Risk substitution in cryptocurrencies: Evidence from BRICS announcements. *Emerging Markets Review*, 54, 100938.

Hancock, J., Naaman, M. & Levy, K., 2020. AI-mediated communication: Definition, research agenda, and ethical considerations. *Journal of Computer-Mediated Communication*, 25(1), pp. 89–100.

Hein, A. et al., 2020. Digital platform ecosystems. *Electronic Markets*, 30, pp. 87–98.

Hodapp, D. & Hanelt, A., 2022. Interoperability in the era of digital innovation: An information systems research agenda. *Journal of Information Technology*, 37(4), pp. 407–427.

Holiday, S., Norman, M. & Densley, R., 2022. Sharenting and the extended self: Self-representation in parents' Instagram presentations of their children. *Popular Communication*, 20(1), pp. 1–15.

Howson, P. & de Vries, A., 2022. Preying on the poor? Opportunities and challenges for tackling the social and environmental threats of cryptocurrencies for vulnerable and low-income communities. *Energy Research & Social Science*, 84, 102394.

Jain, V., Mogaji, E., Sharma, H. & Babbili, A., 2022. A multi-stakeholder perspective of relationship marketing in higher education institutions. *Journal of Marketing for Higher Education*, pp. 1–19.

Jain, V., Rai, H., Subash, P. & Mogaji, E., 2023. The prospects and challenges of ChatGPT on marketing research and practices. *SSRN Electronic Journal*. http://dx.doi.org/10.2139/ssrn .4398033, pp. 1–16.

Jelovac, D., Ljubojević, C. & Ljubojević, L., 2022. HPC in business: The impact of corporate digital responsibility on building digital trust and responsible corporate digital governance. *Digital Policy, Regulation and Governance*, 24(6), pp. 485–497.

Kandampully, J., Bilgihan, A. & Li, D., 2022. Unifying technology and people: Revisiting service in a digitally transformed world. *The Service Industries Journal*, 42(1–2), pp. 21–41.

Khalil, A., Abdelli, M. & Mogaji, E., 2022. Do digital technologies influence the relationship between the COVID-19 crisis and SMEs' resilience in developing countries? *Journal of Open Innovation: Technology, Market, and Complexity*, 8(2), pp. 100–109.

Koohang, A. et al., 2023. Shaping the metaverse into reality: A holistic multidisciplinary understanding of opportunities, challenges, and avenues for future investigation. *Journal of Computer Information Systems*, 63(3), pp. 1–31.

Kopalle, P., Kumar, V. & Subramaniam, M., 2020. How legacy firms can embrace the digital ecosystem via digital customer orientation. *Journal of the Academy of Marketing Science*, 48, pp. 114–131.

McKinsey, 2022. Marketing in the metaverse: An opportunity for innovation and experimentation [Online] Available at: https://www.mckinsey.com/capabilities/growth-marketing-and-sales/ our-insights/marketing-in-the-metaverse-an-opportunity-for-innovation-and-experimentation

Miric, M., Boudreau, K. & Jeppesen, L., 2019. Protecting their digital assets: The use of formal & informal appropriability strategies by App developers. *Research Policy*, 48(8), 103738.

Mogaji, E., 2021. *Brand Management*. Cham: Springer.

Mogaji, E. & Nguyen, N., 2022. Managers' understanding of artificial intelligence in relation to marketing financial services: Insights from a cross-country study. *International Journal of Bank Marketing*, 40(6), pp. 1272–1298.

Mogaji, E., Olaleye, S. & Ukpabi, D., 2020. Using AI to personalise emotionally appealing advertisement. In: *Digital and Social Media Marketing: Emerging Applications and Theoretical Development*. Cham: Springers, pp. 137–150.

Mogaji, E., Restuccia, M., Lee, Z. & Nguyen, N., 2023. B2B brand positioning in emerging markets: Exploring positioning signals via websites and managerial tensions in top-performing African B2B service brands. *Industrial Marketing Management*, 108, pp. 237–250.

Mogaji, E., Soetan, T. & Kieu, T., 2020. The implications of artificial intelligence on the digital marketing of financial services to vulnerable customers. *Australasian Marketing Journal*, 29(3), pp. 235–242.

Mogaji, E., Wirtz, J., Belk, R. & Dwivedi, Y., 2023. Immersive Time (ImT). *International Journal of Information Management*, 72, 102659.

Morgan-Thomas, A., Dessart, L. & Veloutsou, C., 2020. Digital ecosystem and consumer engagement: A socio-technical perspective. *Journal of Business Research*, 121, pp. 713–723.

Olson, E., Olson, K., Czaplewski, A. & Key, T., 2021. Business strategy and the management of digital marketing. *Business Horizons*, 64(2), pp. 285–293.

Oosthuizen, K., Botha, E., Robertson, J. & Montecchi, M., 2021. Artificial intelligence in retail: The AI-enabled value chain. *Australasian Marketing Journal*, 29(3), pp. 264–273.

Ponzoa, J. & Erdmann, A., 2021. E-commerce customer attraction: Digital marketing techniques, evolution and dynamics across firms. *Journal of Promotion Management*, 27(5), pp. 697–715.

Rasool, A., Shah, F. & Islam, J., 2020. Customer engagement in the digital age: A review and research agenda. *Current Opinion in Psychology*, 36, pp. 96–100.

Sağkaya Güngö, A. & Ozansoy Çadırcı, T., 2022. Understanding digital consumer: A review, synthesis, and future research agenda. *International Journal of Consumer Studies*, 46(5), pp. 1829–1858.

Schneider, J., 2023. Levi's to use AI-generated models to 'increase diversity' [Online] Available at: https://petapixel.com/2023/03/24/levis-to-use-ai-generated-models-to-increase-diversity/

Sharma, H., Soetan, T., Farinloye, T. & Noite, M., 2022. AI adoption in universities in emerging economies: Prospects, challenges and recommendations. In: Emmanuel Mogaji, Varsha Jain, Felix Maringe, Robert Ebo Hinson, eds. *Re-imagining Educational Futures in Developing Countries: Lessons from Global Health Crises*. Cham: Springers, pp. 159–174.

Sheth, J., 2020. Impact of Covid-19 on consumer behavior: Will the old habits return or die? *Journal of Business Research*, 117, pp. 280–283.

Soetan, T., Mogaji, E. & Nguyen, N., 2021. Financial services experience and consumption in Nigeria. *Journal of Services Marketing*, 35(7), pp. 947–961.

Thomas, I., 2021. Planning for a cookie-less future: How browser and mobile privacy changes will impact marketing, targeting and analytics. *Applied Marketing Analytics*, 7(1), pp. 6–16.

Vrontis, D., Makrides, A., Christofi, M. & Thrass, K., 2021. Social media influencer marketing: A systematic review, integrative framework and future research agenda. *International Journal of Consumer Studies*, 45(4), pp. 617–644.

Whittaker, L., Letheren, K. & Mulcahy, R., 2021. The rise of deepfakes: A conceptual framework and research agenda for marketing. *Australasian Marketing Journal*, 29(3), pp. 204–214.

Wirtz, J., Kunz, W., Hartley, N. & Tarbit, J., 2023. Corporate digital responsibility in service firms and their ecosystems. *Journal of Service Research*, 26(2), pp. 173–190.

Index

Acts: Americans with Disabilities Act 200; California Consumer Privacy Act (CCPA) 58; California Consumer Privacy Act (USA) 167; California's Consumer Privacy Act 224; Children's Online Privacy Protection Act (USA) 172; Data Protection Act (Ghana) 168, 170; Data Protection Act (Kenya) 168, 170; Data Protection Act (Nigeria) 168, 170; Data Protection Act (Tunisia) 168; Digital Services Act 167; Dodd-Frank Act (USA) 171; Information Technology Act (India) 168; Personal Data Protection Act (Malaysia) 167; Personal Data Protection Act (Singapore) 167; Personal Information Protection and Electronic Documents Act (Canada) 167; Privacy Act (Australia) 167; Protection of Personal Information Act (South Africa) 167

antitrust laws 112, 174–175, 196

artificial intelligence 2, 36, 47, 51, 54, 65–66, 69, 86, 110–111, 146, 150, 212; increased automation 226

augmented reality 66, 71, 214–215, 222

B2B *see* business-to-business

B2C *see* business-to-consumer

beyond business to consumers 39–40

boutique developer: B2B arrangement 126

boutique developers: data privacy 126; tailored solutions 126; technical expertise 127

brand awareness 75–76

brand reputation 66, 75, 225

brands: brand reputation 66, 75, 84, 215–216; business needs and research 83–84; communication with consumers 85; competitor behaviour 70; competitors 68; consumer engagement 65; consumer trust 84; content customisation 134; data-driven decisions 86; definition of 5; developing mobile apps 77; digital attacks and threats 204; digital consumer preferences 133; digital presence 77; digital transformation 66; evaluation and analysis 85, 86; financial capabilities 78; inclusive design 134; intellectual property rights 134; investments in platforms 78; investments in the ecosystem 66; key considerations for 76; key digital consumption considerations 113; long-term business strategy 135; managing dark sides 204; market research 78; monitoring of third-party developers 135; online presence and capabilities 81; platform and developer selection 84, 85; platform-related costs 134; priorities 135; quality control 134; regulatory requirements on platforms 82; research 83; resource considerations 114; risk assessment 135; security measures 135; social media 71; social media and consumer updates 77; strategic direction 83; strategic directions for 86; suitability of platforms for 66; technical capabilities

for digital platforms 81; technical requirements and needs 80
brands and platforms: alignment of values and philosophy 82–83
business-to-business (B2B) 39–41, 113, 130
business-to-consumer (B2C) 113

C2B *see* consumer-to-business
C2C *see* consumer-to-business
co-created platforms: customer-brand collaboration 74; dark sides 198–200; earned/owned platforms 74; managing 74
collaboration: brands and platforms 106
computer-generated models: drawbacks of 215
consumer behaviour 2, 7–9, 14, 29, 38, 41, 46, 61, 146; digital environments 16; information overload 36; IoT AI and VR 2; marketing purposes 10; online brands 2; social media platforms 2
Consumer Culture Theory (CCT) 19
consumer engagement: digital environment 1
consumer-brand relationship 69
consumer-to-business (C2B) 39, 41; digital platform 40
consumer-to-consumer (C2C) 39; interactions 40
contemporary issues 228; 5G 214; AI-generated content 215; AI-powered virtual assistants 219; aspirations and stakeholders 228; authenticity and ownership 214; blockchain and cryptocurrency 212; blockchain and decentralisation 226; central bank digital currencies 217; computer-generated influencers 216; considerations for staff and organisations 224; crossfunctional collaboration 213; decentralised finance 217; decentralization of data storage 216; deepfakes 214; digital addiction 221; digital currencies 216; digital transformation 213; digital wellness 221; disfinformation 214; ethical considerations for companies 224; fake news 221–222; implications for developers 227; implications for staff and organisations 223; implications for start-ups 219–222; implications for students 217, 219, 226; implications of 228; implications on stakeholders 218; IoT 215; metaverse 214; misuse of AI 214; Natural Language Processing 219; ownership and control of data 216; privacy and anonymity 214; public interest in 229; regulatory environments 229; revenge porn 214; understanding of 217; virtual and augmented reality 214
content moderation policies 172, 197

cookies-less world 224
corporate digital responsibility 35, 53, 221
cryptocurrency: implications of 216
customer feedback 4, 30, 151, 220
customer loyalty: 50, 65, 75, 225; and trust 65, 86
Cybersecurity Law (China) 167, 169

dark side management and stakeholders 206
dark sides of digital consumption: possible solutions 195, 196
data analytics: anti-money laundering programs 142; benefits of 148–149; competitive advantage 139, 149; consumer behaviour 148, 155; context reasoning 142; customer loyalty 148; data mining 141; data-driven management 144; data storage and management 153; definition of 141; descriptive analytics 144–145; diagnostic analytics 145; drawing patterns 140; employee retention 143; energy consumption 142; enhanced product development 149; goal of 141; improved decision-making 148; IoT applications 142; limitations 152; marketing 144; operational optimisation 149; optimisation models 142; optimization of business processes 148; precision immuno-profiling 144; predictive analytics 146; predictive modelling 140; prescriptive analytics 147; techniques of 150; techniques used 139; types of 139, 144; understanding of customers 148; use in different sectors 142, 143; use in recruitment 143; value of 156
data analytics issues: data privacy 152–153; data security 153; lack of skilled workforce 153, 154; poor data quality 152; regulatory compliance 154; transparency 154
data analytics techniques: bibliometric analytics 151; data mining 150; machine learning 150; social network analysis 151; text analytics 151; web analytics 151
data collection: first-party 225; personal/private 172
data: extraction 139; generation 9, 26; harvesting 189; partnerships 225
data privacy 13, 38, 58, 60, 71, 80, 82–83, 216, 218, 226; law and regulations 153; security and 104
data privacy and security 224, 227; regulatory challenges 212
data protection laws 14, 84, 111, 166
data protection regulations 169, 170
data quality: informed business decisions 152
data-driven decisions 10, 139, 145, 219–220; trends and technologies 10

descriptive analytics: limitations of 145; strengths of 144

devices: handling of platforms 52; and platforms 50

diagnostic analytics: limitations of 145–146; strengths of 145

Digital Advertising Alliance 176

digital analytics tools 140; customer needs and preferences 140

digital consumer: definition of 11, 27, 28; engagement 84, 212

digital consumer experience 8, 162

digital consumer management 1, 9, 11, 22–23, 25; competition in marketplace 2

digital consumers: age 28; background of 28; brands and tech companies 12; cancel culture 33; communication with brands 68–69; content creators 32; convenience 31; dark activities 54; dark sides 200; definition of 5; definition of 8, 25; devices 52; digital noise 40; empowerment 33; engagement of 40; engagement with brands 55; engagement with digital platforms 45; gender 28; geographical limitations 38, 39; globalisation 33; information overload 36; internet access 56, 57; managing data 35–36; personalisation 32; separated ecosystems 34; tech-savvy 32

digital consumers and consumption 1; experience 20

digital consumption: addiction 212; assistive technologies 29; being connected 30; brands and developers 28; components of 7; conceptual framework for 11; consumer trust 164; contemporary issues 211; customer feedback 30; dark side exploitation 38; dark side of 162, 187; dark sides 205; dark sides of 212; data 59; data privacy and security 211; democracy 163; developers companies and regulators 10; digital divide 211; digital platforms 45; disinformation 163; effects on society 15; enhanced firm-consumer engagement 188; government policies 14; internet 12; management of 7; managing consumer engagement 166; manipulation of public opinion 163; problems of 162–163; psychological effects of 38; purchasing decisions 2; regulation of 161–162, 175; social media influencers 215; stakeholders 2, 5, 20; success of 6; tech companies 6; theoretical underpinnings 16

digital consumption and digital management 1, 7

digital consumption behaviour 8–9

digital consumption dark sides 189–190; definition of 188–189

digital consumption ecosystem 2, 6

digital consumption negative impacts: carbon emissions 192; decline in revenue 193; depression and loneliness 191; digital divide 190–191; on environment 191; e-waste 192; extraction activities 192; inequality 191; job loss 191; lack of transparency 194; layoffs 193; loss of trust 194; market dominance 192; outsourcing 193; on people 190; on profit 192; waste 191

digital consumption problems: harms affecting adults 165; harms affecting children 164–165; harms affecting organisations 165–166; interference in elections 166, 173; regulation against 166

digital divide 13, 36, 37, 56; adverse effects of 37; developed and developing countries 103; digital consumption 37; digital literacy 37; education 37; geographical locations 56

digital ecosystem: consumers and stakeholders 4

digital environment: consumer engagement 28

digital experience: role of brands 65

digital experiences 10, 12; navigation of 227

digital landscape 2, 20, 26, 41, 48, 50, 65, 114, 115; adaptation to 2; challenges and opportunities 2; evolution of 86

digital marketing 8: definition of 8; digital consumption 8

digital marketing strategies 10, 21, 34

digital platform: consumer engagement 106; definition of 8, 27, 47, 48; development and management challenges 106; devices 47; internet access 49; provider 92; regulations 182; regulatory bodies 182; social media platforms 48

digital platform and devices: characteristics between 51

digital platforms 28, 30; ability to use 57–58; access to 49; action plans dichotomies 79; brand awareness 10; brands 19; brights sides of 188; challenges and actions 60; challenges with 55; consumer challenges 61; consumer engagement 59; consumers as regulators 177–178; consumers with disabilities 12; customer behaviour analysis 67; dark activities 54; dark sides 15; data analytics 49; data collection 54; data collection ethics 53; data collection techniques 61; data control 58; data generation 53; devices 52; digital consumption 9; digital devices 50; digital divide 56; engagement evaluation 54; engagement optimisation 70; engagement with customers 69; features of 48; government as regulator 174–175; kinds of 48; knowledge and skills 57; legal/regulatoty requirements 58; needs and preferences 12; organisations as regulators 177; parents/guardians as regulators 178, 179; presence on 67; regulatory bodies as regulator 175; role of brands 65; self-regulation 176, 177; selling on 71

digital presence 13, 15, 26, 78; brands 86; improvement of 85; platform managers 114

digital regulation reasons 168; avoiding misinformation 172; digital well-being 168, 171; ethical considerations 171–172; financial well-being 171; national security 173–174; promoting competition 172–173

digital technologies: consumers and brands 1

digital technology: dichotomies 77–78

earned platforms 72–73; content creation 72; dark sides 197, 198

ecosystem loyalty: implications of 105

emerging technologies: developers 227; implications of 213–215

equitable access and safety 223; definition of 223; marginalized communities 223

EU Platform to Business Regulation 2019/1150 167

European Electronic Communications Code 167

Federal Trade Commission (FTC) 173, 175

FTC see Federal Trade Commission

GAFAM see Google (Alphabet) Amazon Facebook (Meta) Apple and Microsoft

GDPR see General Data Protection Regulation

General Data Protection Law (Brazil) 167

General Data Protection Regulation 112, 154–155, 166, 172, 224

General Data Protection Regulation (GDPR) 14, 58, 112, 155, 166, 169, 172, 224

Global Anti-Social Media Policy 83

Global E-waste Statistics Partnership 192

Global Initiative on Ethics of Autonomous and Intelligent Systems 176

Google (Alphabet) Amazon Facebook (Meta) Apple and Microsoft (GAFAM) 13, 92, 122; ecosystem 107

innovative idea: definition of 108

intelligence analysis 143; implications of 143

intention to use technology 17–18; effort expectancy 17; facilitating conditions 17; performance expectancy 17

International Telecommunication Union 190

Internet of Things (IoT) 2, 12–13, 55, 66; devices and platforms 13; devices and services 13

interoperability: brands and platforms 80; challenges for users 97; definition of 80; platform developers 96–98

IoT see Internet of Things

location-based advertising 31

low user engagement 95, 222

machine learning algorithms: customer behaviour 150, 220, 225; customer data analysis 220; optimization of logistics 220

managing consumer engagement 1, 35, 53, 101, 179

market competition 18; regulators 6

market research 4, 9

marketing insights: definition of 9; digital consumption 10

metaverse: new forms of digital interaction 226

monetization of content 215

monetization of digital information 172

National Cyber Security Centre 174

online brand activism 225, 228

Online Safety Bill (UK) 14, 163, 167, 169, 175–176

owned platforms: 14, 71, 75, 78; dark sides 199, 203

Paid Earned Shared Co-Created and Owned 12, 71–72, 92; paid platforms 72

paid platforms 72, 92, 127, 197, 201; dark sides 194

Payment Services Regulations 2017 171

PESCO see Paid Earned Shared Co-Created and Owned

PI see predictive intelligence

platform dark sides and solutions 201–203

platform design 46; content optimisation 46

platform developers: acquisitions and mergers 100; artificial intelligence and machine learning 110; awareness of dark sides 204; business operations of 93; competitors 108; consumer engagement 115; creating ecosystem 104–105; creating own devices/platforms 103–104; data collection 111; definition of 6; developing innovative ideas 108; digital consumption 91; enhancing digital consumption 115; environmental considerations 111; ethical stance 111; ethics and dark sides 204; e-waste considerations 205; funding for development 100–101; growth strategies 99; innovative 96; innovative ideas 106; intense competition 109; job of 93; management of operations 112–113; marketing the platforms 94, 99–100; platform monitoring and evaluation

112; pre-installation on devices 102–103; protecting the platform 96; provision of upgrades 101; regulatory engagement 98–99; regulatory requirements 112; responsibilities 94; responsibilities of 92; sponsoring 94; transparency and accountability 99; user engagement 109–110

platform development: bringing users 94; chatbot integration 93; components of 93; enabling brand engagement 95; human resources 110–111; push notifications on mobile phones 95; range of skills needed 110

platform owners: ongoing engagement 101–102

platform provider: safety of consumers 96

platforms: choosing target audience 76; considerations for students 114–115; difference between media and 72; differences between 75; management of 76; presence and financial capability 78; understanding of consumers on 76–77

precision targeting 36; digital data 69

predictive analytics 139, 141, 155; limitations of 147; and predictive intelligence 147; and predictive models 146; real-world applications of 143; strengths of 146

predictive intelligence (PI) 141–143, 146–147, 151, 155

prescriptive analytics 147; and consumer behaviour 147

regulating digital consumption: challenges 179; constant change 180; costs and complexity 180, 181; developer hostility 179; digital liberty 181; government responsibilities 181; role of stakeholders 180

regulators: regulation of dark sides 205

revenue growth 75, 147

robotics process automation 66

shared platforms 14, 73–74, 95–96; dark sides of 198; functionality and user experience 734; vulnerabilities on 73

Social Cognitive Theory 19

start-ups: AI tool 220; brand reputation 220; growth strategies 99; platform developers 221

supervised learning techniques 141

Task-Technology Fit (TFF) 18

tech developers: definition of 13; ecosystem 35; third-party developers 13

Technology Acceptance Model 17

technology adoption 16–18, 26; attitudes and behaviours 20; environmental factors 18; factors for 18; innovation 19; organisational factors 18; technological factors 18; understanding 19; use 20

Technology Organization and Environment (TOE) 18

Theory of Planned Behaviour 16–17; attitudes 16; perceived behavioural control 16; subjective norms 16

third-party developers 13, 92, 112, 121, 127, 129, 227; accreditation 130; advantages of 127; affodability 129; agency developer 126; anti-competitive behaviour 103; boutique developers 126–127; communication challenges 131; contract developer 125; customisation 127, 129; custom-made needs 123; cybersecurity risks 131; definition of 122, 123; digital consumption 123; disadvantages of 130; features of 123; flexibility 129–130; flexible engagement 124; freelance developer 125; jeopardising credibility 131; managing commitments 130–131; managing consumer engagement 124; opportunities for 122; personalization of services 129; personalized solutions 129; quality control 131; security breaches 131; size of 123; specialisation 124; speed of 123–124; strategic operations 124; suitability 127; summary of types of 128; symbiotic relationship 124; technology ecosystem 135; types of 125; verification of competencies and expertise 130

Tinder for Vegetarians 197

TOE see Technology Organization and Environment

TOE framework 18–19, 110

TPB see Theory of Planned Behaviour

triad of digital consumption 5

triple bottom line 15, 111, 187, 190, 194–195; framework 188

TTF see Task-Technology Fit

UK Competition and Markets Authority 173

Unified Theory of Acceptance and Use of Technology (UTAUT) 17–18

user engagement: Instagram 109

UTAUT see Unified Theory of Acceptance and Use of Technology

virtual and augmented reality 222

web analytics: definition of 9; digital marketing strategies 9; tools 70

white labelling 121–122, 132; advantages of 132; brand recognition and customer loyalty 132; customization issues 133; definition of 132; disadvantages of 132; ethical/legal issues 133; managing consumer engagement 133; overdependence issues 133; quality control measures 132; resources and expertise 132

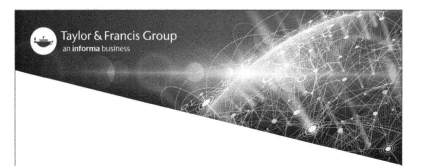

For Product Safety Concerns and Information please contact our EU
representative GPSR@taylorandfrancis.com
Taylor & Francis Verlag GmbH, Kaufingerstraße 24, 80331 München, Germany

www.ingramcontent.com/pod-product-compliance
Ingram Content Group UK Ltd.
Pitfield, Milton Keynes, MK11 3LW, UK
UKHW051835180425
457613UK00023B/1266